AF575191

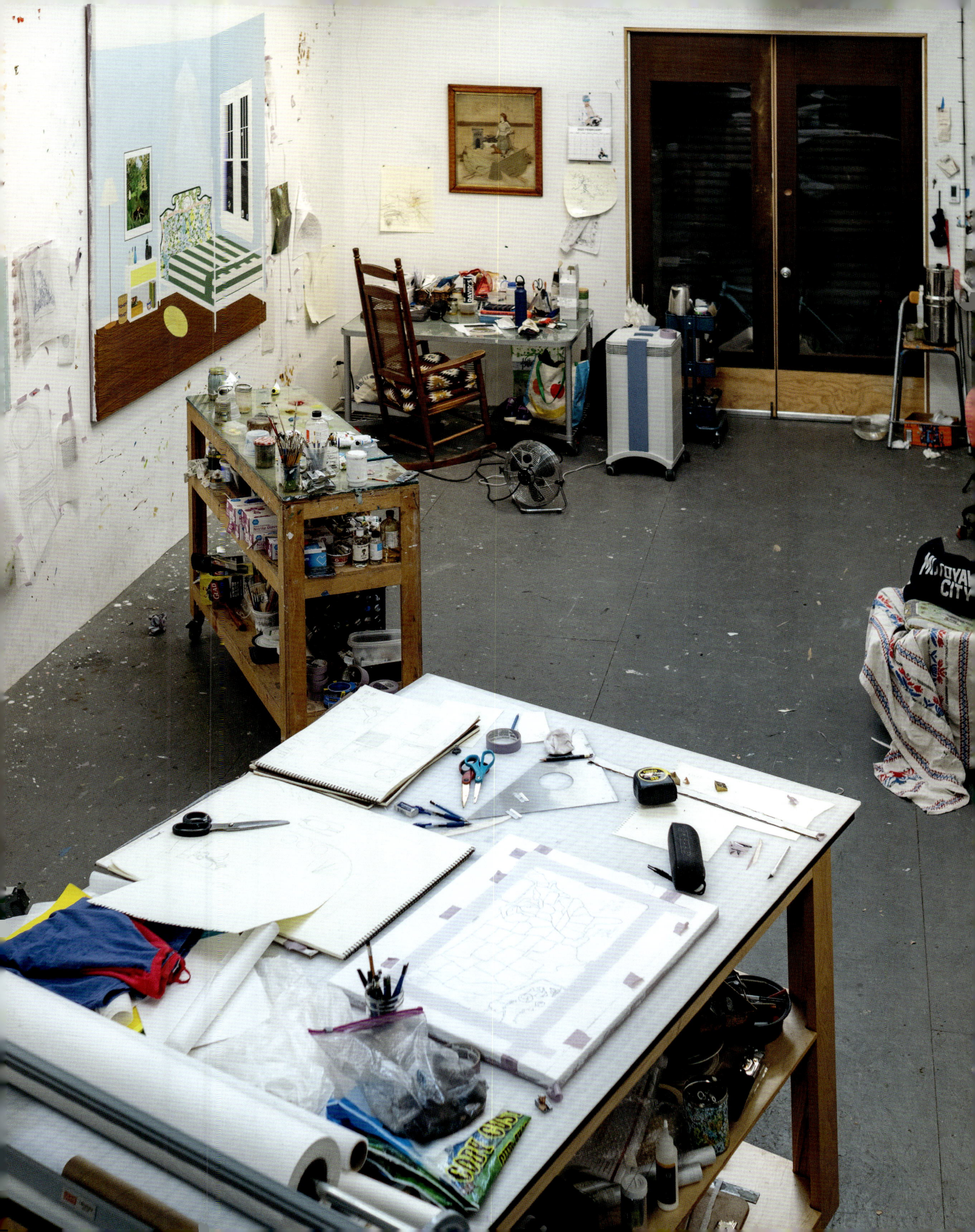
CORN NUTS

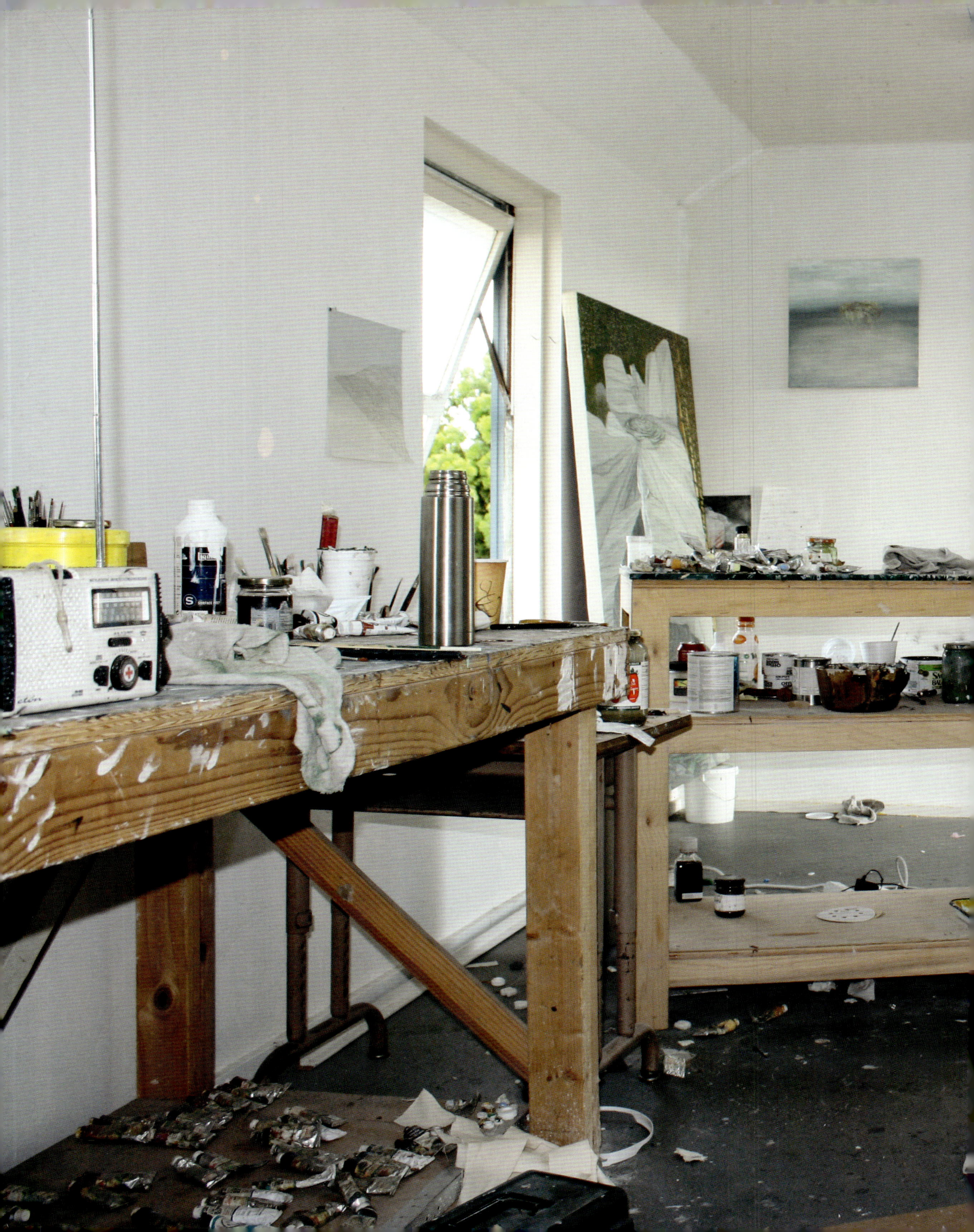

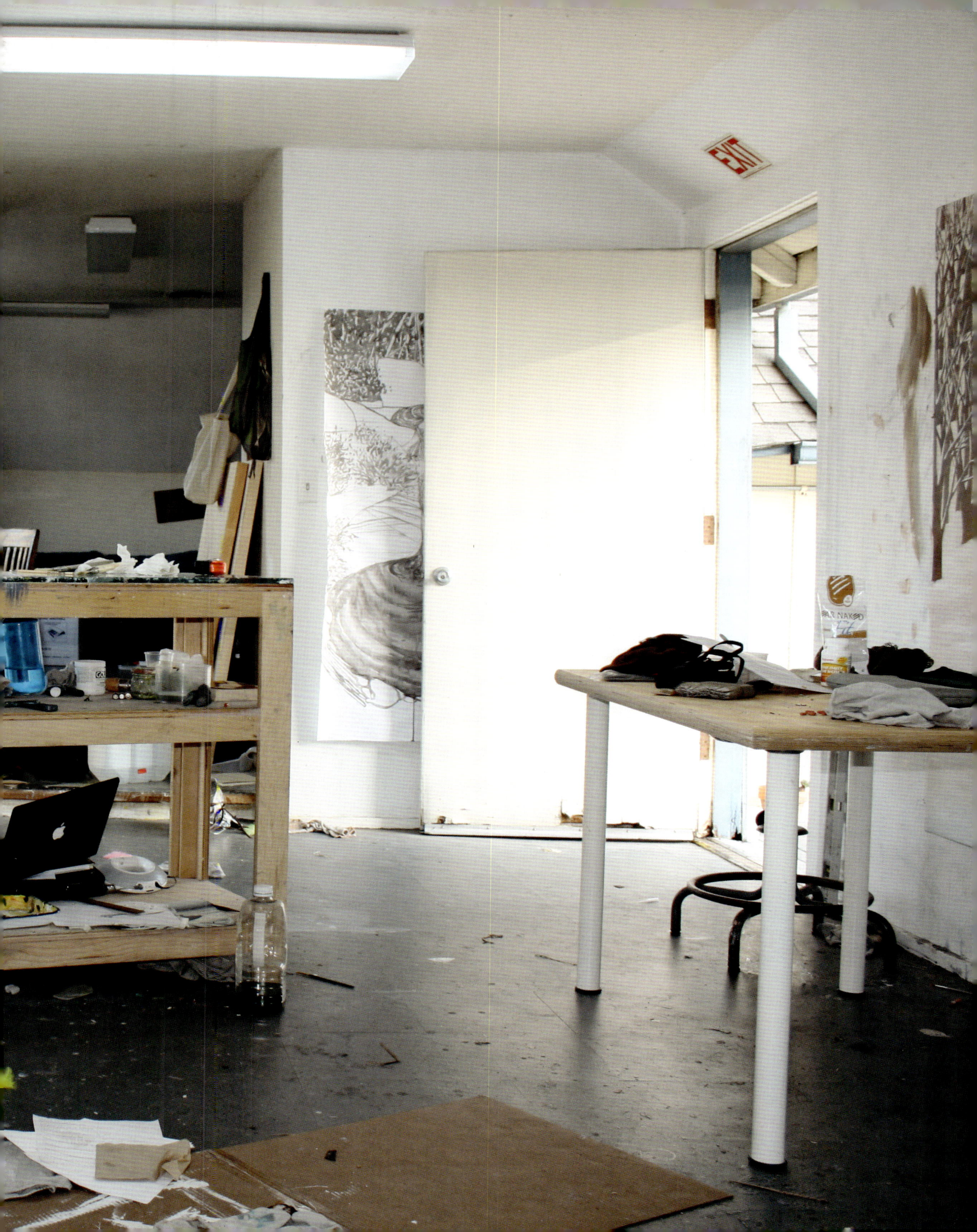
EXIT

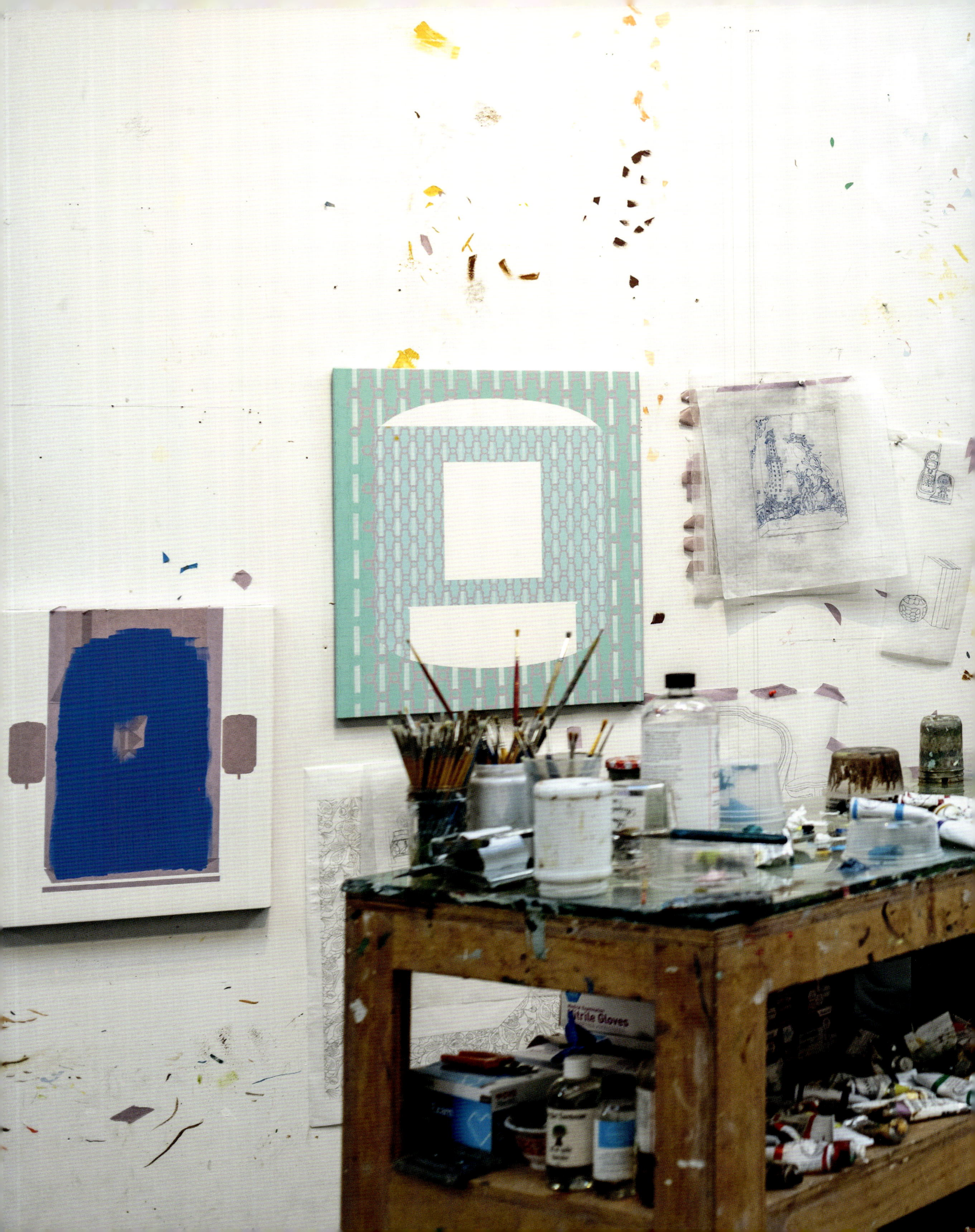
Gloves

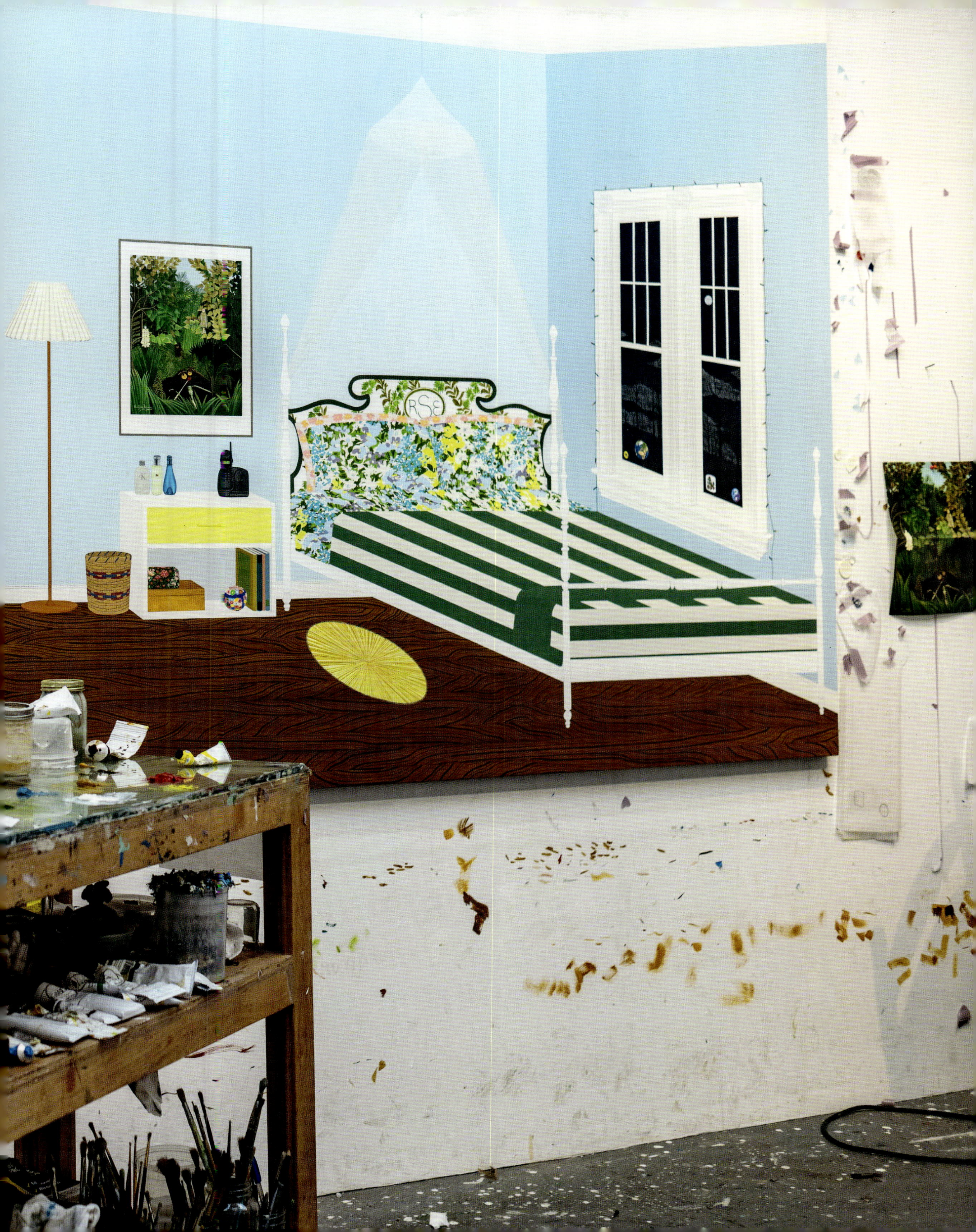

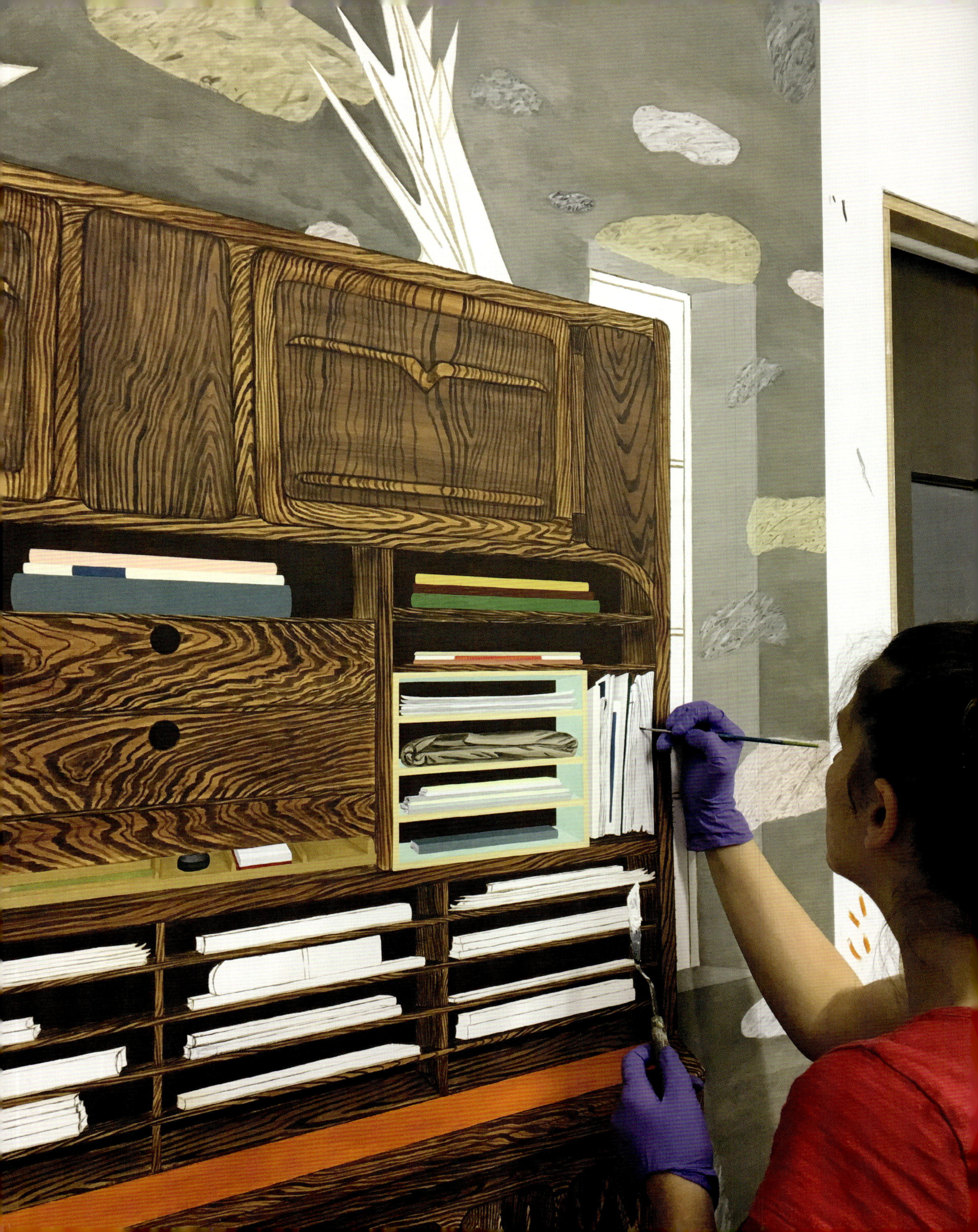

Becky Suss

SKIRA

for my mom

The home of Becky Suss's grandparents, c. 2011. The living room window served as inspiration for *76 Meadow Woods Road*, 2012
Courtesy of Becky Suss

76 Meadow Woods Road, 2012
oil on linen, 72 × 120 inches
Pennsylvania Academy of the Fine Arts, Philadelphia

because nothing can bring back the home or the humans once within their walls. Rather, they are a form of commemoration and a continuation of imperfect memory.

In her book recalling a childhood spent in a midcentury home built in rolling green hills an hour south of Edinburgh, Scottish author Shelley Klein reflects on its own "see through" quality. In this house, called High Sunderland, the picture window gives way to walls of glass. Klein's descriptions of the passages of light, thought, and recollection in and through this place resonate with Suss's own layering and movement between painted planes. A Jewish emigre from the European continent, Klein's father, the renowned textile designer Bernat Klein, built his home as an experiment in partnership with the young architect Peter Womersley. Beri, as he was affectionately known, kept photographs of the generations he left behind in Yugoslavia as a teenager during World War II. Leafing through these family archives after her father's death, his daughter alights upon pictures of long-gone relatives and traces the features of her forebears with her fingertip.

Her attention goes to the rooms in which they are posed, ones she never stepped into herself but that come alive through the attention to the objects within them: "a lace cloth . . . a small collection of glass and silver jars alongside an ornate, silver-backed hairbrush," tiled floors, "candelabras and gilt-framed paintings," furniture "upholstered in richly patterned chintzes and velvets," and "huge potted ferns with leaves coiled tight as clock springs."[2] Just as evocative as the paintings of Meadow Woods Road, Klein writes of the smells and sounds of her ancestors manifesting in her mind. It is, she says, the closest thing to discovering an attic within an otherwise flat-roofed, brightly-lit modernist home.

***

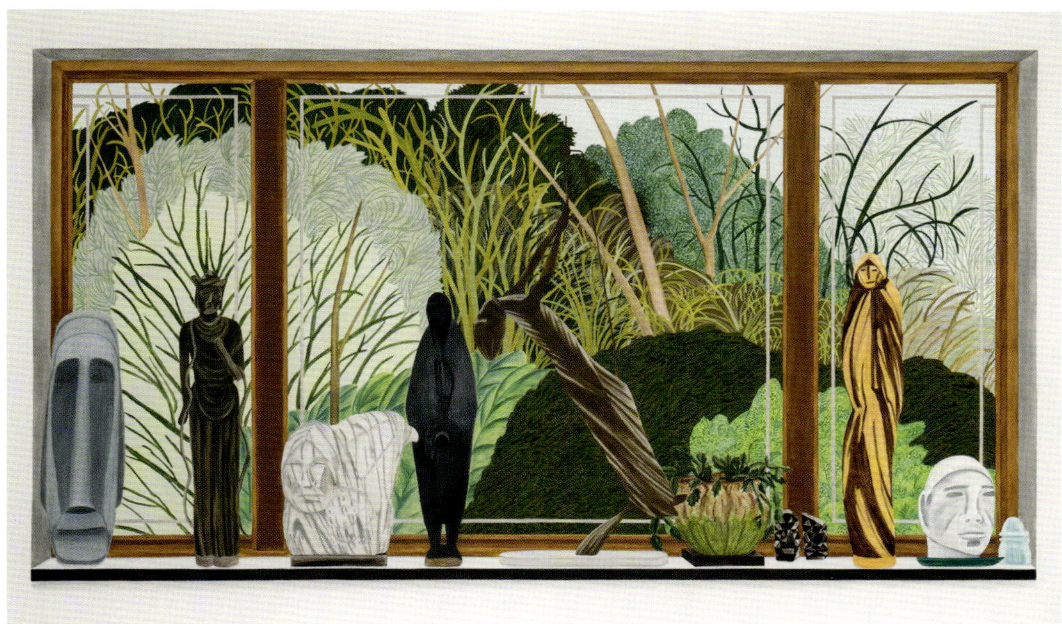

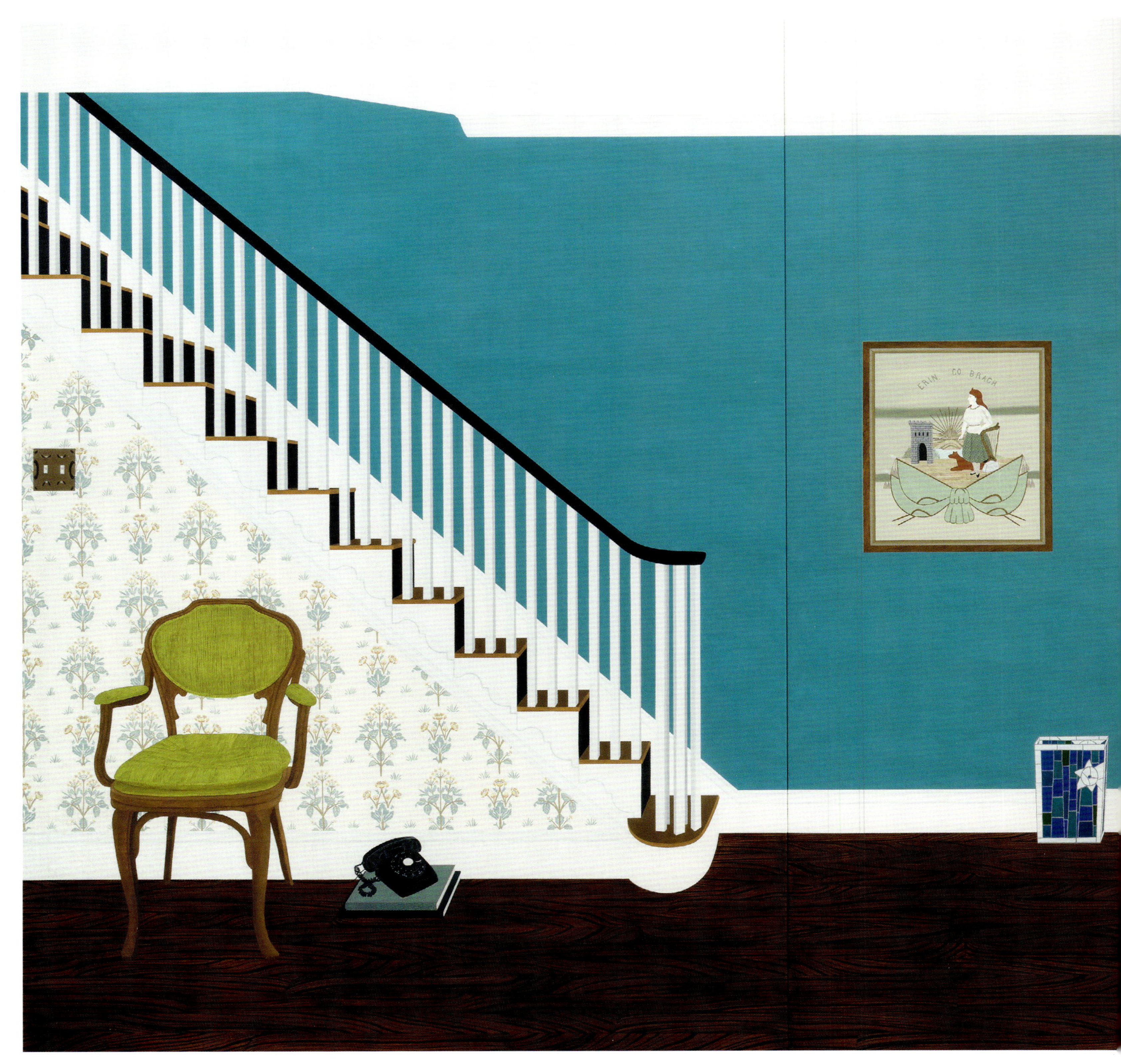

Hallway, 2017
oil on canvas
84 × 180 inches

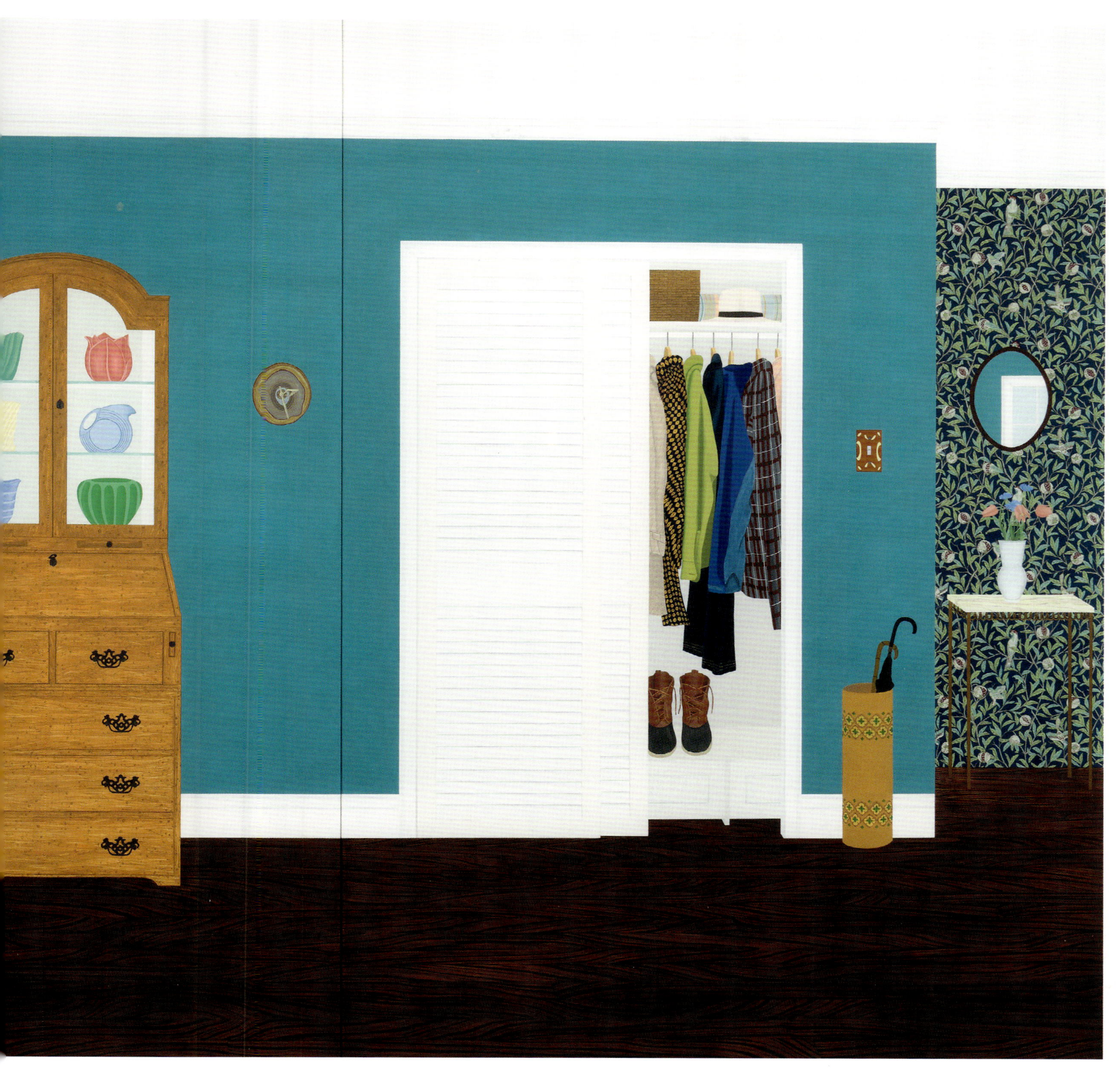

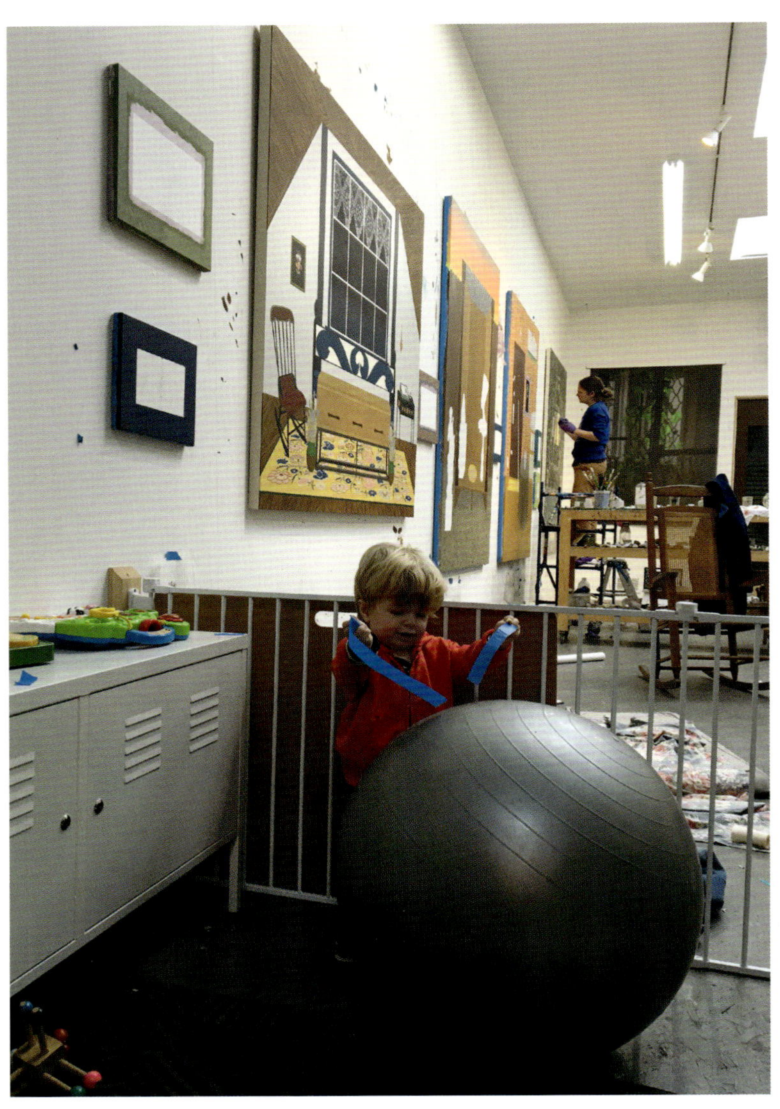

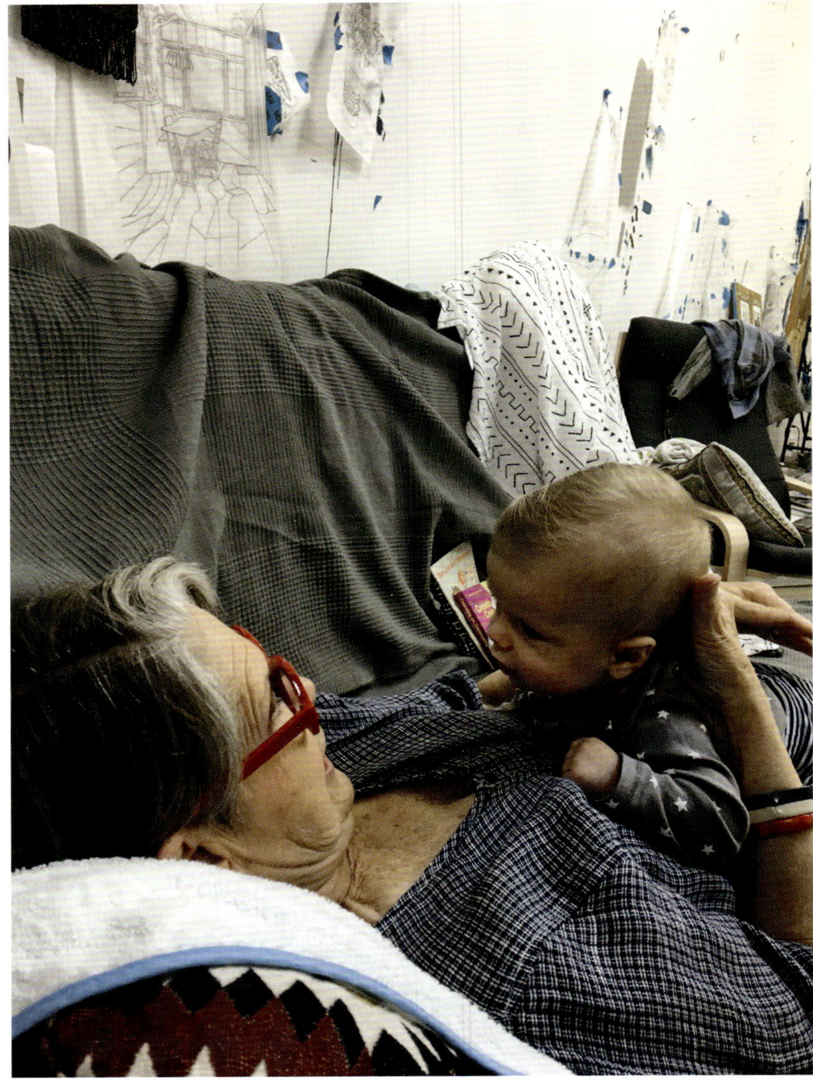

Becky Suss's son, Sid, in her studio while she paints, c. 2019
Courtesy of Micah Danges

Becky Suss's mother, Paula Suss, caring for her grandson, Sid, in the artist's studio, 2018
Courtesy of Becky Suss

Like the photographs of so many homes deemed of architectural note, Suss's paintings are not peopled. Unlike their celluloid cousins, however, it is plain to see that these spaces have been lived in. Indeed, they are portraits of those who have occupied them, those who have settled in easy chairs, balanced half-read books on side tables, and placed their coats on hooks and slippers by the door. The artist has chosen these vignettes deliberately because they are less *House Beautiful* and more "home, sweet home."[3] In *Hallway* (2017), three layers of space collide: stairs in the left foreground invite the viewer into an unseen upper realm, an open closet offers a peek into the sartorial lives of the home's occupants, and patterned wallpaper indicates a hallway beyond. Suss's work argues for the relevance of the humanity and mundanity of the home. Her attention lingers on the lived-in domestic landscapes created by ordinary people.

Her work is created in such conditions. Many of the recent paintings that I know of Suss's were made in a studio that accommodated a playpen where her young son, Sid, spent his first year or so of his life watching his mother work on canvases. There, Suss broke from the careful labor of painting to undertake another equally arduous and detailed task when he needed to be fed or tended to. While she painted, her own mom watched and fed and played with Sid tirelessly, a form of intimate, generational and familial support without which none of Suss's work as an artist would have been realized. Different-but-related types of labor percolated side-by-side out of necessity and informed one another. Her studio was the site of a type of work that, over the last century in particular, has been associated with the household, and has often been shunned in the places where fine art is made and displayed. Yet, in a pre-industrial world, as poet and writer Adrienne Rich reminds us, the home and the workplace were always intertwined. The home "was not a refuge, a place of leisure and retreat . . . it was a part of the world, a center of work, a subsistence unit."[4] These words come from Rich's chapter titled *The Sacred Calling*, and in it she refuses the stereotypical and essentialized division of space into the domestic feminine and the public masculine. She reminds us that home is forged in the tensions between its wider cultural construction and what we ourselves determine it and need it to be. The latter requires our constant vigilance and effort to build in ways that offer creativity, freedom, and joy.

***

The worldwide coronavirus pandemic, with its attendant lockdowns that kept many alternately within or estranged from the confines of domestic spaces, created a profound shift in many of our individual and collective relationships with physical and emotional notions of where we live. Years before, Suss had already presciently focused on an aspect that is only more recently being paid attention to: the matrilineal heartbeat of the home. As she put it when describing some of her earliest paintings of her grandparents' house,

> I really started thinking about my legacy in terms of the women in my family. I always used to think, "Oh, my grandfather, he fought in the war and then he went back to school and became a stockbroker. And then my other grandfather was a doctor.

> A cardiologist. And my great great grandfather was an inventor. This was the narrative of my family, as opposed to the generation after generation after generation of women who kept these homes."[5]

When she presented a suite of paintings of interiors at Jack Shainman Gallery in 2017, the artist titled the exhibition *Homemaker*. It was a noun that gave both her and her gallerist pause for the potential to pigeonhole her work but was ultimately chosen as a deliberate provocation. It's a term that is dismissed and derided, unloved and undervalued by social and cultural preference for systems of validation that are more firmly public. It's a word that invokes the drudgery of mundane maintenance and routines of care. It describes one of the only full time jobs that is unpaid, receives no retirement savings, and is undertaken predominantly (though not exclusively) by women.

If I flip to the back of my well-worn copy of Rich's 1976 masterpiece, *Of Woman Born: Motherhood as Institution and Experience*, the index reveals that "home" is mentioned in four distinct strands: *history of*, 46–52; *as an institution*, 44; *loneliness and*, 53; *socialism and*, 54–55. As ever, Rich parses something complex and opaque into its constituent parts with ease. In her dexterous descriptions, the home is simultaneously a product of culture, a construction subject to interpretation and change, a place of emotion, and (always) a political project. But, as Rich says when she writes about motherhood and its environs, "the social institutions and prescriptions for behavior created by men have not necessarily accounted for the real lives of women . . ."[6]

As a student of architectural history, I dutifully studied the work of Great Men and their many model homes fed to me by most of my undergraduate instructors. I learned of Gaudi and Gropius and Le Corbusier and Mies. Such received wisdom tells us that homes are built by men and then tended to by women. But we know better. Women build worlds. They are the very foundations of the built environment. In the words of Ursula K. LeGuin, women form whole new geographies: "We are volcanoes. When we women offer our experiences as our truth, as human truth, all the maps change. There are new mountains."[7]

At Glasgow University, I found my refuge in a class titled Domestic Landscapes taught by (in my biased estimation) the most impactful design historian of her generation, Juliet Kinchin. It was in her tutorials that, as in Suss's paintings, material culture connected with real life, women's agency and ideas, and the politics of things. Like the artist, our professor focused our attention on the parts of architecture and design usually overlooked in the archives (if ever saved in the first place), unwritten about in survey texts, and deaccessioned from museum collections (if they had ever found their way in). Suss tends to these anecdotal histories, too—the ones that are passed down to us in the stories we are told and that we retell and re-shape for ourselves as we grapple with how and why we live like we do. As Suss notes, "With objects, it's the way we've chosen them and touch them and care for them and live with them over the years that's tender and secret."[8] Choosing to paint them is perhaps the tenderest act of all.

In Sarah Knott's reflections on maternity, *Mother Is a Verb*, which is as well-worn on my bookshelf as Adrienne Rich's texts, the scholar reminds us of the value of this type of anecdote to history.

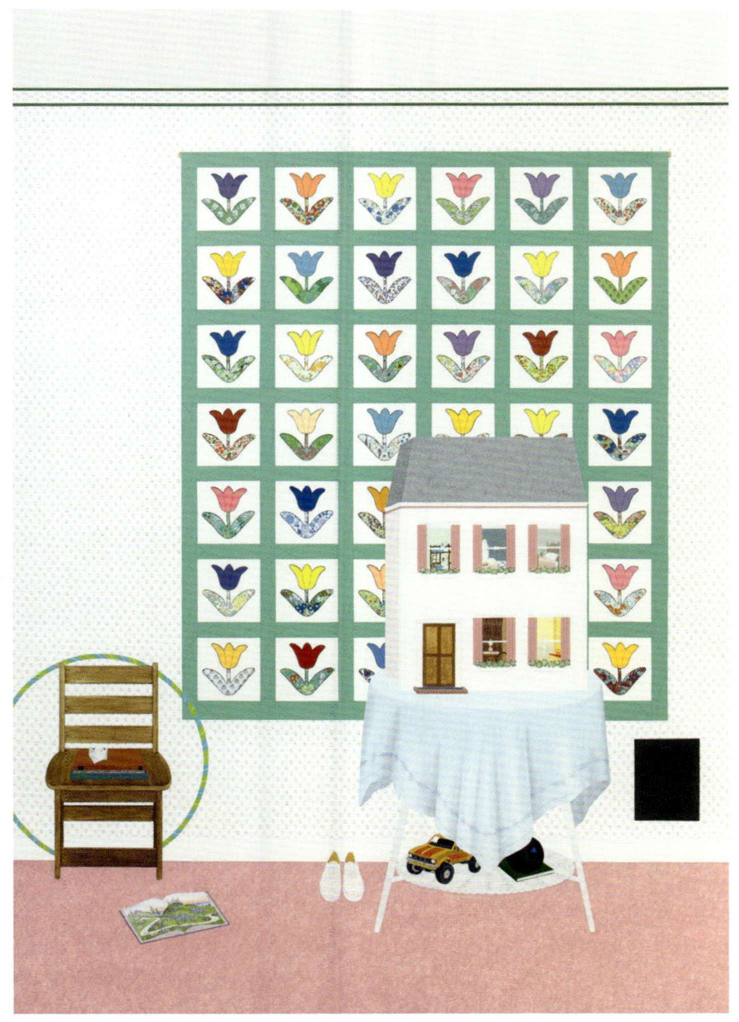

8 Greenwood Place (1985-88), 2021
oil on canvas, 84 × 60 inches

following pages
Installation view of *Homemaker*,
Jack Shainman Gallery, New York, 2017

In her estimation, a focus on the minor detail of everyday life is a form of historical writing that emerged in the seventeenth century. It was a means of "exploring private lives and inner worlds . . . in contrast to conventional preoccupations of the doings of important men." Knott shares that these radical early modern historians were termed "anecdote-graphers."[9]

This odd, satisfying term is one way to describe what Suss does. The material culture that she paints with such painstaking care—the vessels and pieces of furniture and the textures and textiles and wallpapers—are the connective tissue of our histories. Per Knott, far from being throwaway or inconsequential, focusing in this way is an act of "recasting such shards and nuggets of evidence, of turning absence into presence, what's mentioned *en passant* into the main drama."[10] Gather enough of this material and by a process that Knott describes variously as a slow accumulation and an accretion, quiet, persuasive stories emerge from the ether.

***

Suss's most recent series of paintings began during the pandemic when the artist returned to her childhood home in Wyncote, Pennsylvania, a half hour north of Philadelphia. Long leery of taking on a subject so literally close to home, she found herself mining different eras of rooms in which she had grown up and grown out of, including her own childhood bedroom. These places were palimpsests, spaces where furniture had gradually gathered, and that had been updated cosmetically over time. They were of the present and yet connected to everyone who had ever occupied them. Reflecting on their compacted, compounded nature, Suss relates it to the neurological theory of memory reconsolidation, in which the act of remembering causes a small shift in the memory, which then lands on top of and shifts the original.

She went to Wyncote so that her mother could provide childcare for Sid during the pandemic, and so these works materialized while his grandmother, once the artist's own carer, looked after a new generation. Similarly overlapping life cycles are evoked in the wallpaper peeking out from the cupboard in *8 Greenwood Place (1988-93)* (2021) and busily populating the walls *8 Greenwood Place (my bedroom)* (2020). The pattern comes directly from one that the artist excavated from a remnant left hidden in a corner in the house during her stay there. Once uncovered, childhood associations flowed. Suss remembers begging as a birthday present for the pink carpet which shows up on these canvases. A dollhouse appears across works, replicating interiors described in some of the artist's favorite children's books in ways that are, in her words, "familiar but magical."[11]

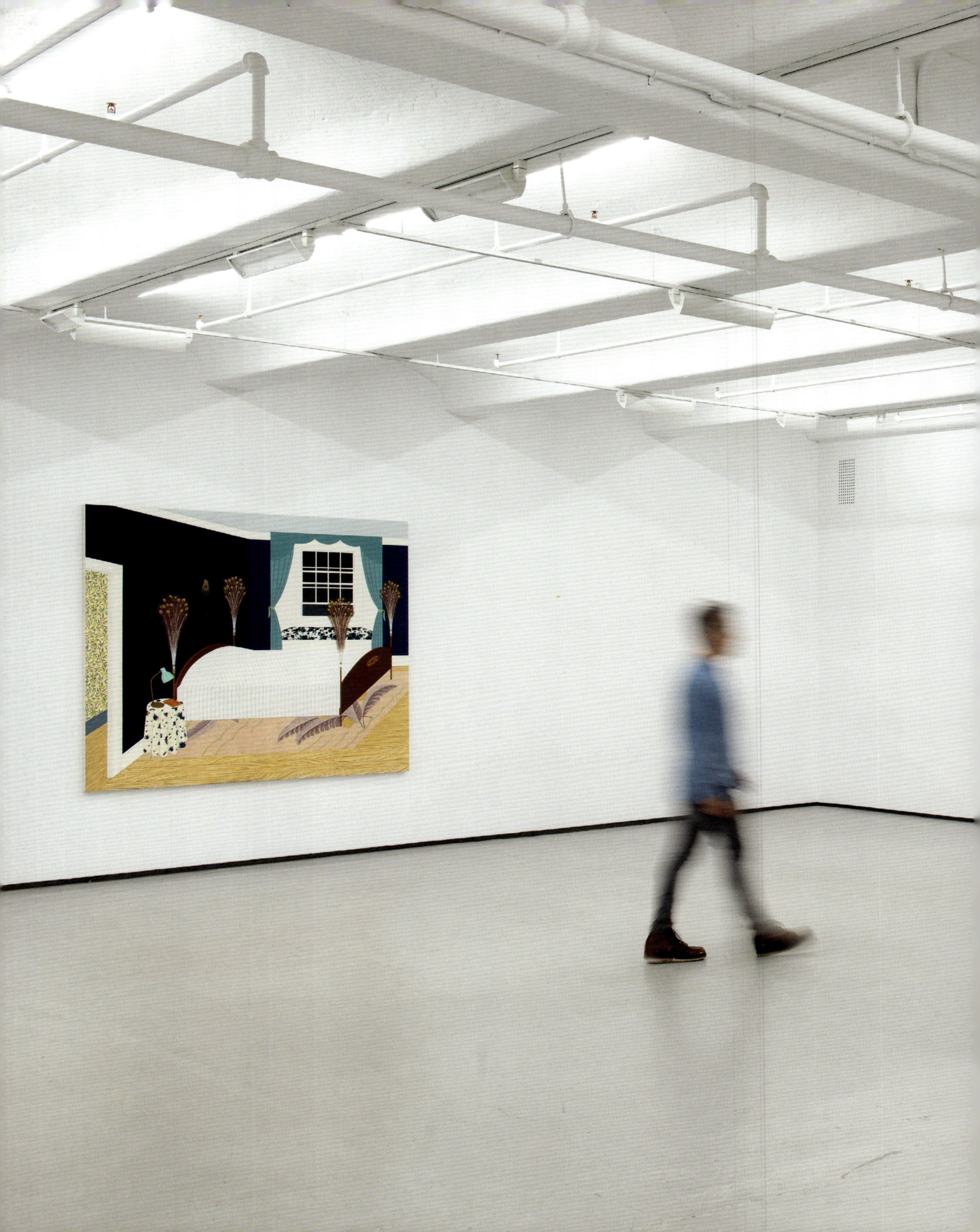

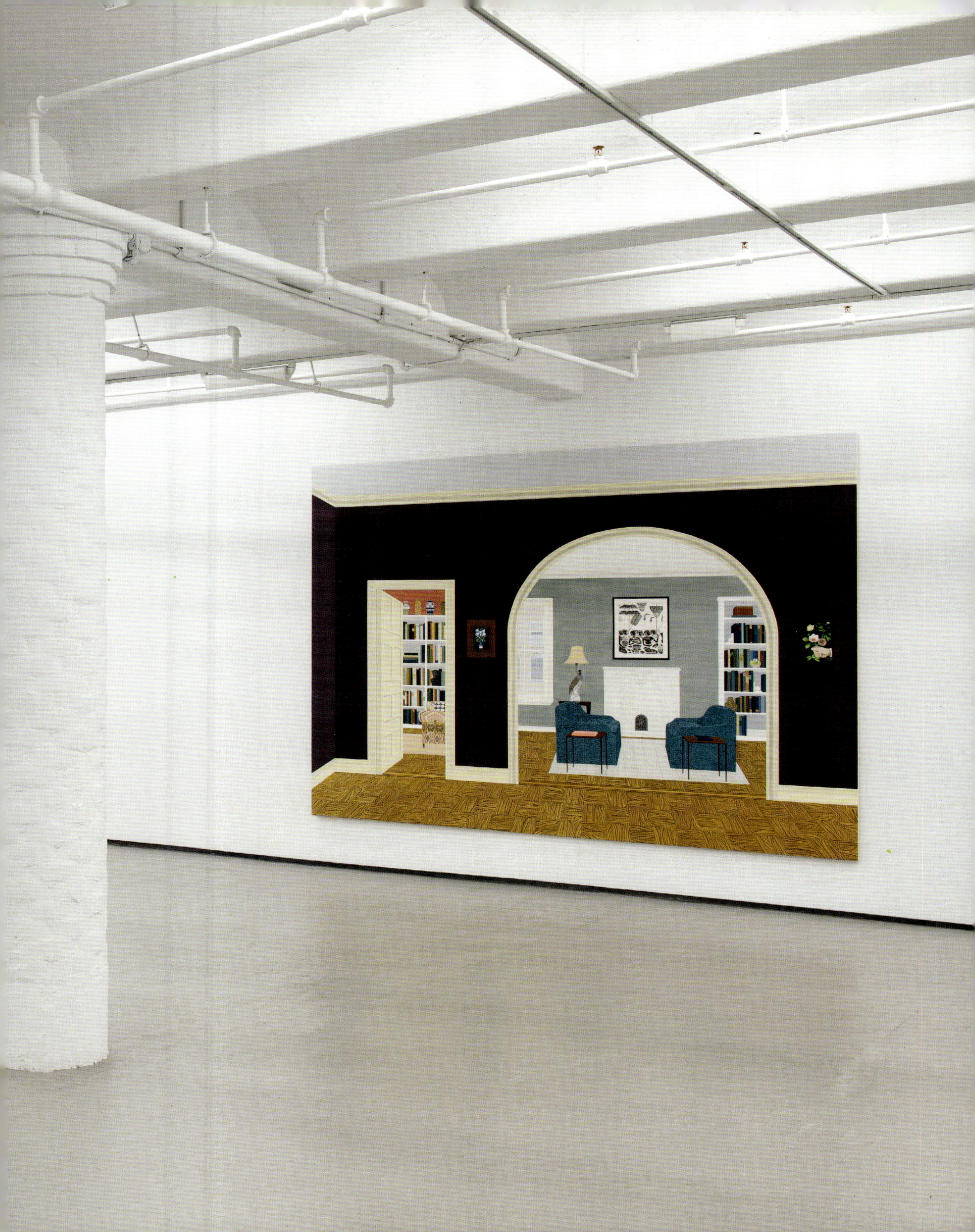

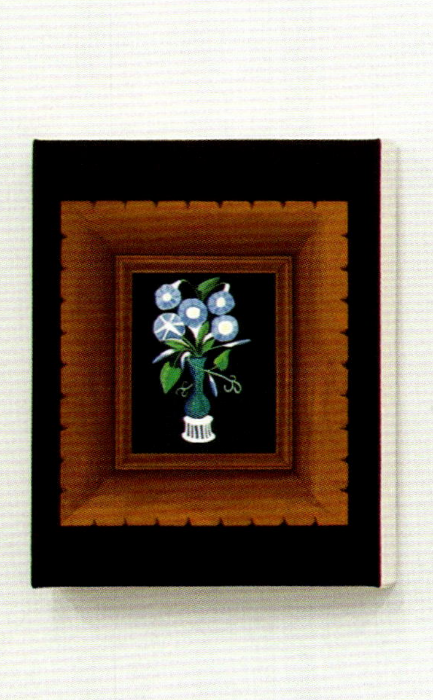

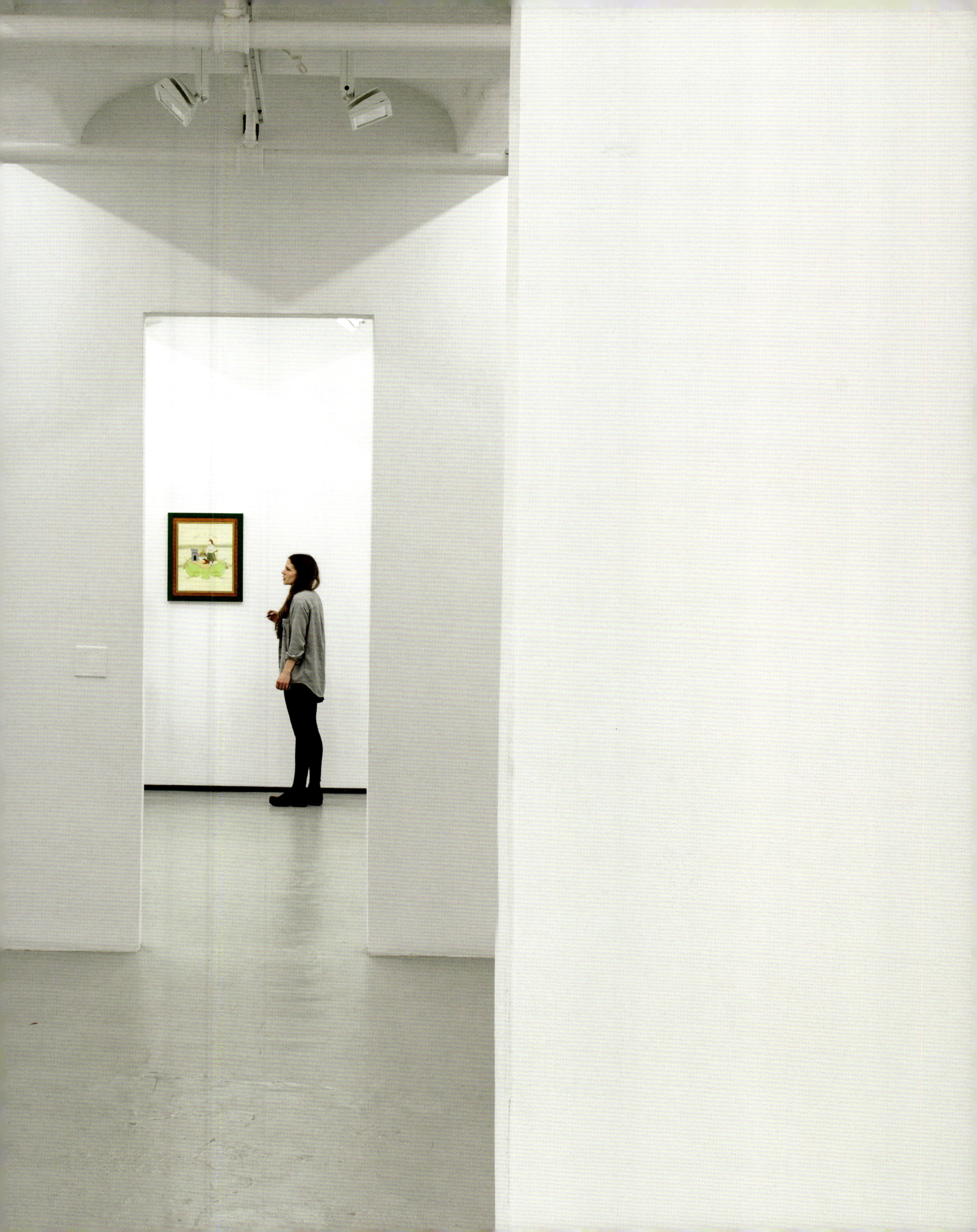

Books appear continually across Suss's paintings. Some of my favorites include towering shelved stacks in her grandparents' home in *Reading Room* (2012), the richly-colored *Book (Chagall, All Saints Church)* (2016), as well as the ceramic book towers that were presented as part of the artist's exhibition at the Philadelphia Institute of Contemporary Art in 2015. As she notes, she treats books as objects to paint because of the "weight that they carry . . . [there's] the content in between the pages, but there's also the idea of the book as a sentimental object . . . [and] what the book or knowledge can represent in society."[12]

From a 2018 suite of large and small scale works titled *Where They Are*, the painting, *WT, TJ, and Blinky* (2020), foregrounds children's literature as a lens through which we learn to live. Inflected by the teaching philosophies of the renowned inquiry-led student-focused training center of Bank Street Education School in New York, the books in this series of paintings are both titles handed down from the artist's own family and new ones she has sought out to read to Sid. Her small book paintings are object portraits that zero in on detail so carefully that they allow us to imagine the object living inside of the depicted space in larger paintings. Their framing as *things* that are touched and used usher them into the realm of craft.

Almost all of us can recall a book read to us as a child, or one of the first we read alone. Even as adults, we have many of them on our bookshelves. I return to them in the moments where I want to remember not only the storyline but the voice of those who brought their pages alive

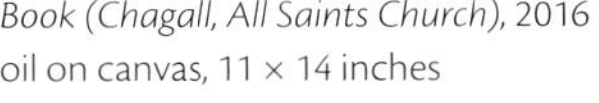

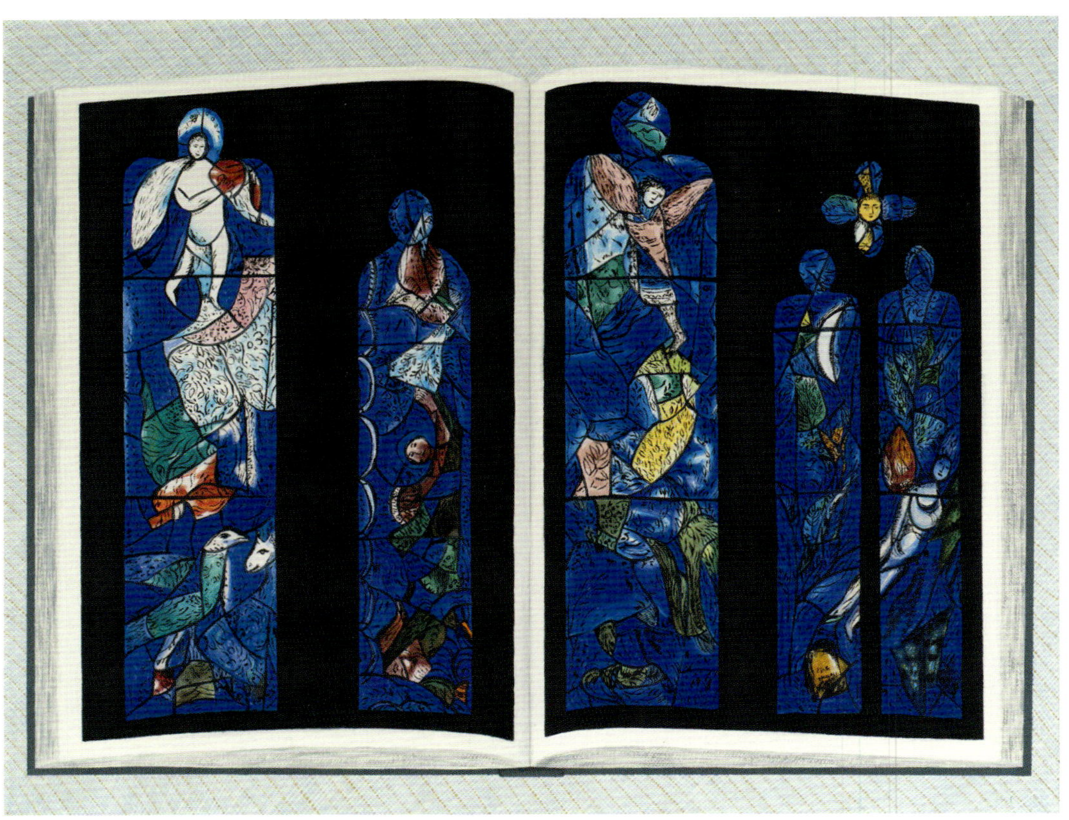

Book (Chagall, All Saints Church), 2016
oil on canvas, 11 × 14 inches

for me, or the illustrations my smaller fingers traced as I listened along. Suss notes that while these texts are so foundational to our lives and the formation of our identities and cultures, they're also rarely heralded in the same way as works of fiction and nonfiction for adults. The works of *Where They Are* ask us to consider children's rooms and literature, places that merge autobiography with fiction, as worthy of capturing and holding our attention, and reigniting our own imaginations.

***

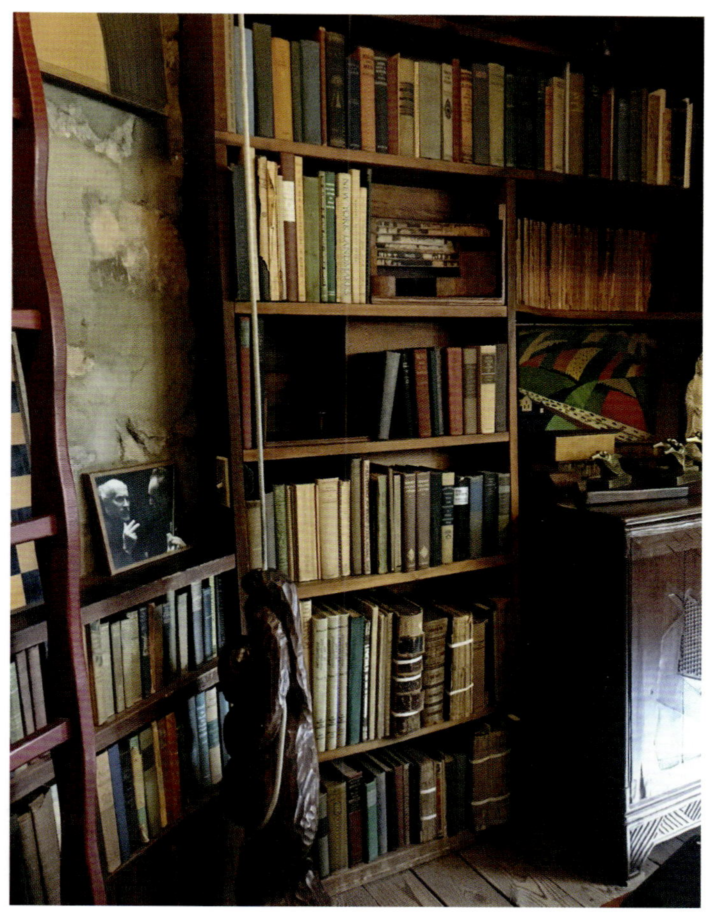

Bookshelf in bedroom
of the Wharton Esherick Museum
Courtesy of Becky Suss

Philadelphia, Suss's home city, is a place that has a proud legacy of craft and a thriving contemporary maker community. Wharton Esherick is one of the city's best kept secrets. He is often dubbed "the father of the American studio craft movement," the bridge between nineteenth century Arts and Crafts traditions and the contemporary renaissance of craft amongst American artists living today. Yet, fewer than might be expected make the pilgrimage to his home and studio a short car ride away in Paoli, Pennsylvania. It's a magical haven of twisted and turned wood forms, carefully preserved interiors, and bucolic peony-laden landscapes. On a visit there a few years ago, Suss's imagination was sparked, resulting in what became an informal artist residency, the first of it's kind in the Museum's history.

The series of paintings she created in response to Esherick's home and studio were exhibited at Fleisher/Ollman in 2018. The presentation firmly rebelled against the artificial distinction between art and craft. Pieces from Esherick's own home on loan for the occasion provided punctuation for the paintings on the walls, from handwrought wooden stools to a maquette of a library.[13] Visitors to Esherick's home and studio are encouraged to run their hands over the works, a tactile impulse that Suss notes is immediately lost when objects are transported from the everyday into a gallery context. By arranging her paintings in relationship with works that can be touched, she made painting accessible, especially to those who did not bring familiarity with art history to the encounter. Her juxtapositions led the paintings to behave like their three-dimensional counterparts.

It feels more germane to contextualize Suss within architecture, design, and craft histories rather than reaching first for precedent in people who have painted or collaged interiors. So many of the obvious compositional comparisons (Hockney, Matisse) or artists dealing in tactility and alterity (Louise Bourgeois) or the politics of the home (Martha Rosler) fall short of the *thingness* of Suss's work. But there is also a profoundly emotional and completely abstract element to this work, too.

***

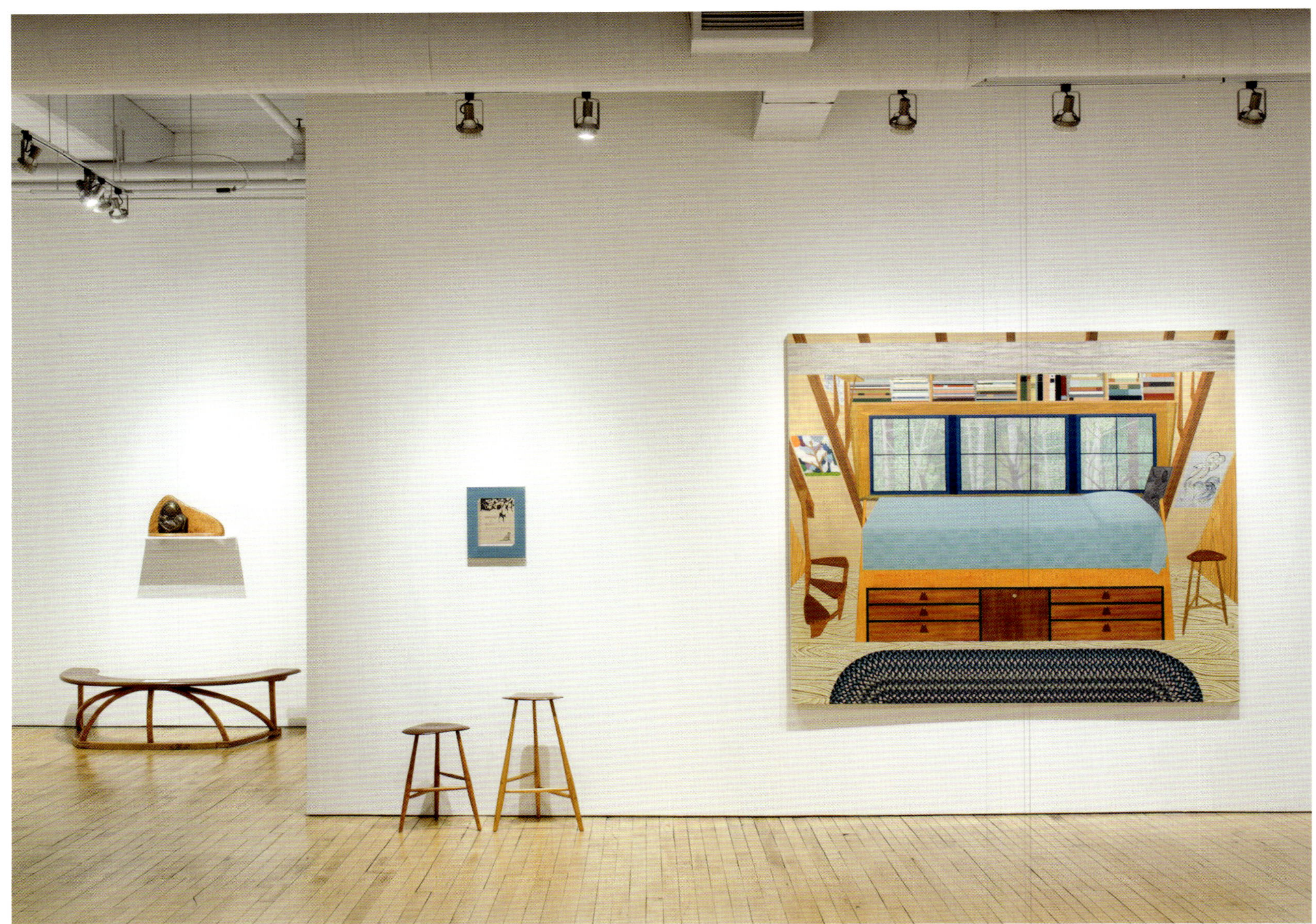

Installation view of *Becky Suss/Wharton Esherick*, Fleisher/Ollman Gallery, Philadelphia, 2018

I turned to Shelley Klein's history of High Sunderland above not just because it is the same age as Suss's grandparent's house or, like the artist's own contingent relationship with the truth and fiction of a place, Klein oscillates between dredged remembrance and matter of fact. I turned to Klein because of her invocation of the Old Norse term "hefting," used by Scottish farmers to imply a deeply-rooted belonging to a landscape. Sheep that are hefted "carry within them an instinctive understanding of their surroundings . . . over the years the land becomes mapped in their blood and intuitively they recognize each stony pathway, each hillside and rocky decline." It is the knowledge that is passed on to their young each generation, an "ancient way of moving through the landscape."[14]

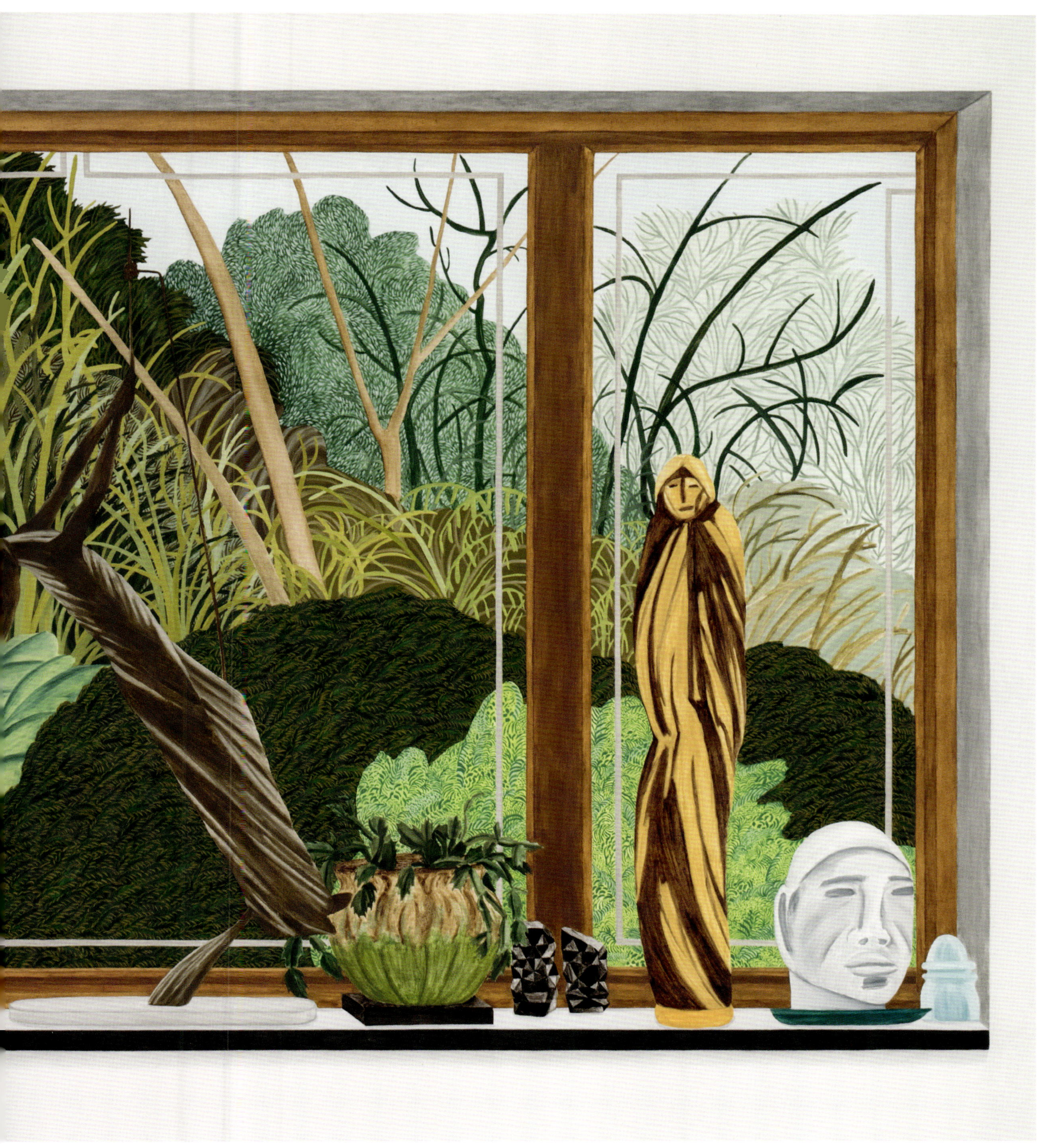

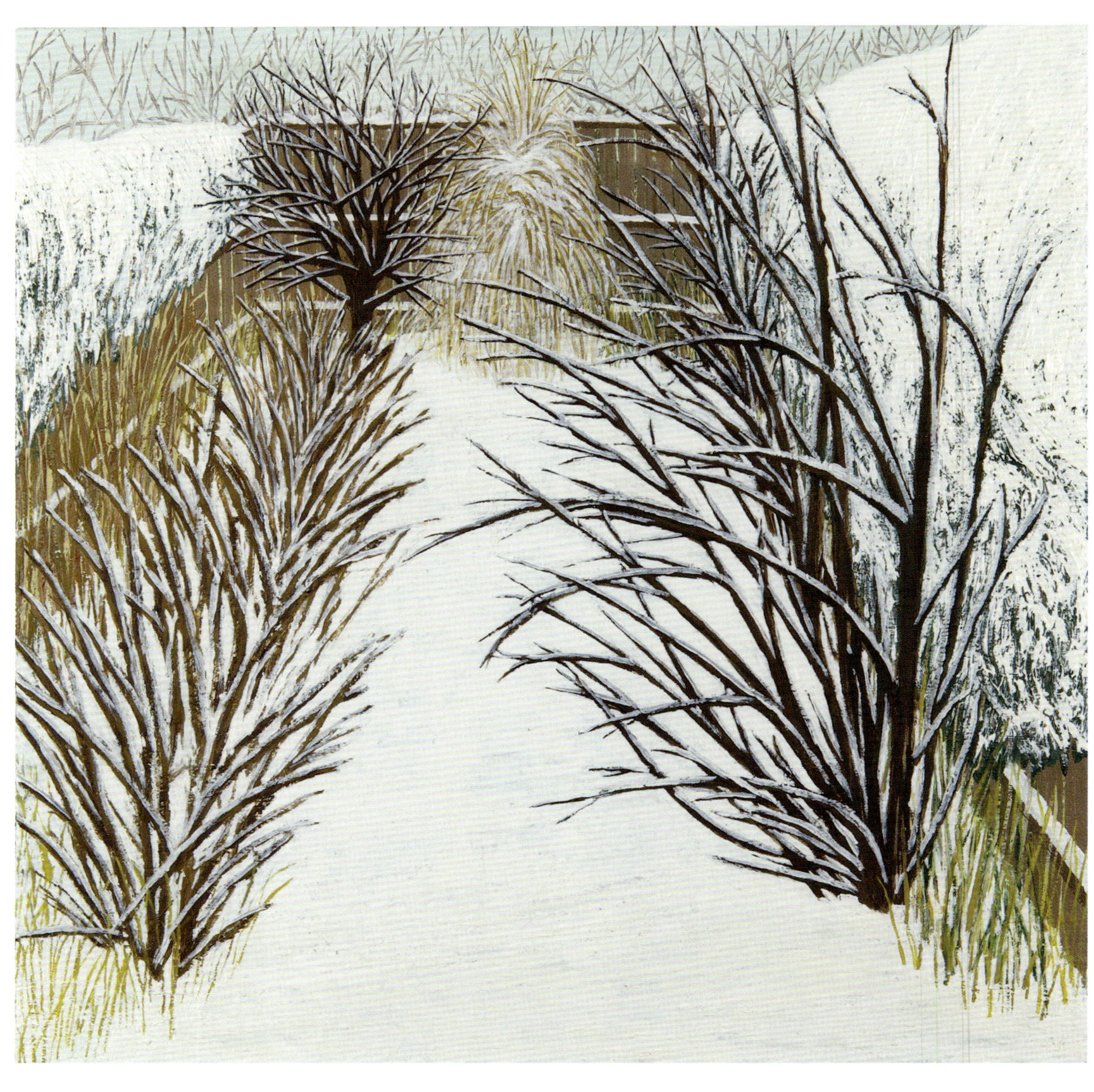

Kensington, Winter, 2010
oil on linen
16 × 16 inches

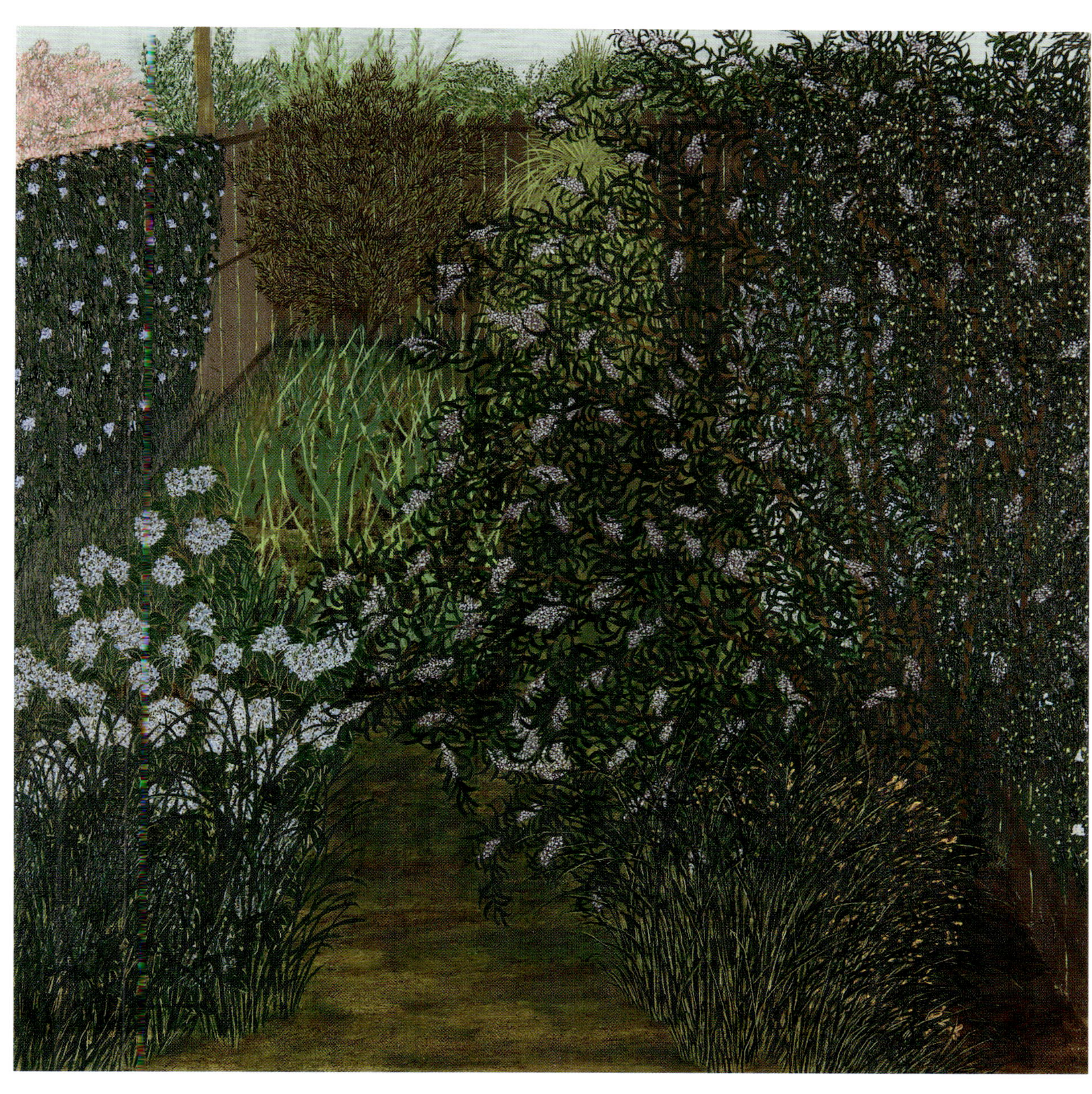

Kensington, Summer, 2010–11
oil on canvas
16 × 16 inches

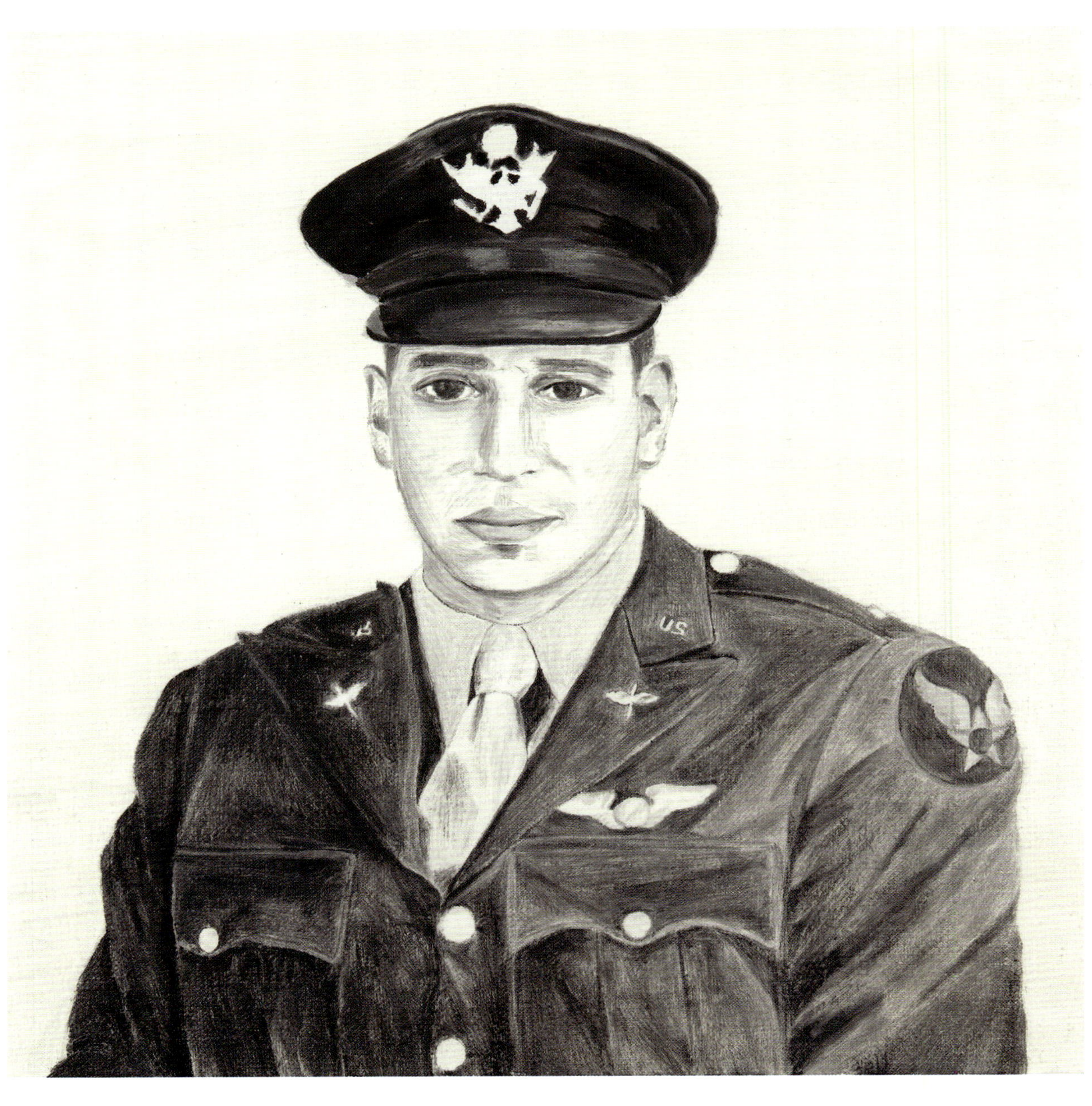

1943-44, 2012
oil on linen
14 × 14 inches

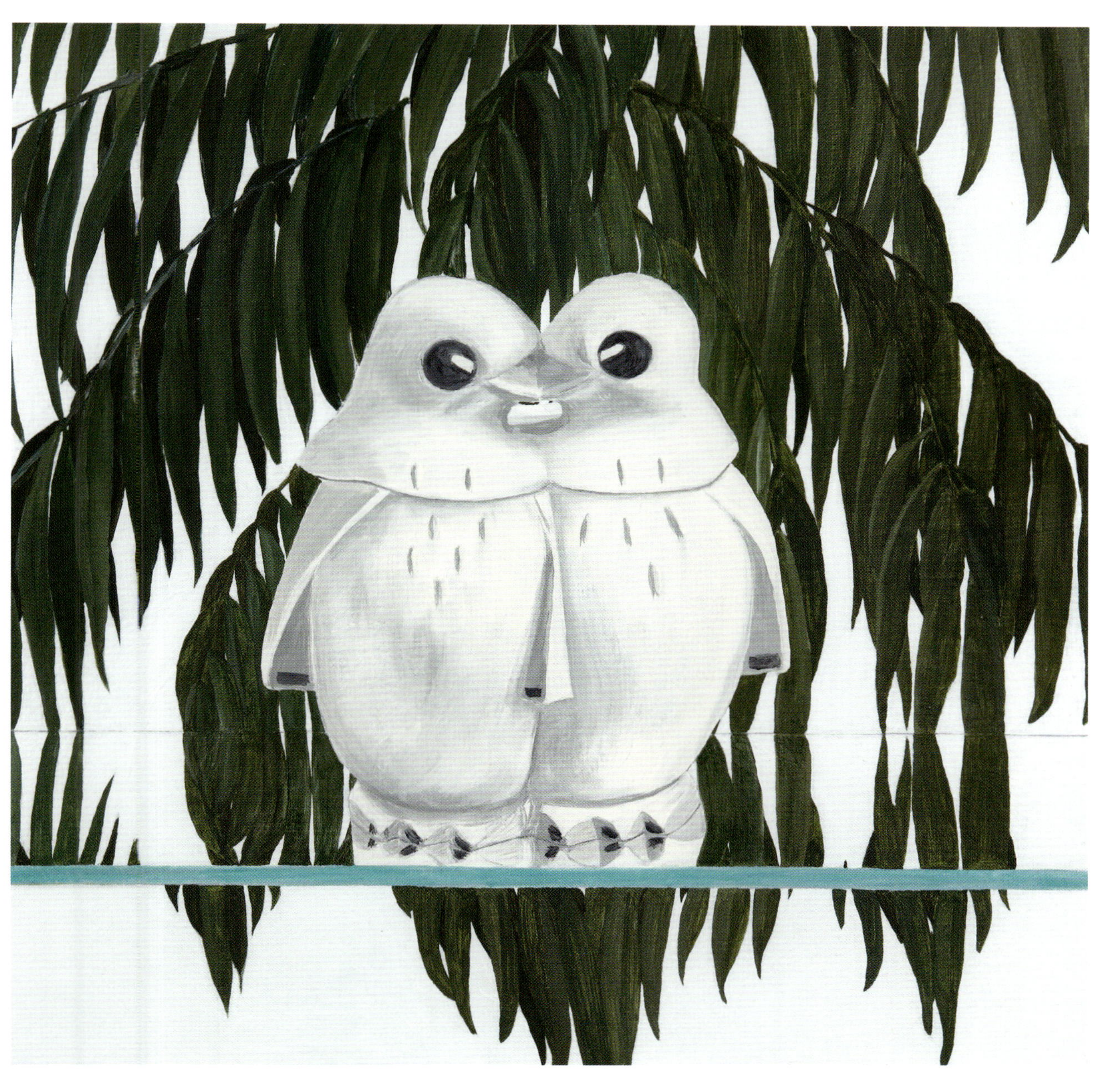

Cookie Jar, 2012
oil on canvas
16 × 16 inches

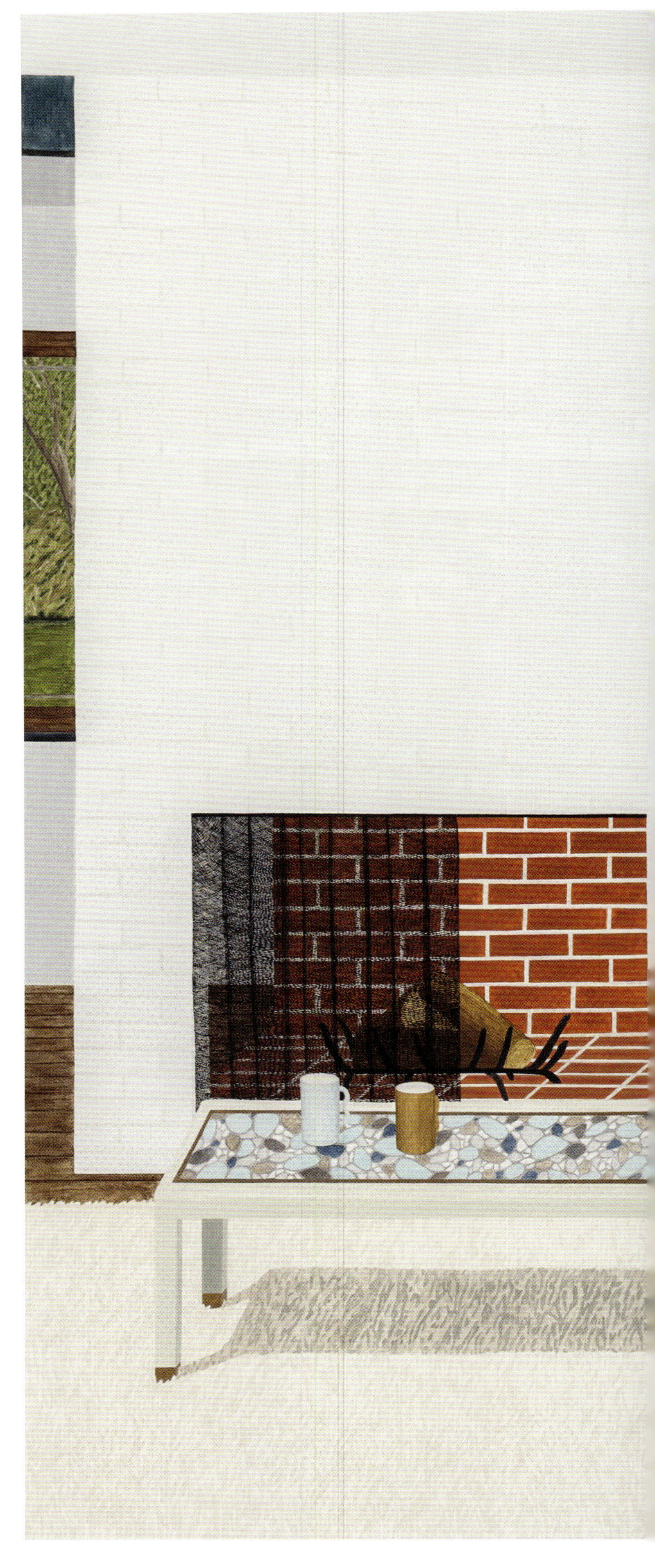

Living Room (blue chair), 2013
oil on linen
60 × 72 inches

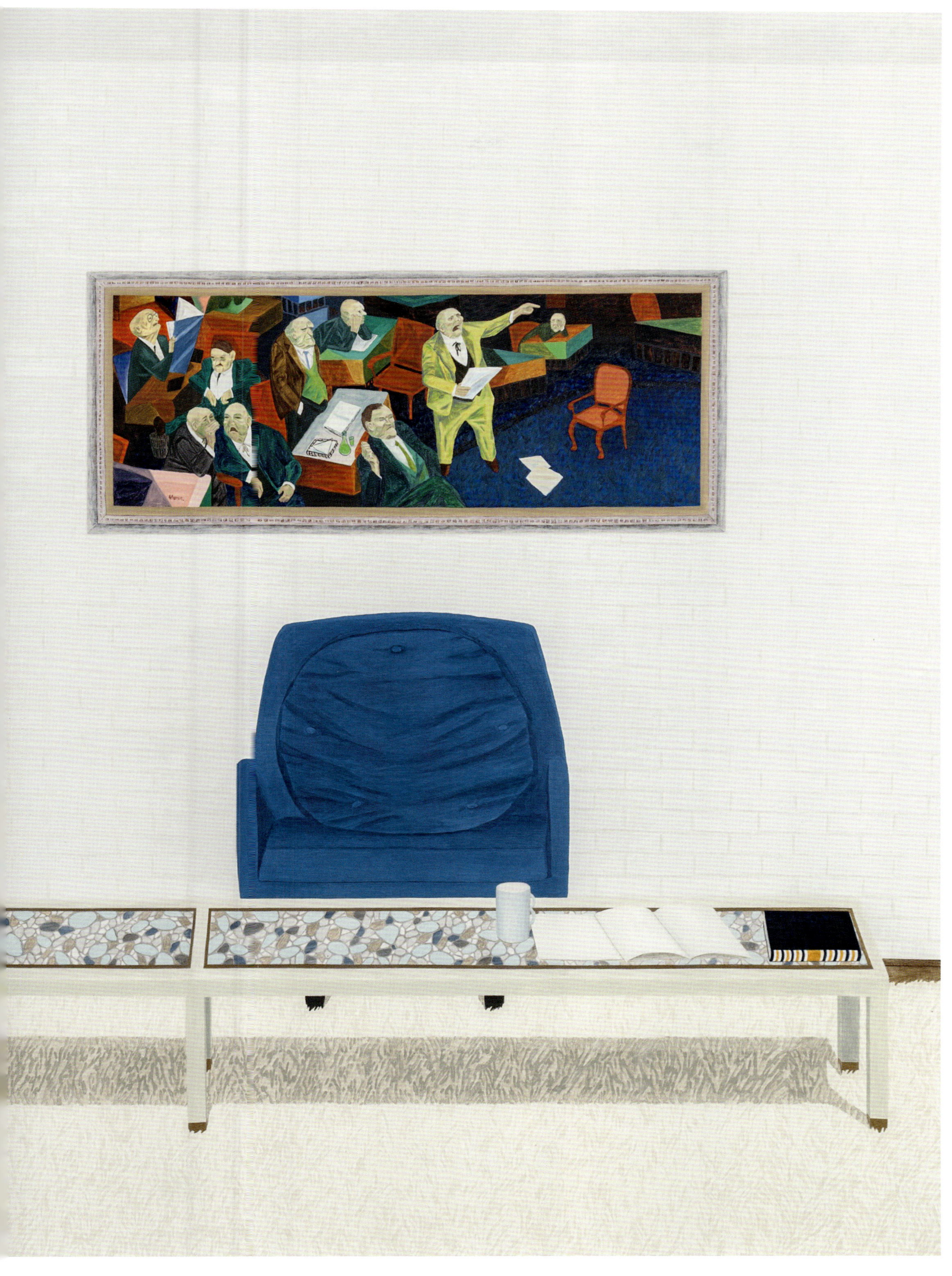

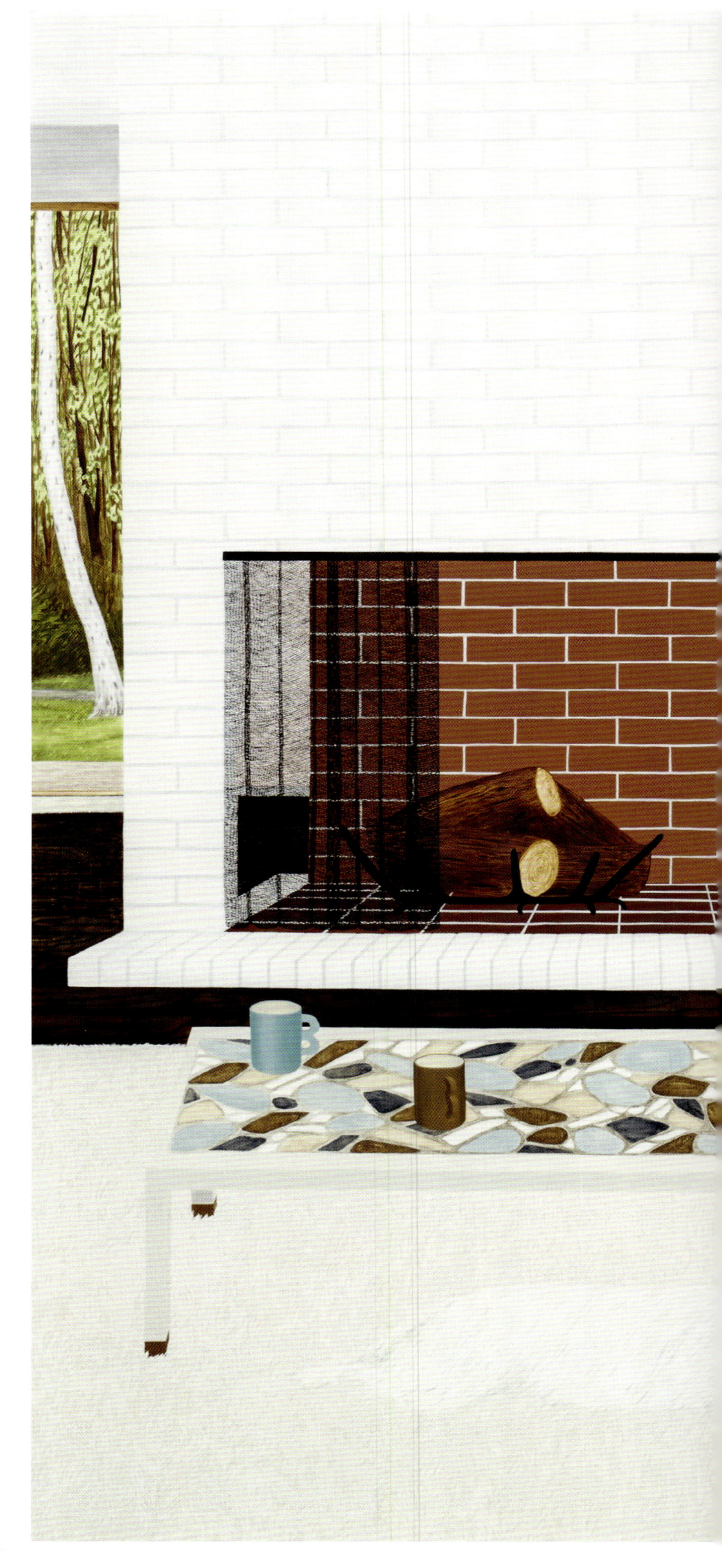

Living Room (Yogi 2), 2013
oil on linen
72 × 96 inches

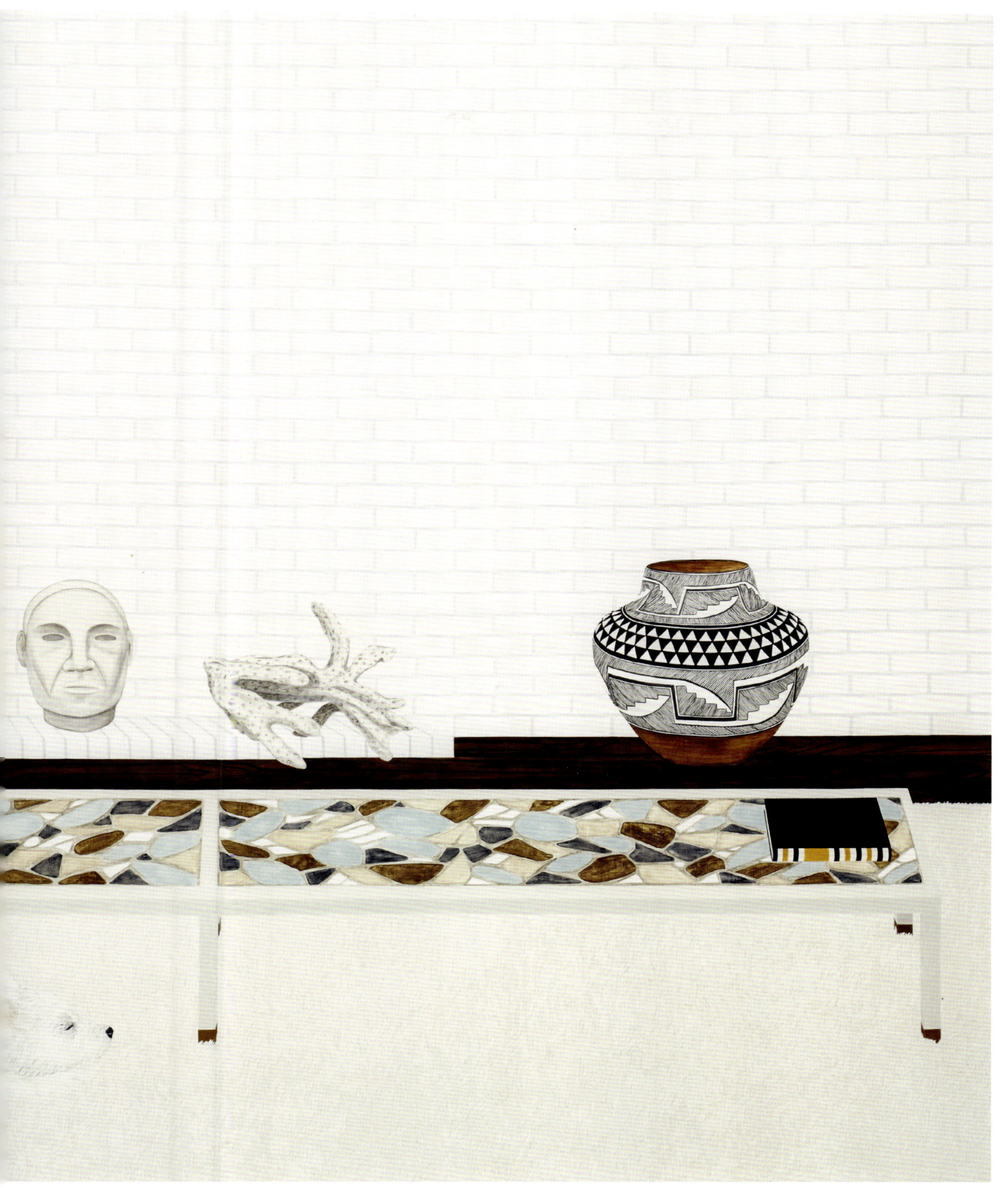

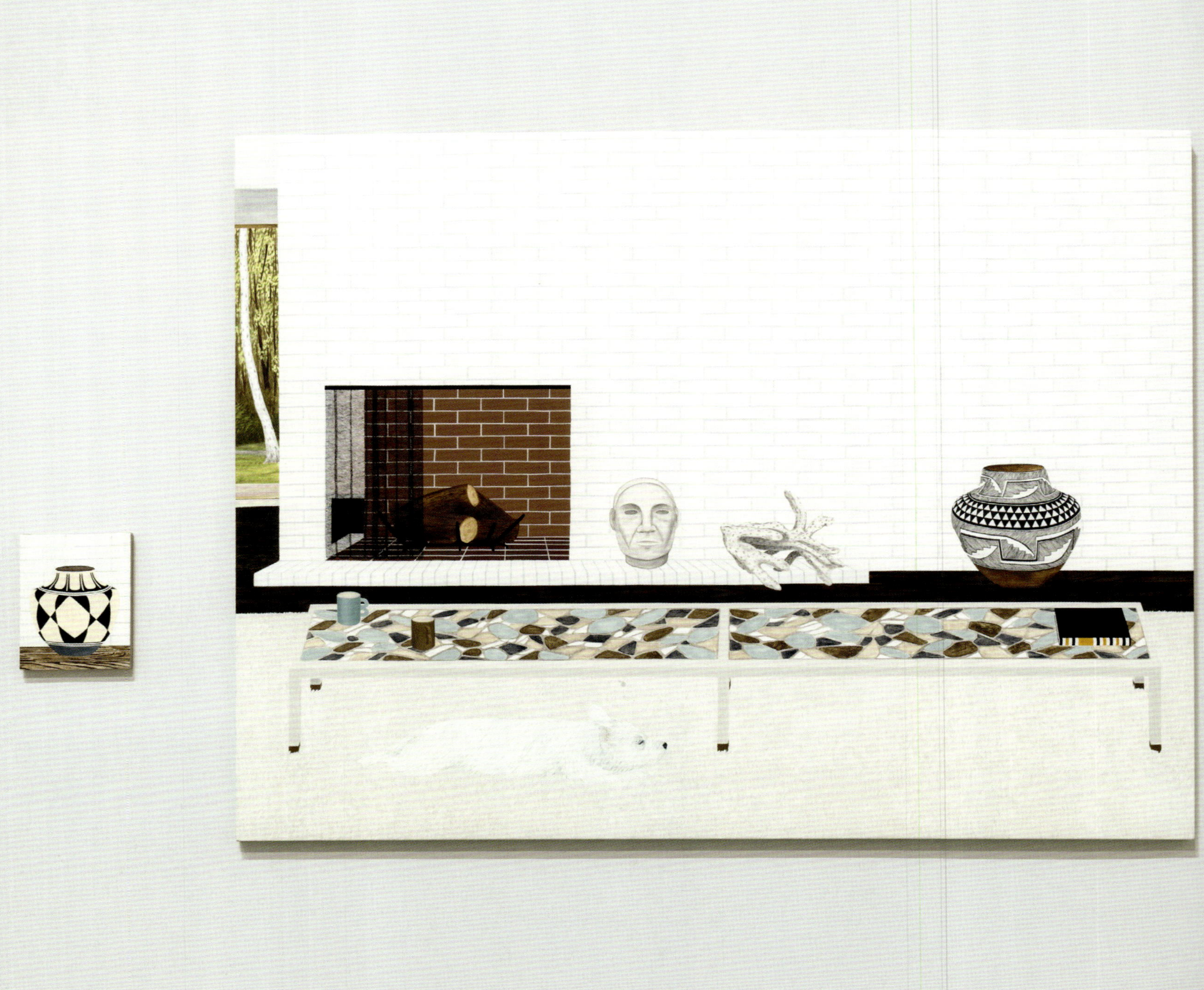

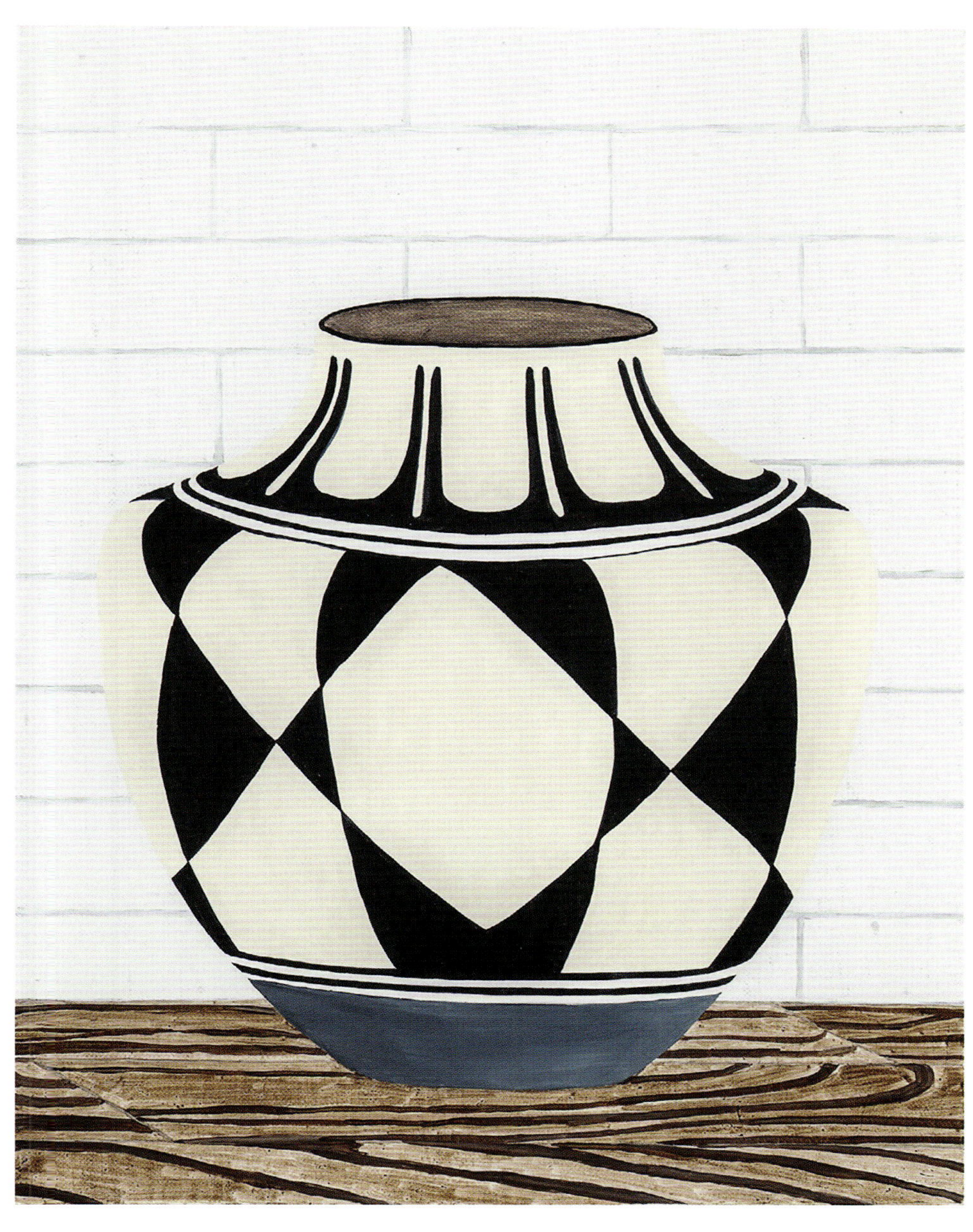

Installation view of *Becky Suss*, Institute of Contemporary Art, University of Pennsylvania, 2015

Pueblo Pot, 2013
oil on linen
14 × 11 inches

1919 Chestnut (Three Cities, Kiddush Hashem, Salvation, the Apostle, Mary, Nazarene), 2015
oil on canvas
84 × 60 inches

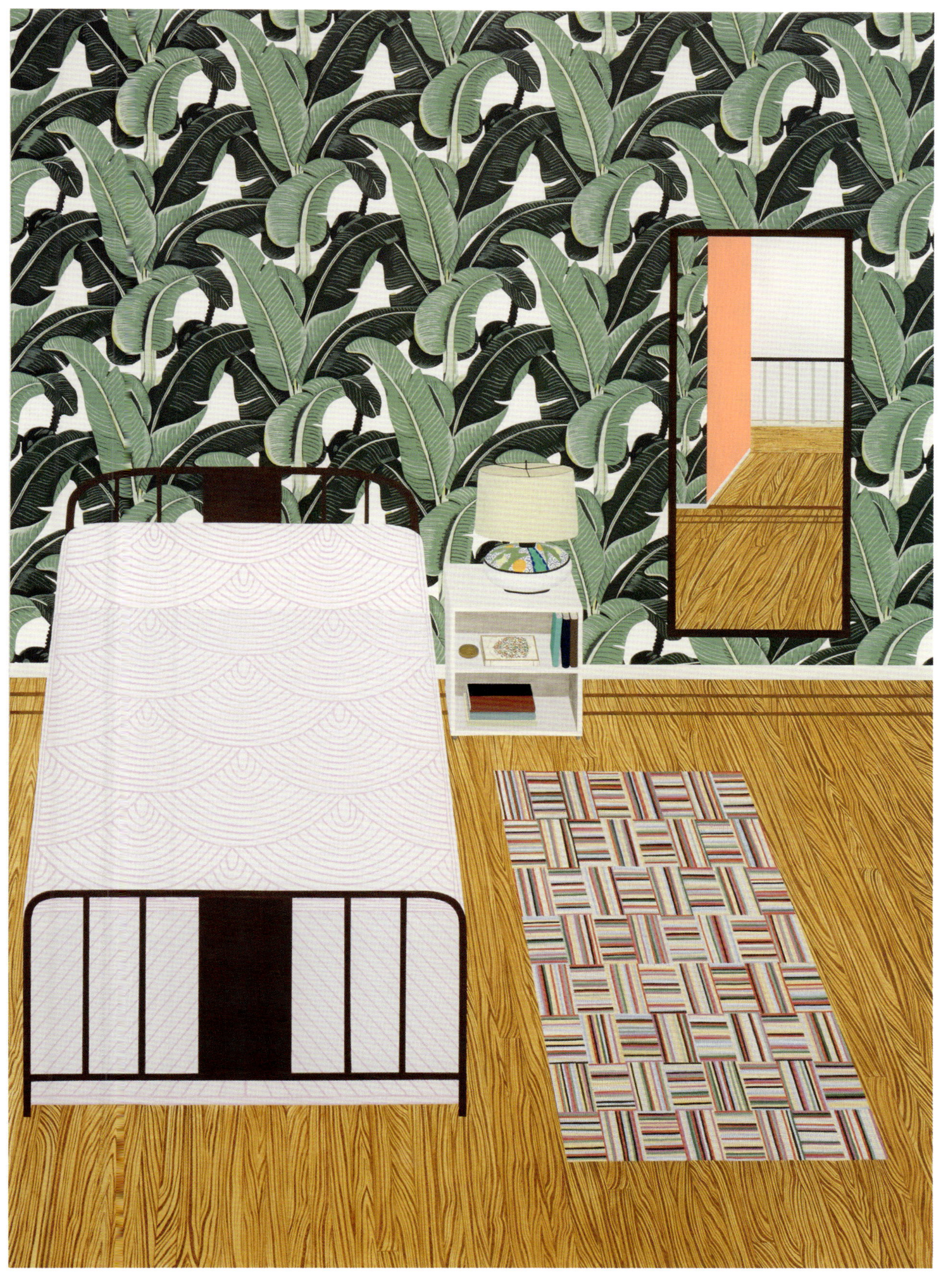

Installation view of *Becky Suss*, Institute of Contemporary Art, University of Pennsylvania, 2015

Bedroom, 2013
oil on canvas
84 × 60 inches

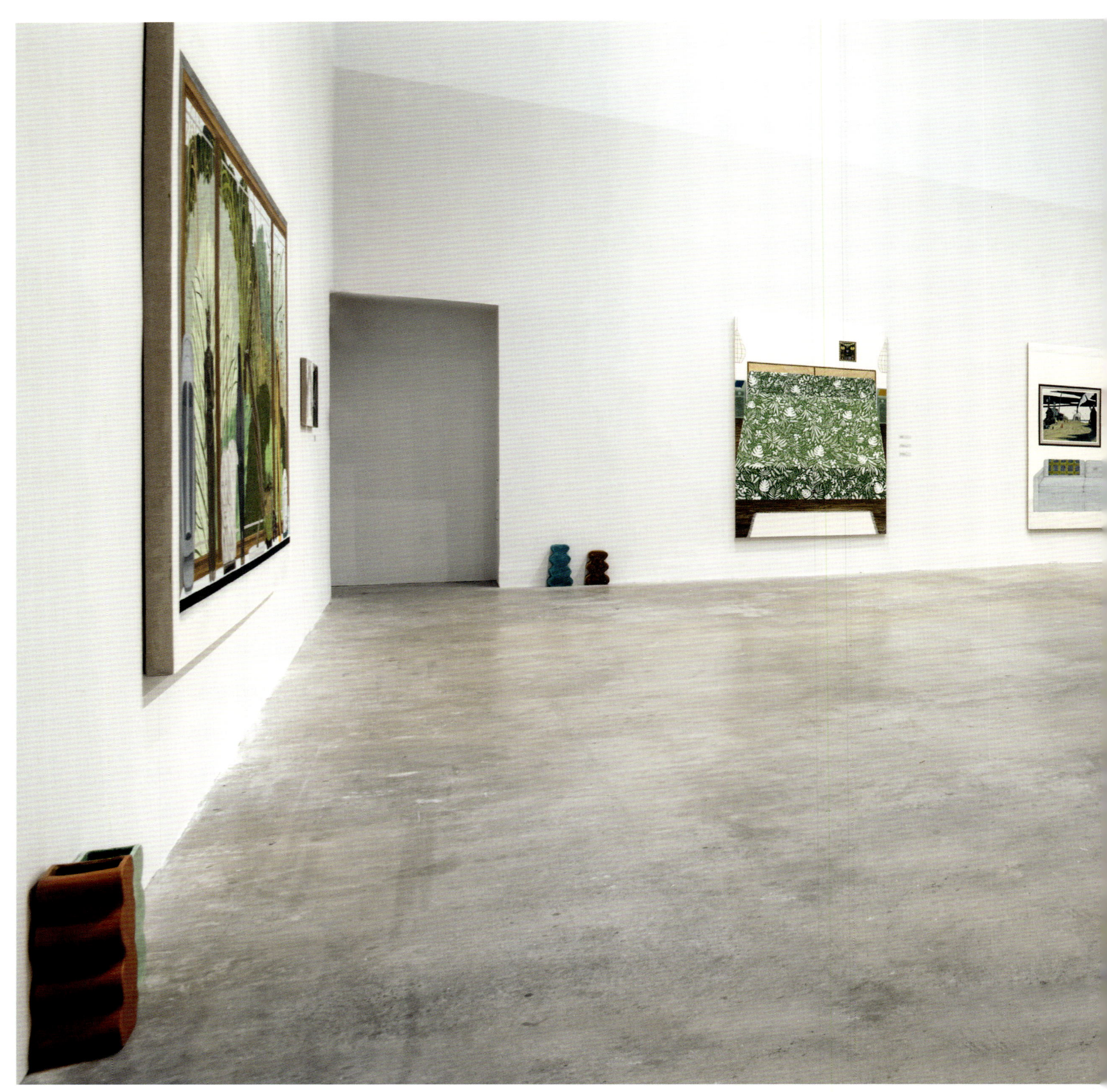

Installation view of *Becky Suss*, Institute of Contemporary Art, University of Pennsylvania, 2015

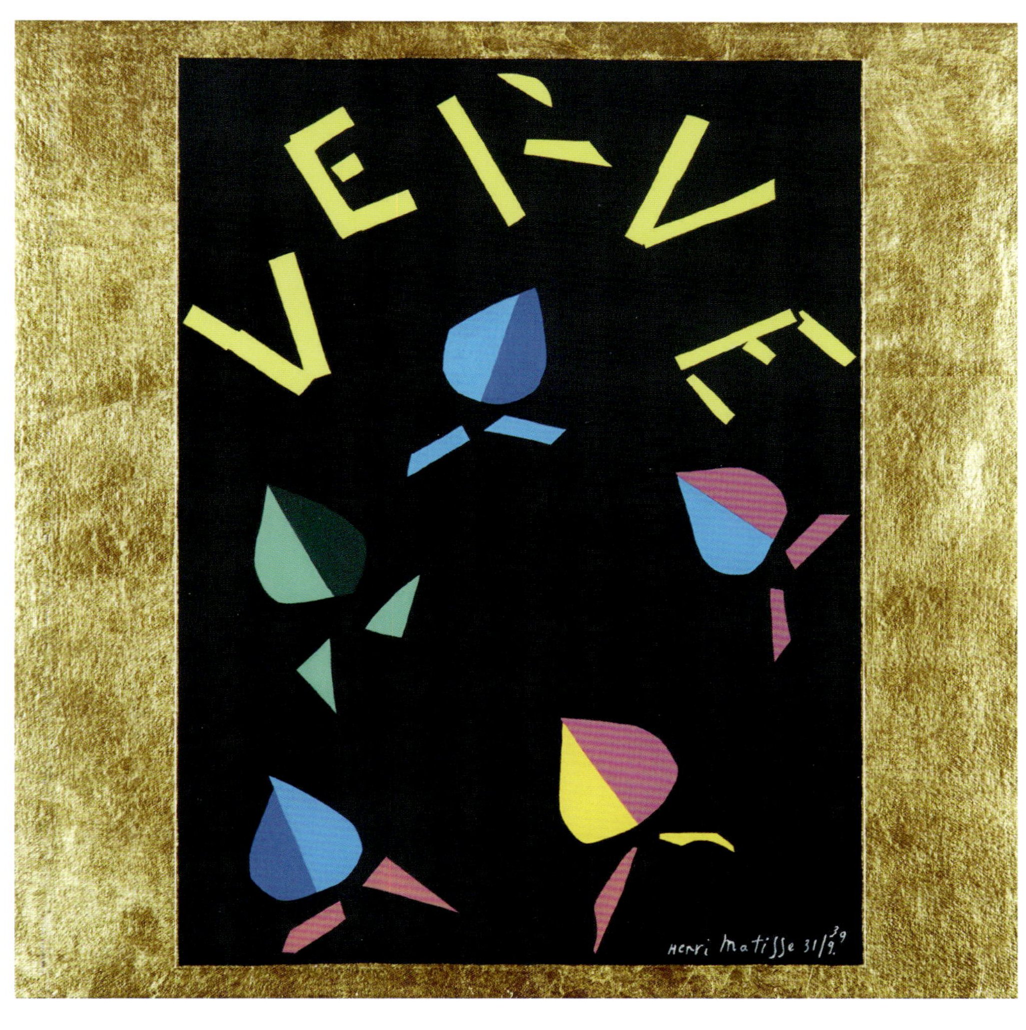

Installation view of *Becky Suss*, Institute of Contemporary Art, University of Pennsylvania, 2015

Wartime Issue (Henri Matisse, Verve Magazine, Vol. 2, No. 8), 2015
oil on canvas with 22-carat gold leaf
14 × 14 inches

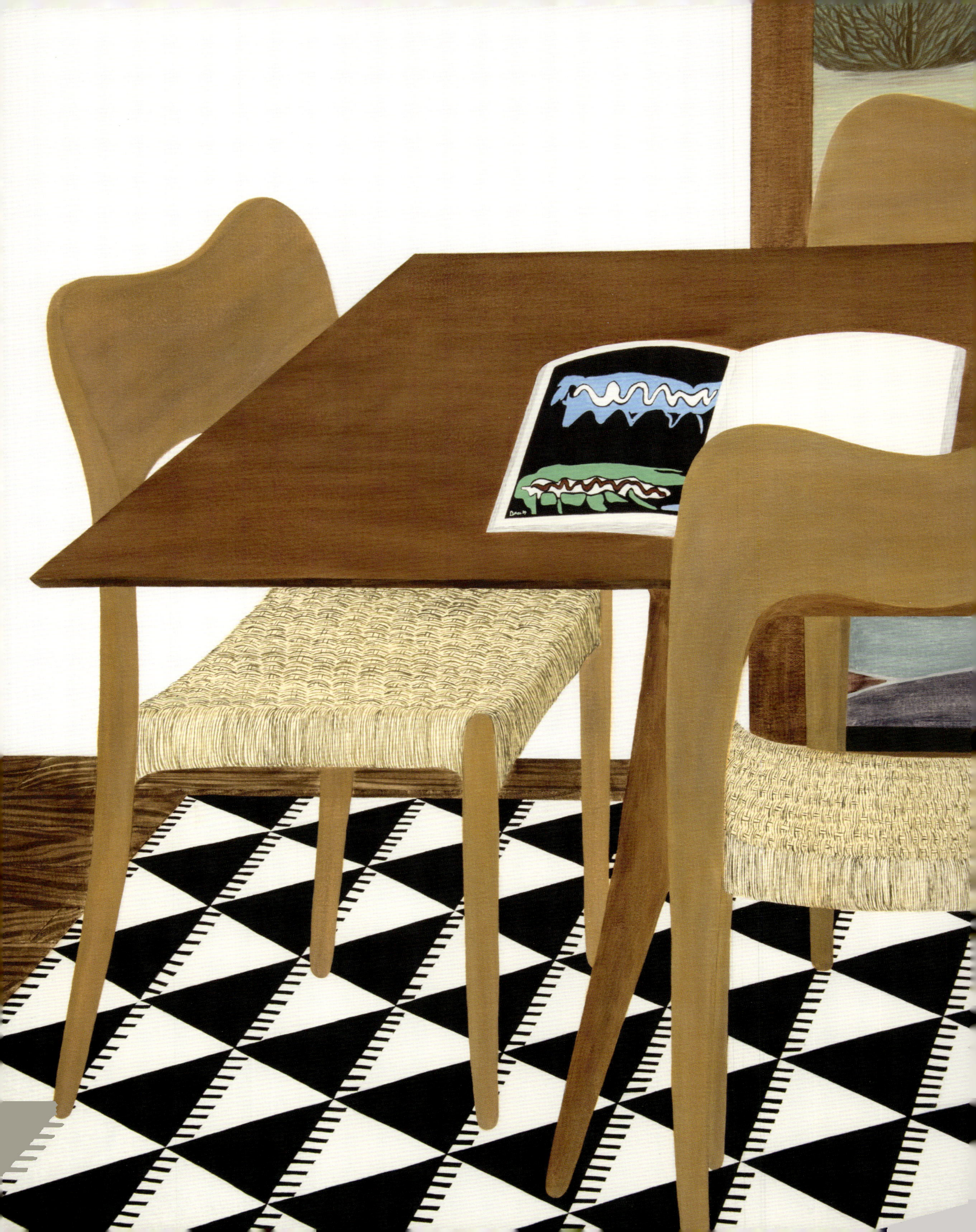

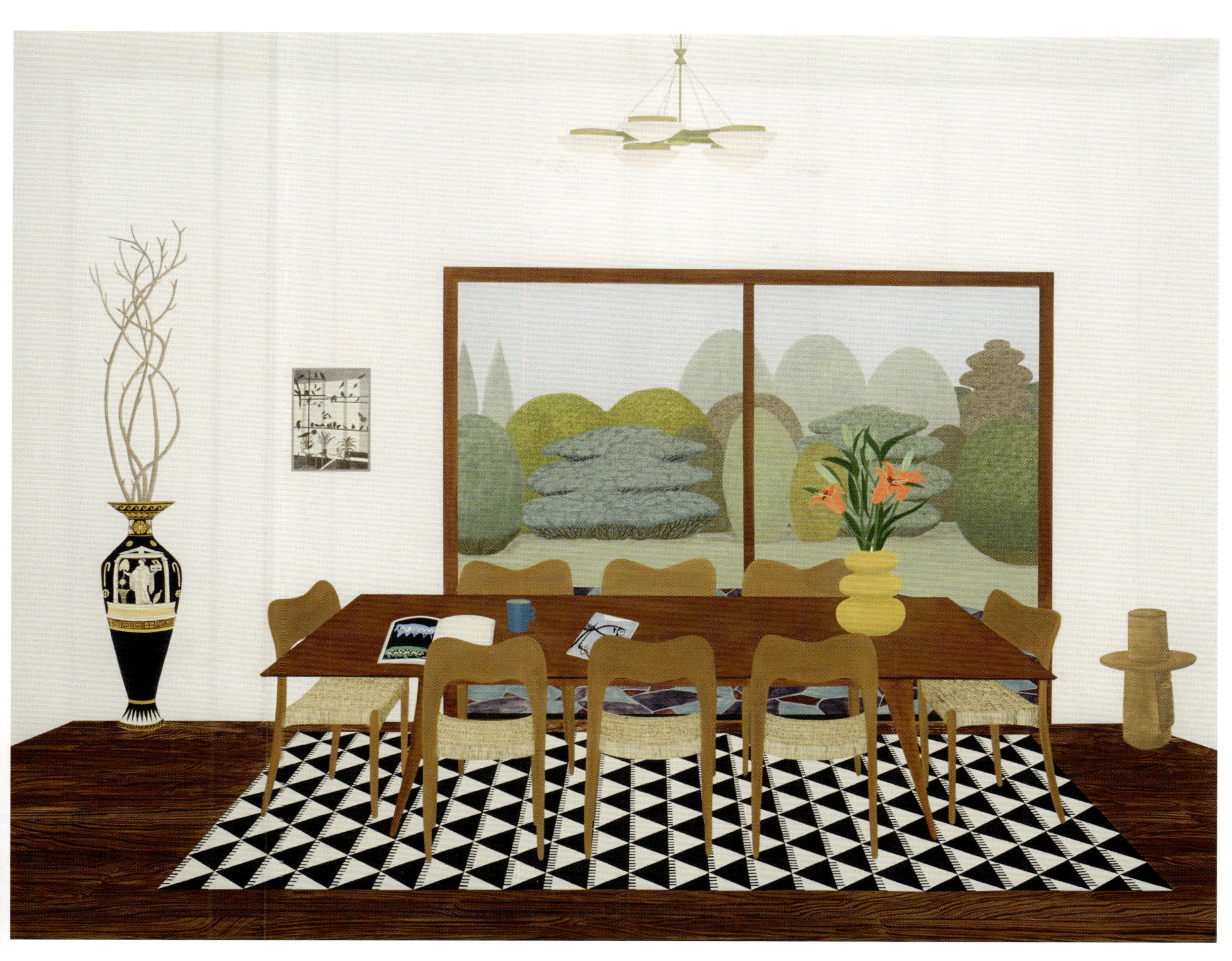

Dining Room (Verve Magazine, Vol. 1, Nos. 1 and 2), 2015
oil on canvas
84 × 108 inches

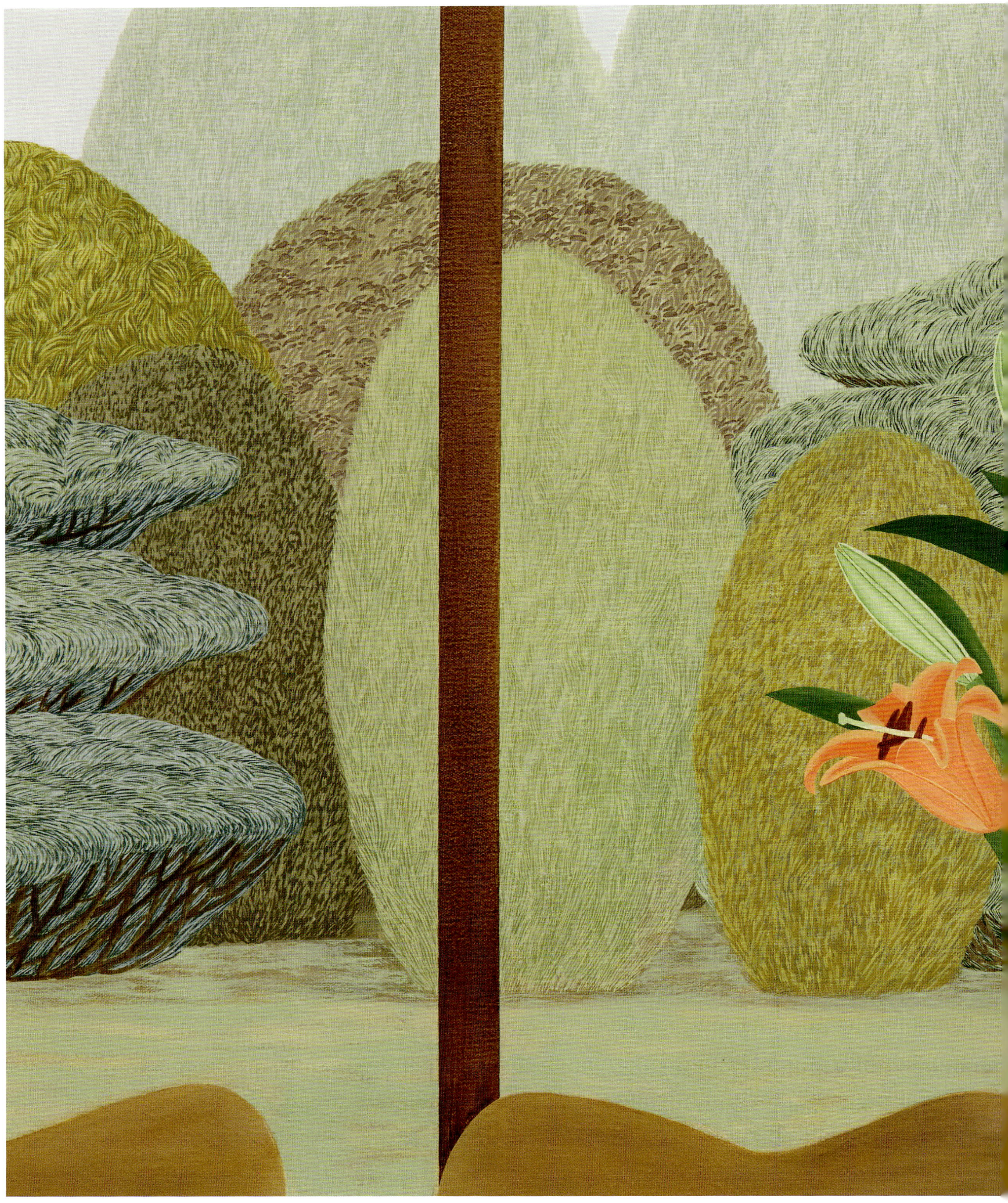

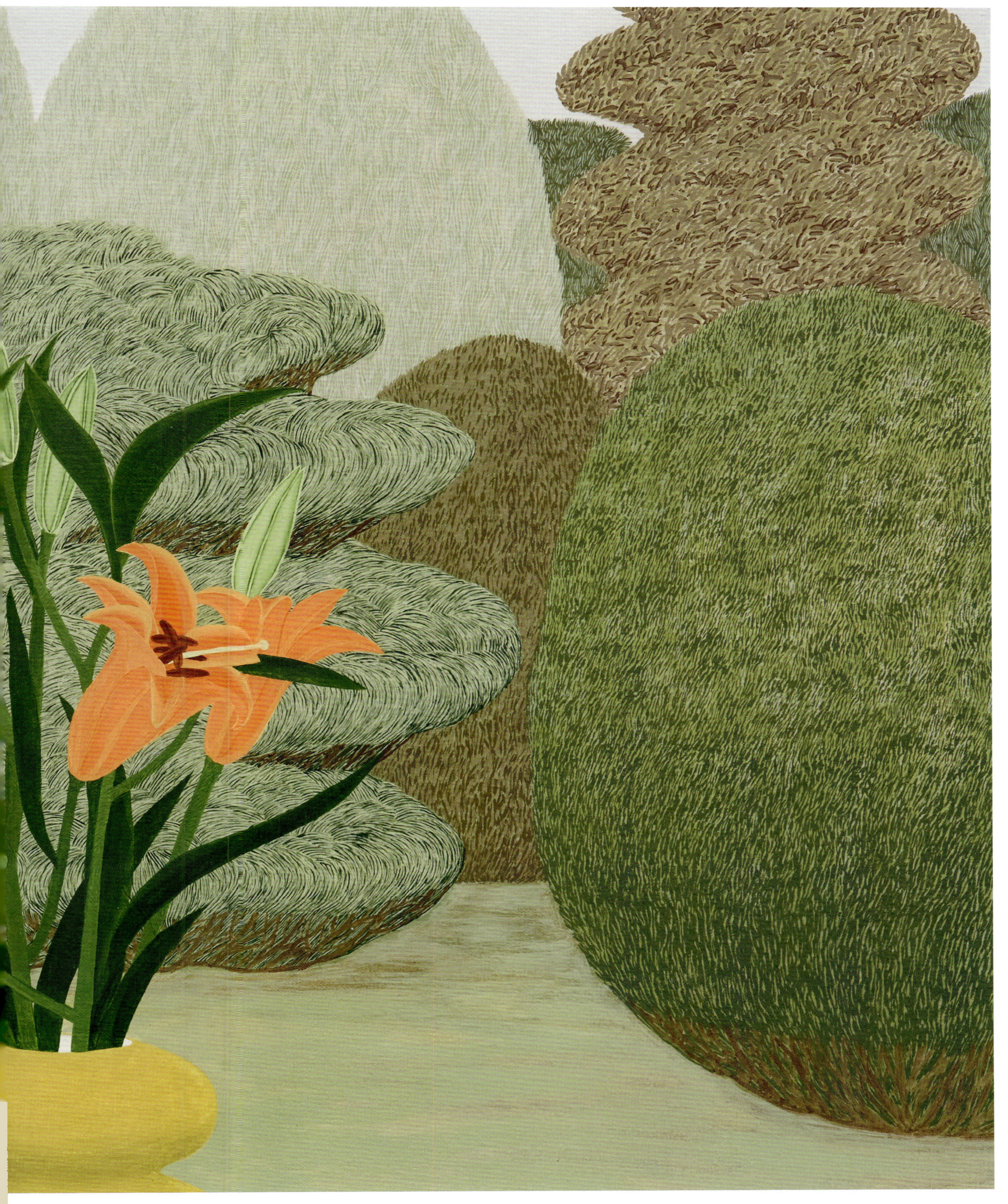

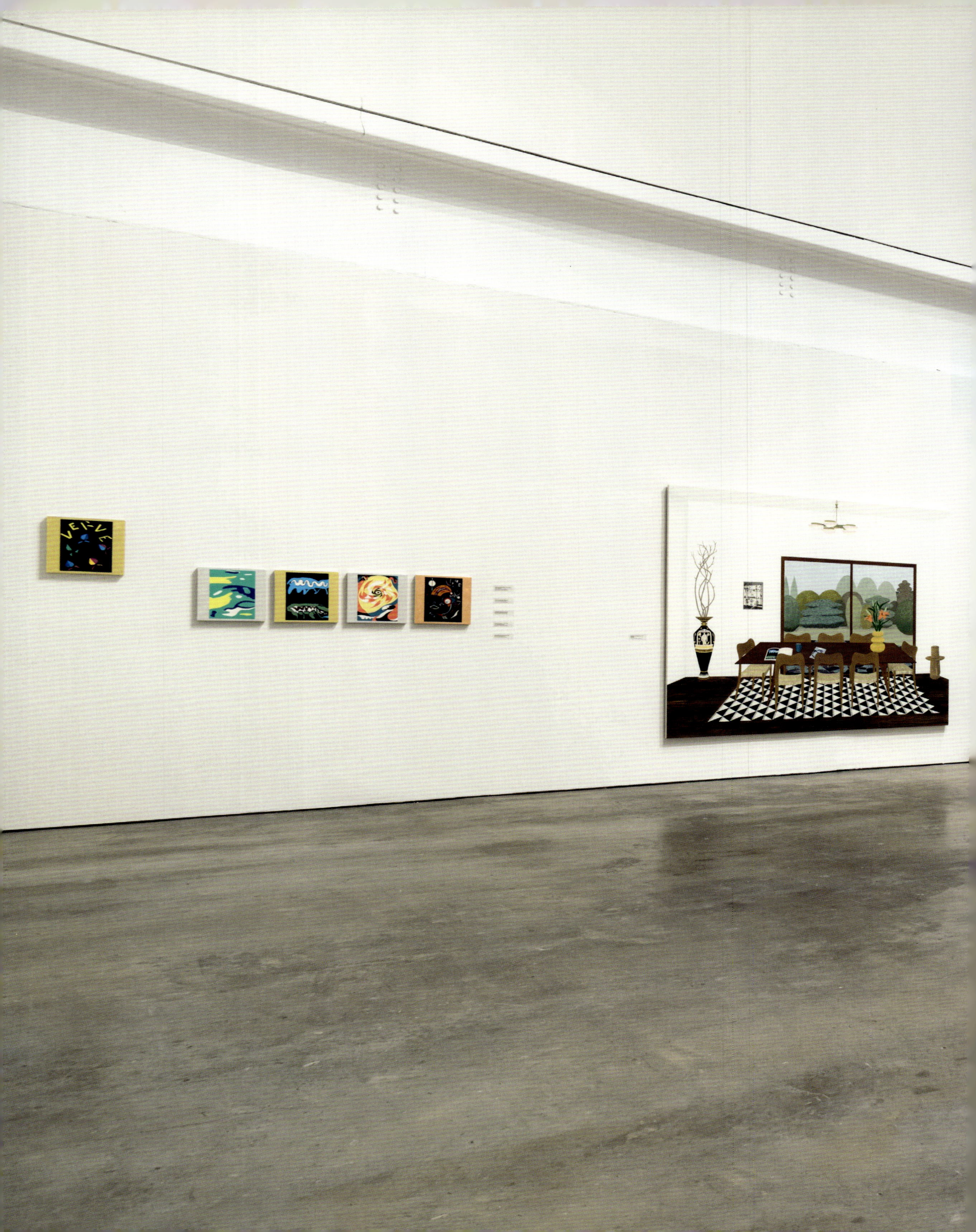

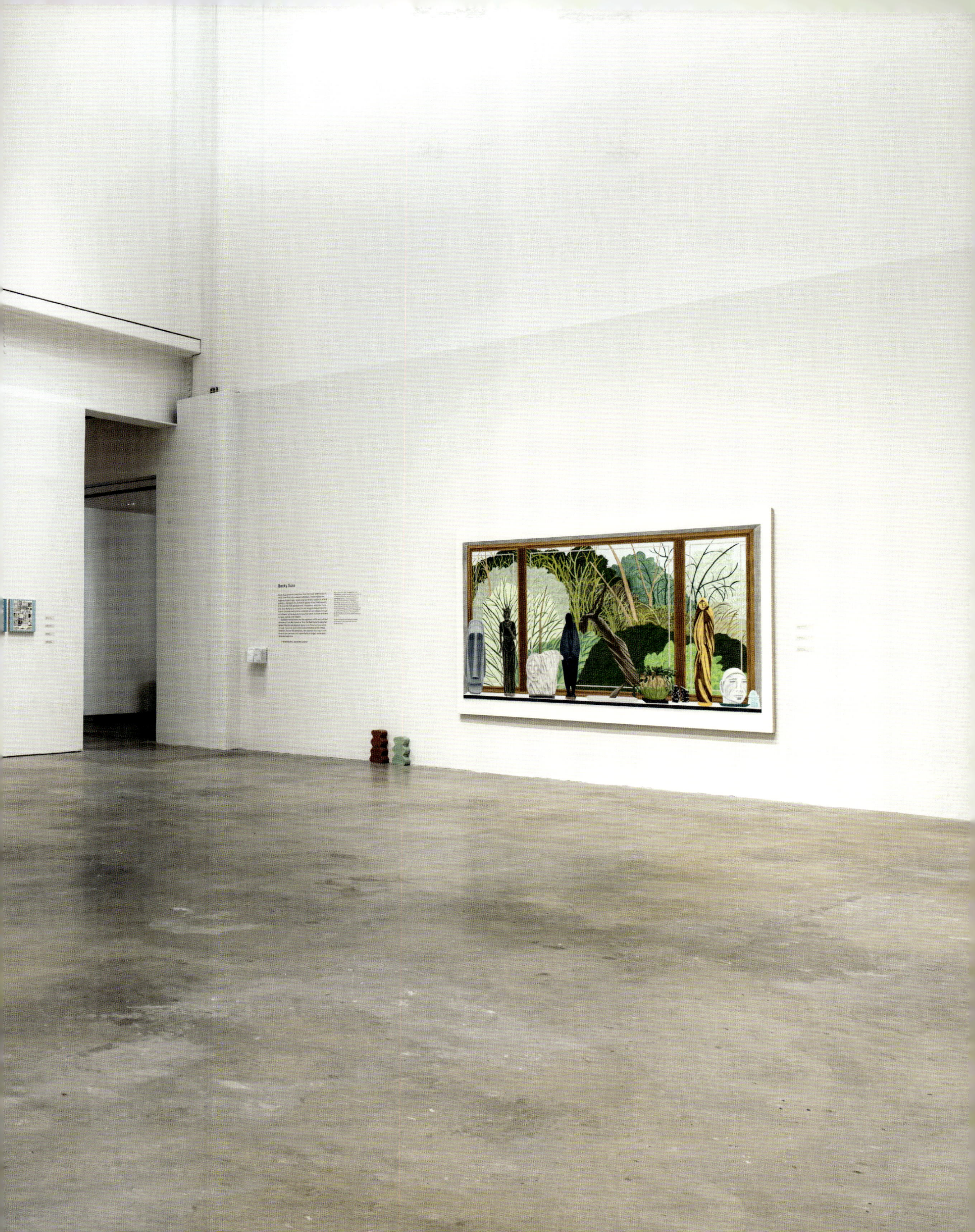

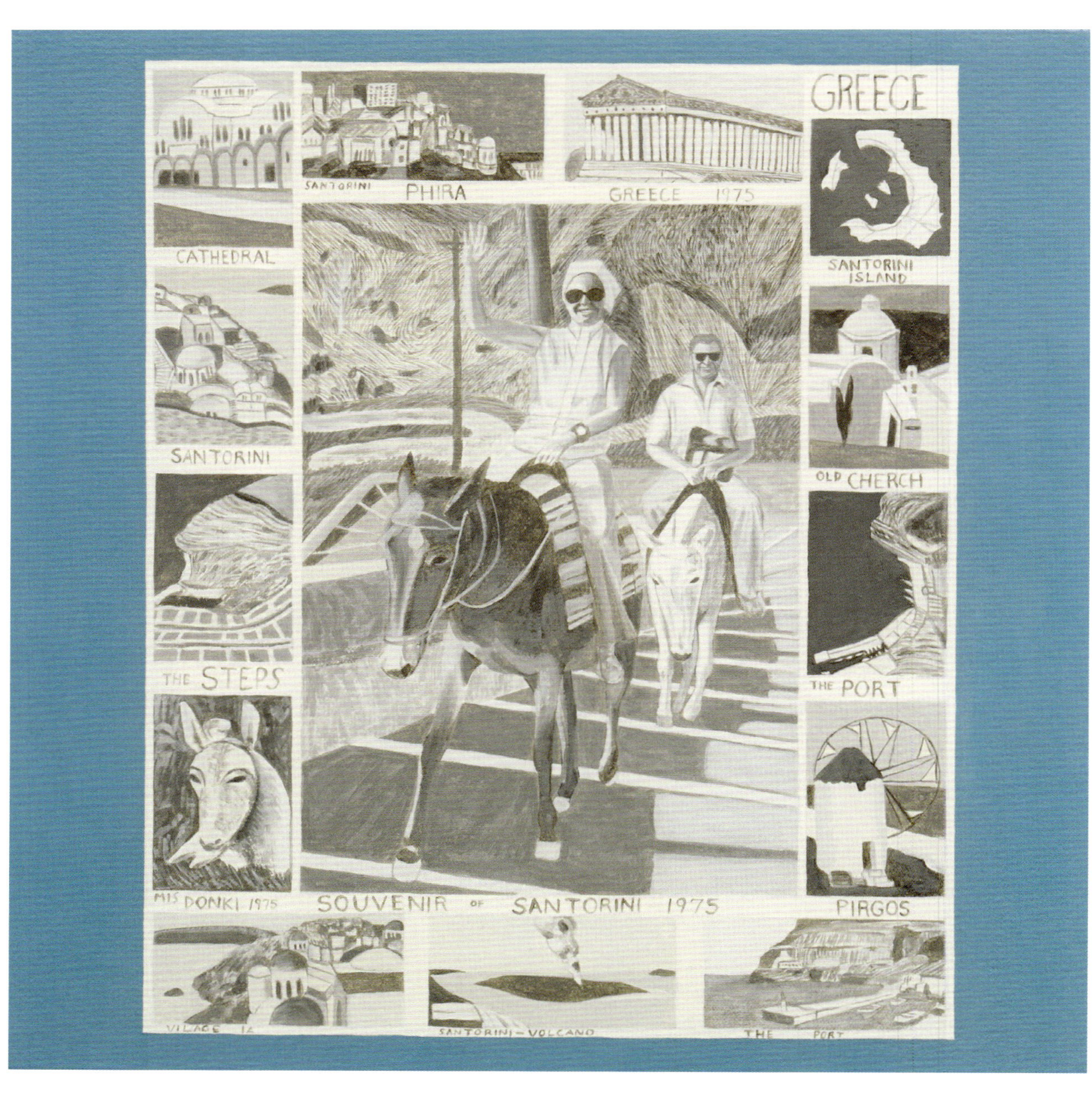

previous pages
Installation view of *Becky Suss*, Institute of Contemporary Art, University of Pennsylvania, 2015

Souvenir of Santorini 1975 (#2), 2015
oil on canvas
14 × 14 inches

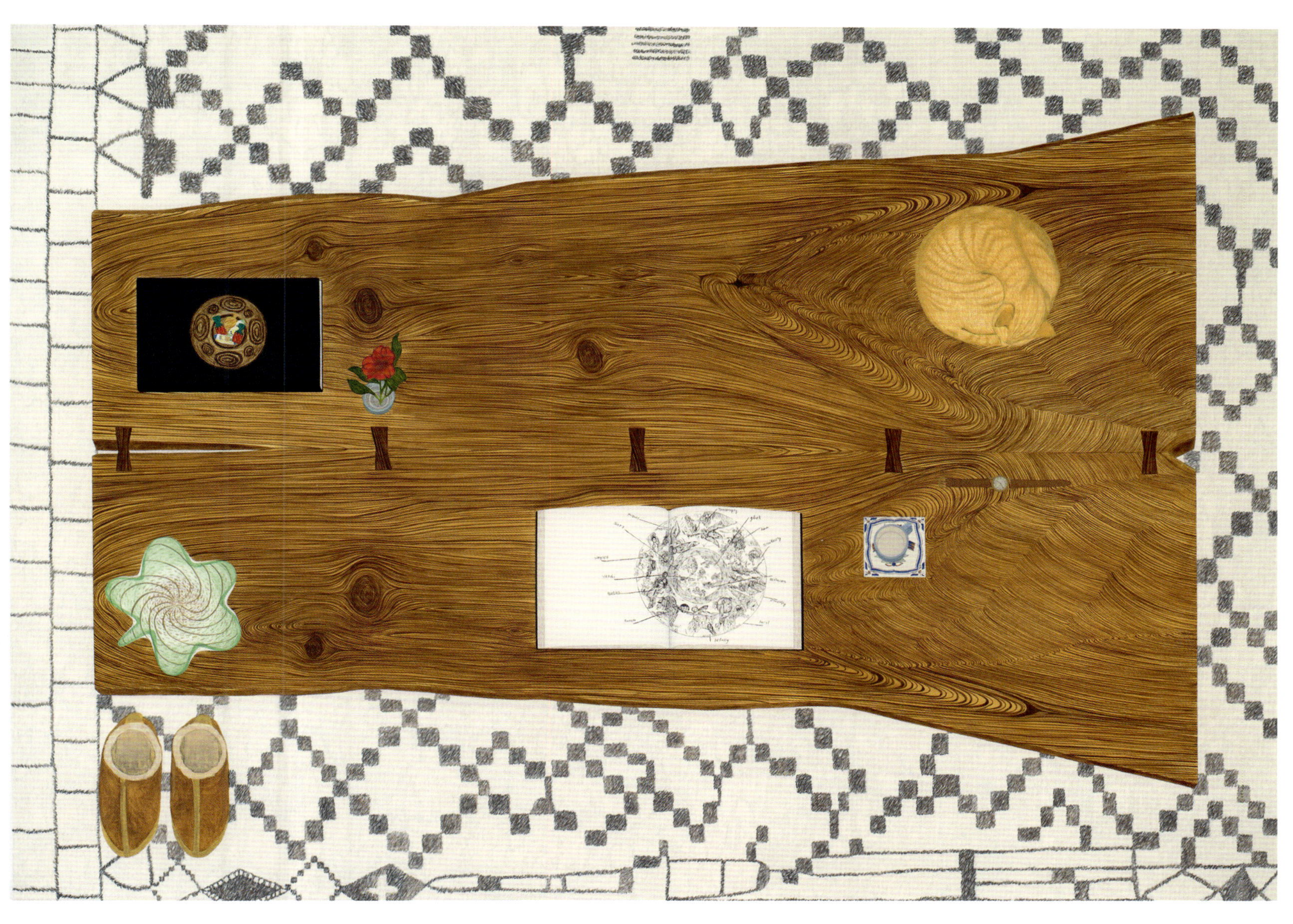

Tabletop, 2016
oil on canvas
60 × 84 inches

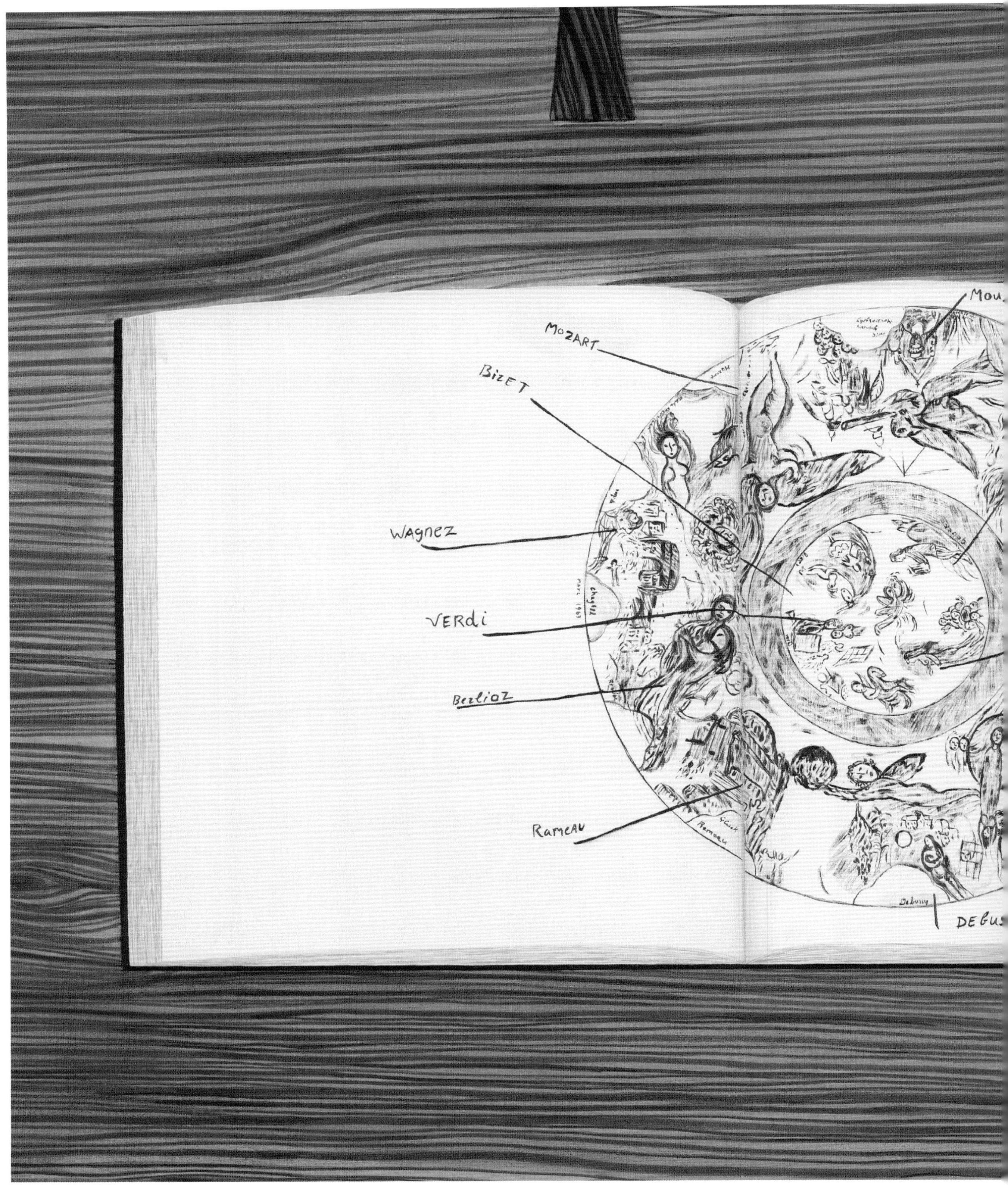

MOZART
BizET
Wagnez
VERdi
Berlioz
Rameau

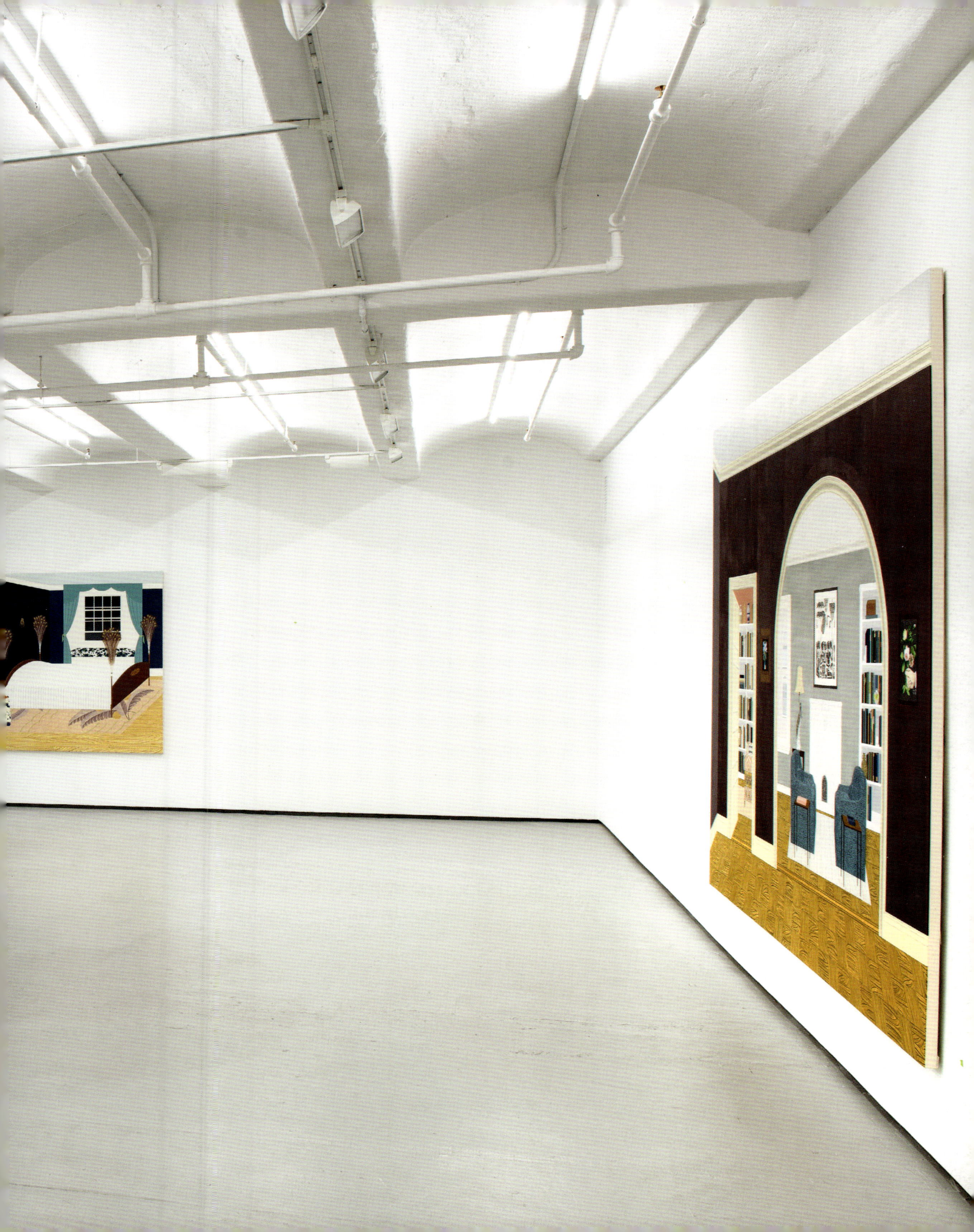

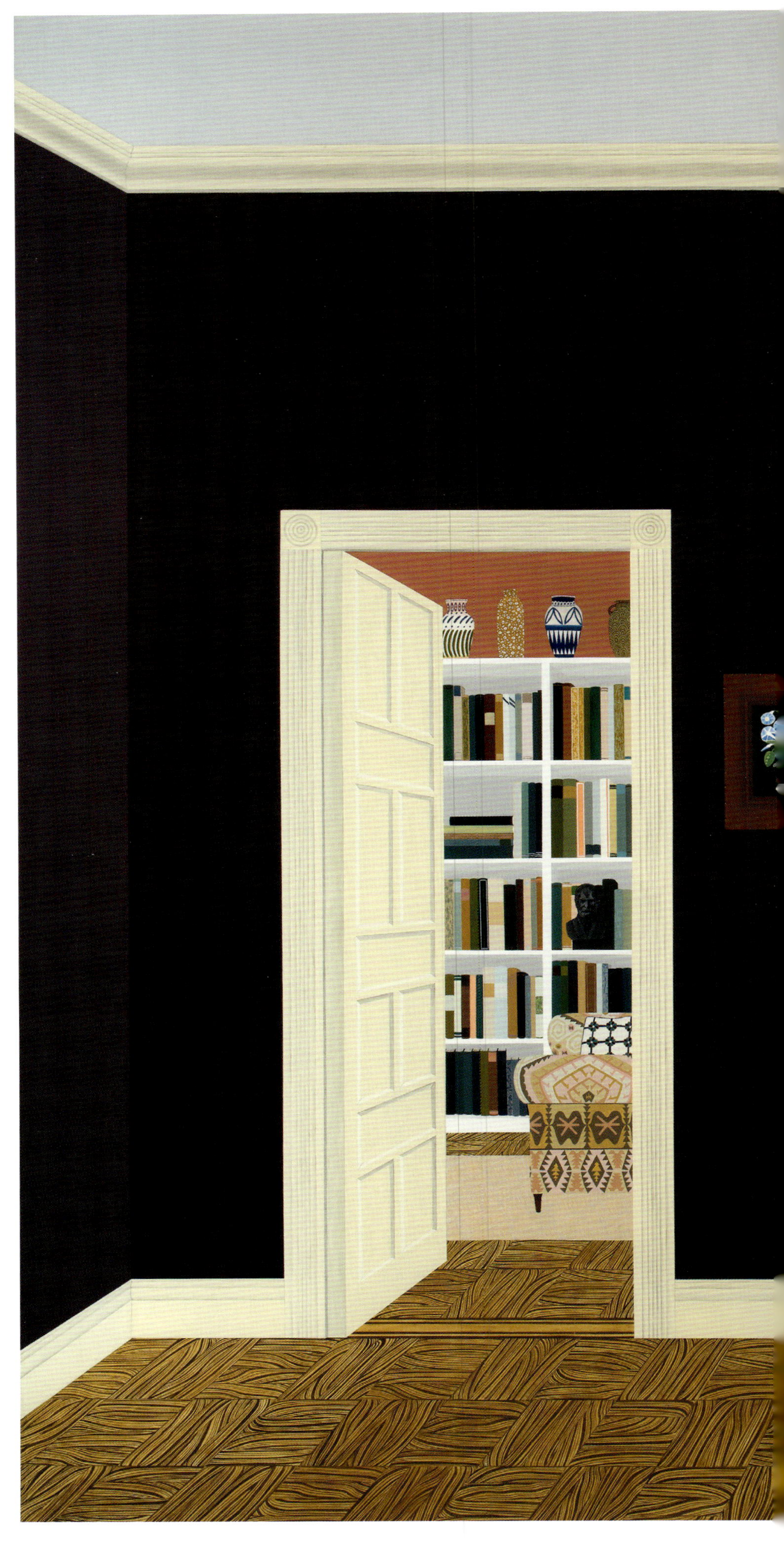

August, 2016
oil on canvas
96 × 132 inches
Princeton University Art Museum.
Gift of Joshua R. Slocum, Class of 1998,
and Sara T. Slocum

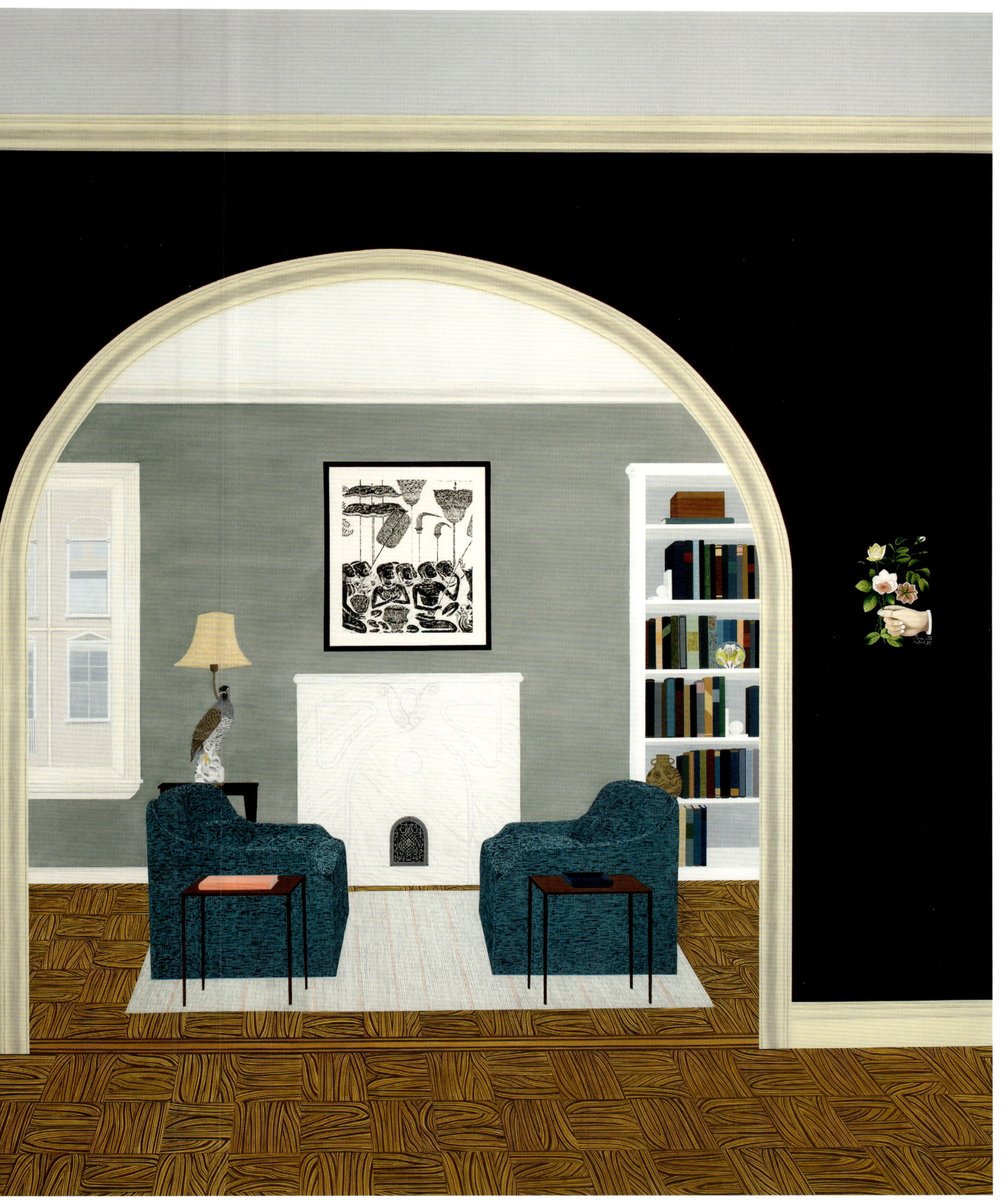

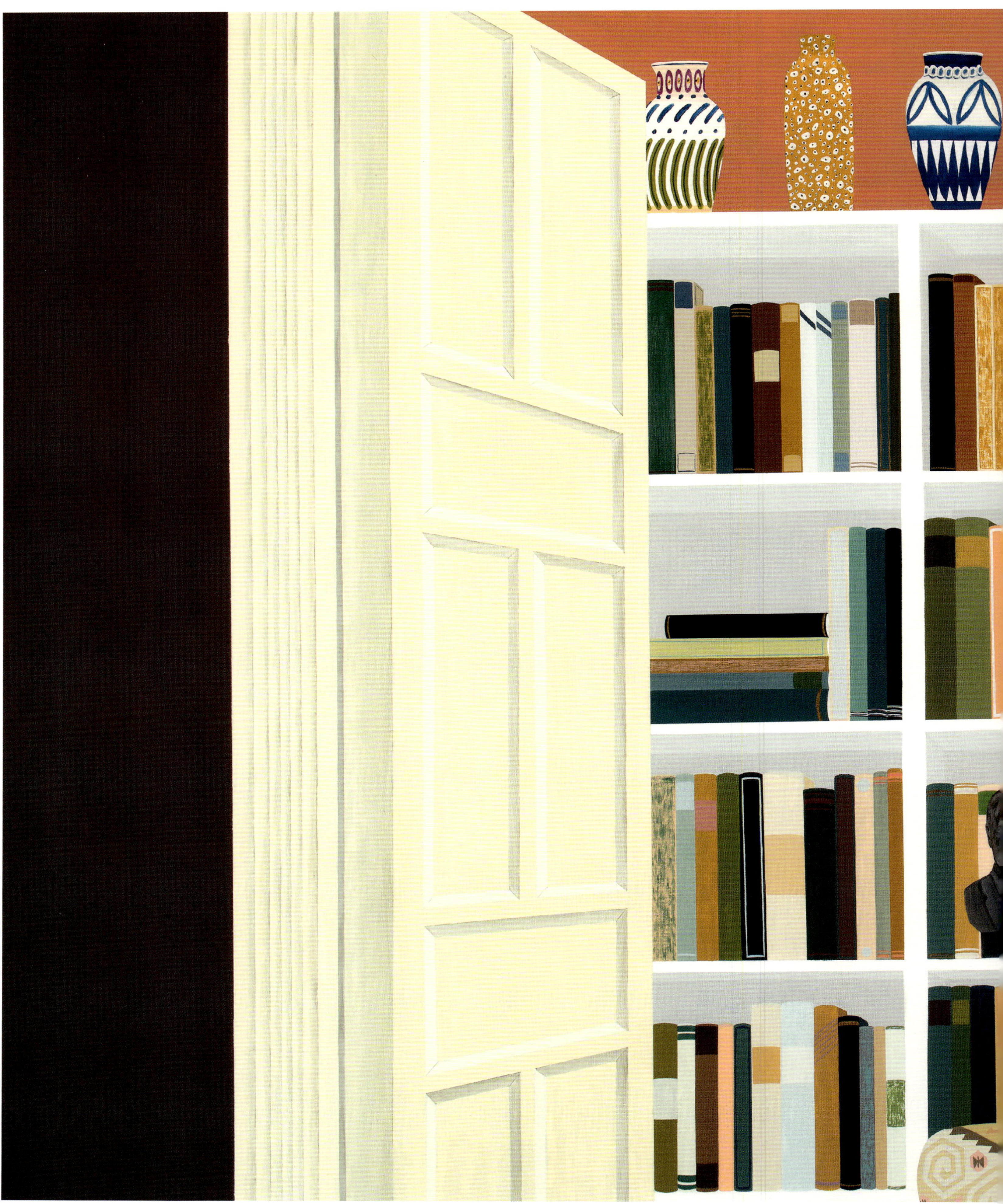

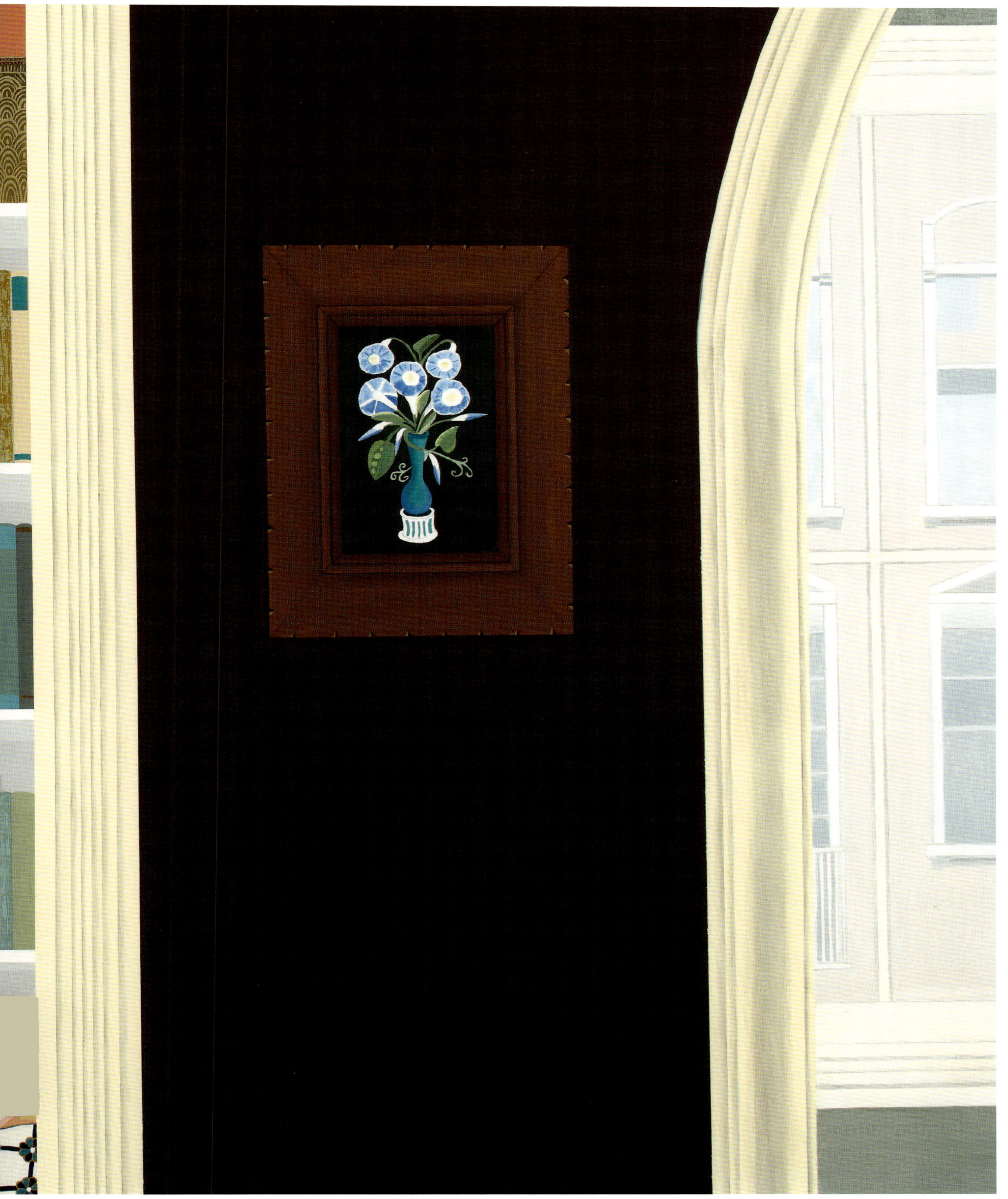

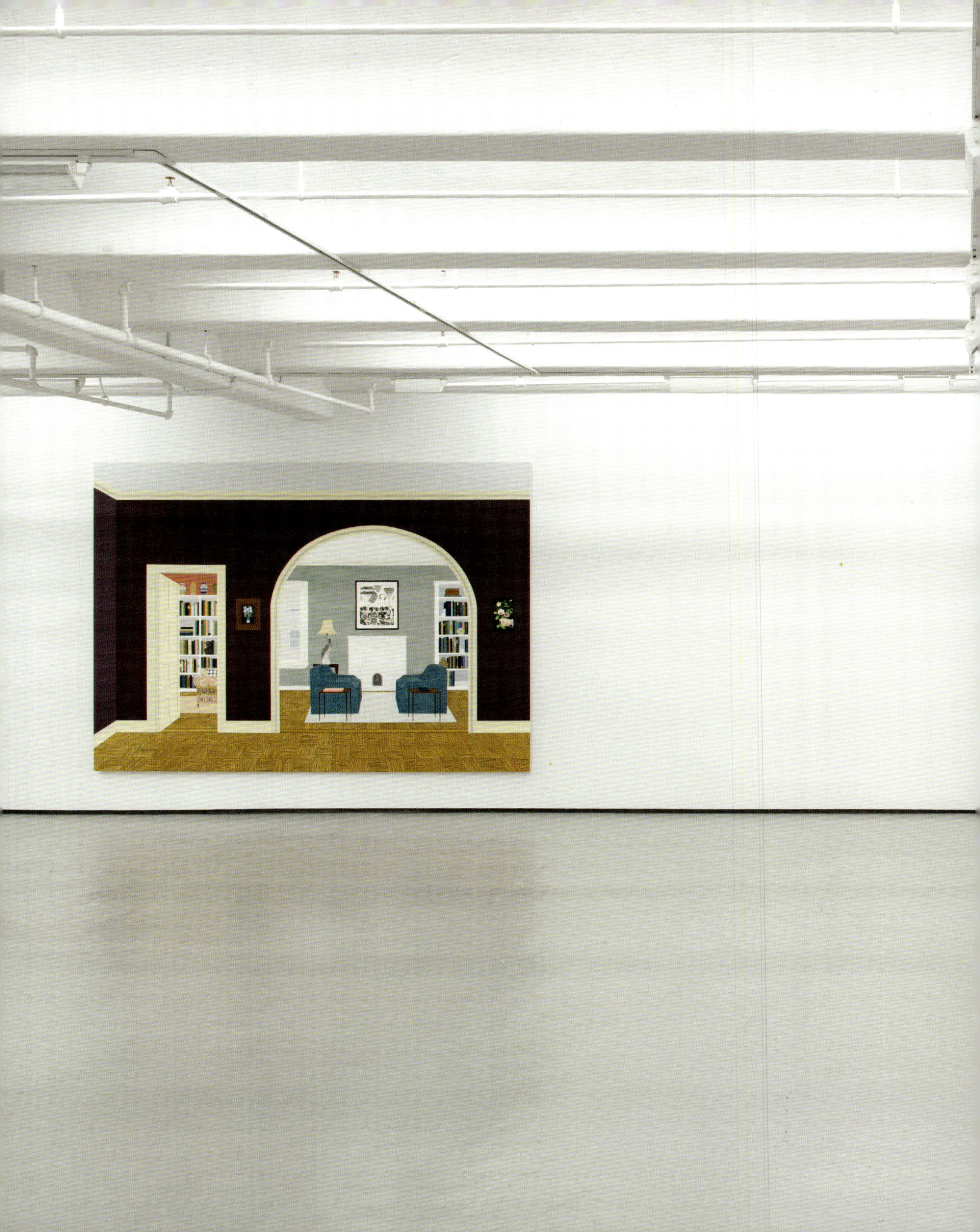

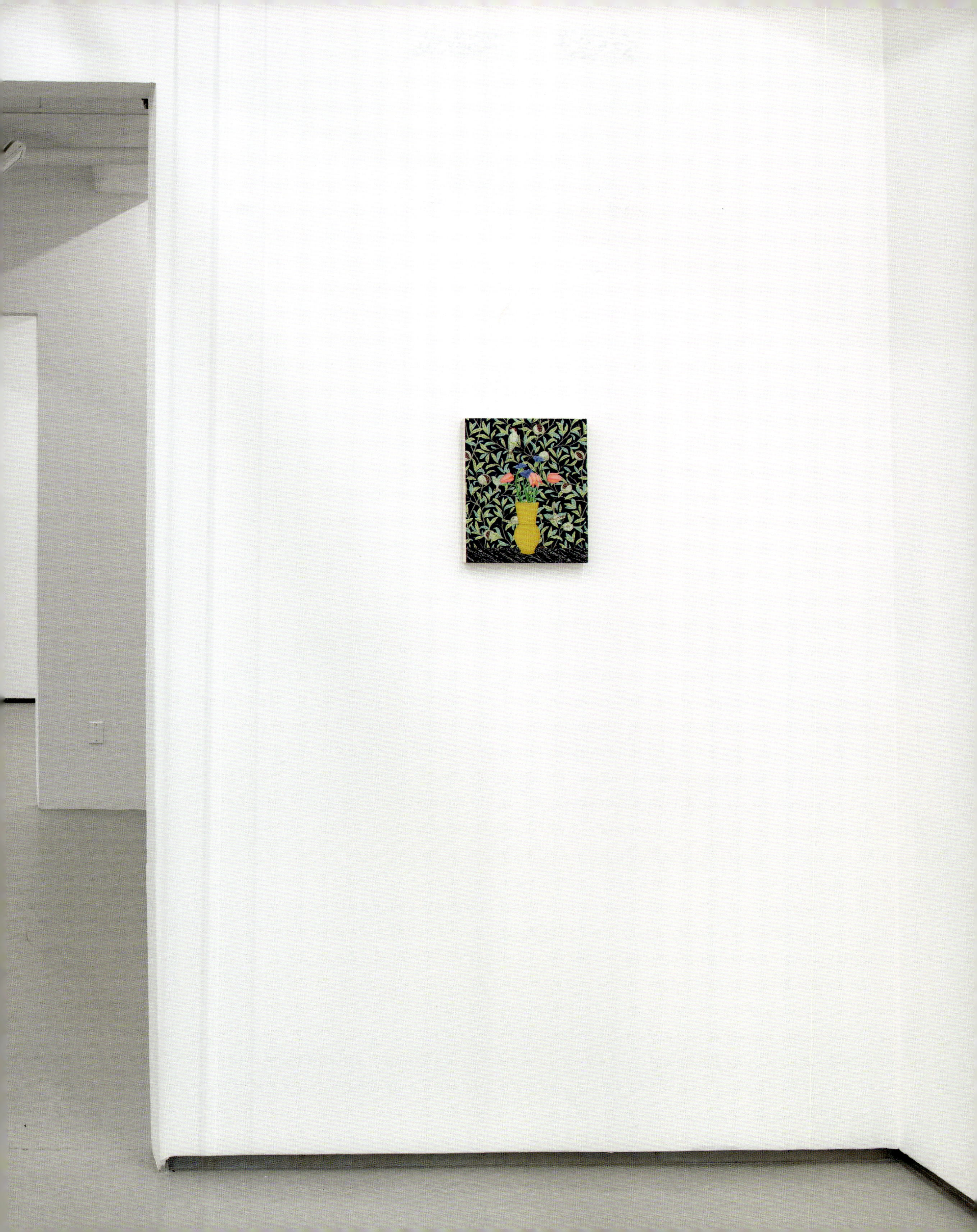

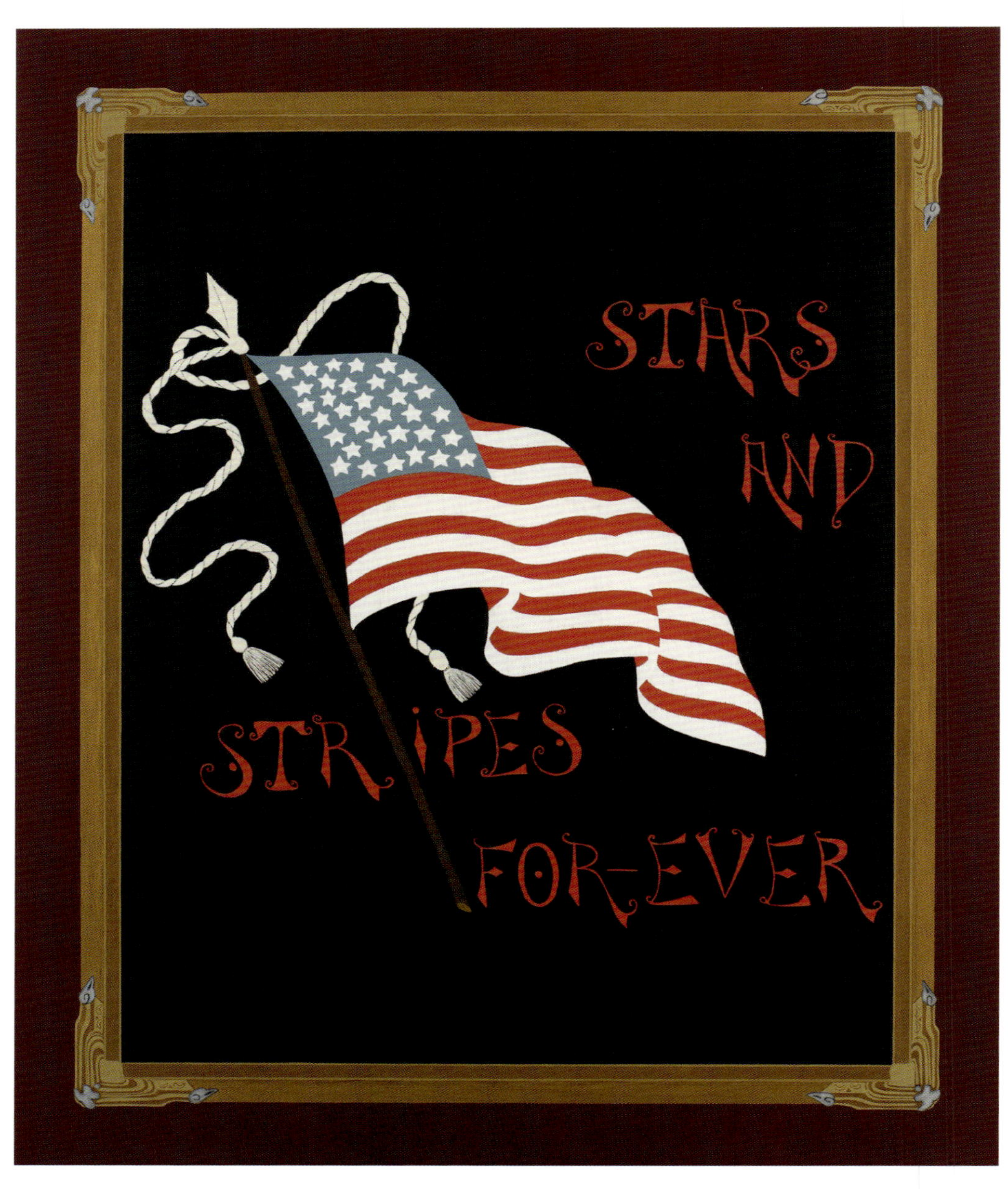

Stars and Stripes For-Ever, 2016
oil on canvas
24 × 20 inches

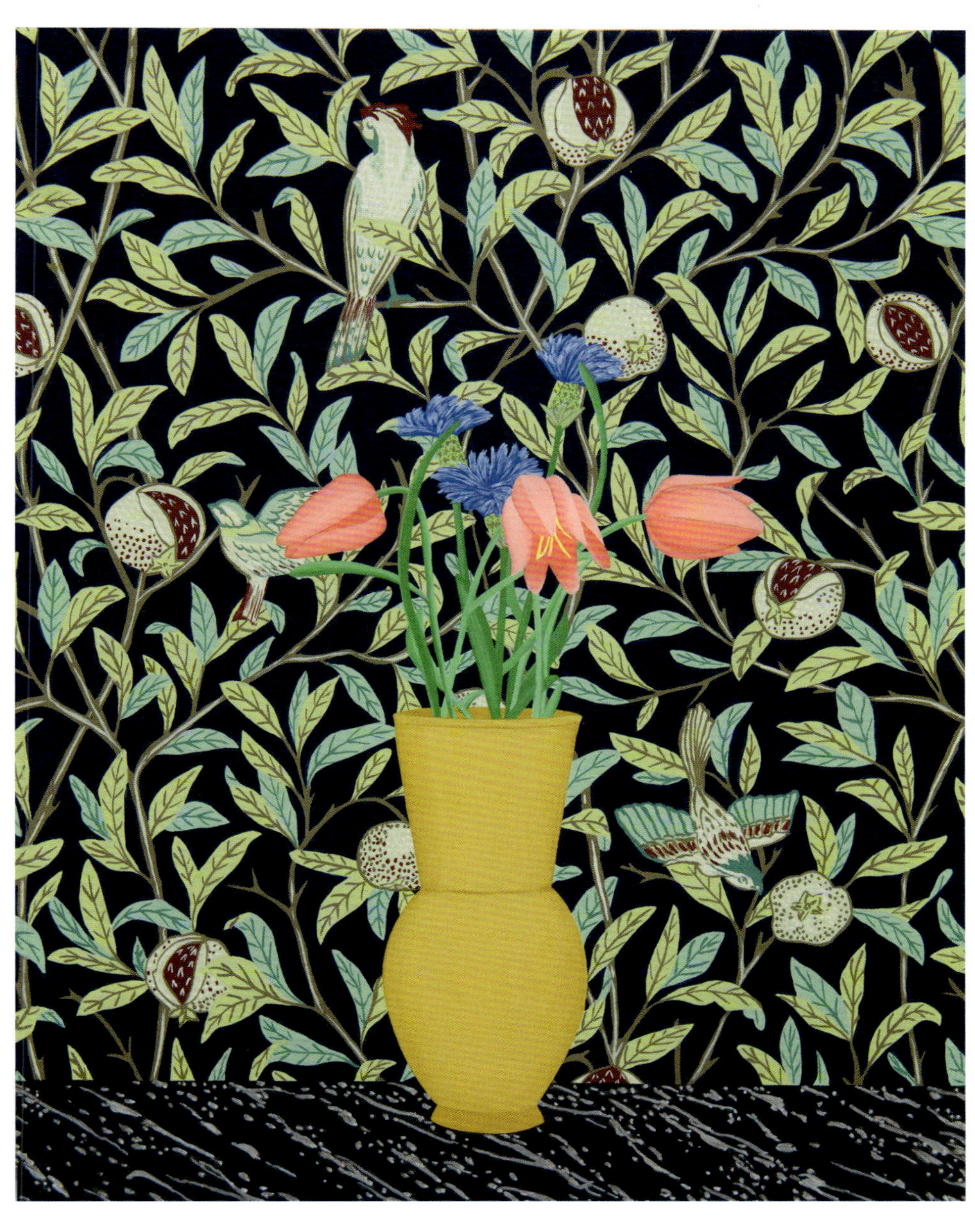

Still Life, 2017
oil on canvas
14 × 11 inches

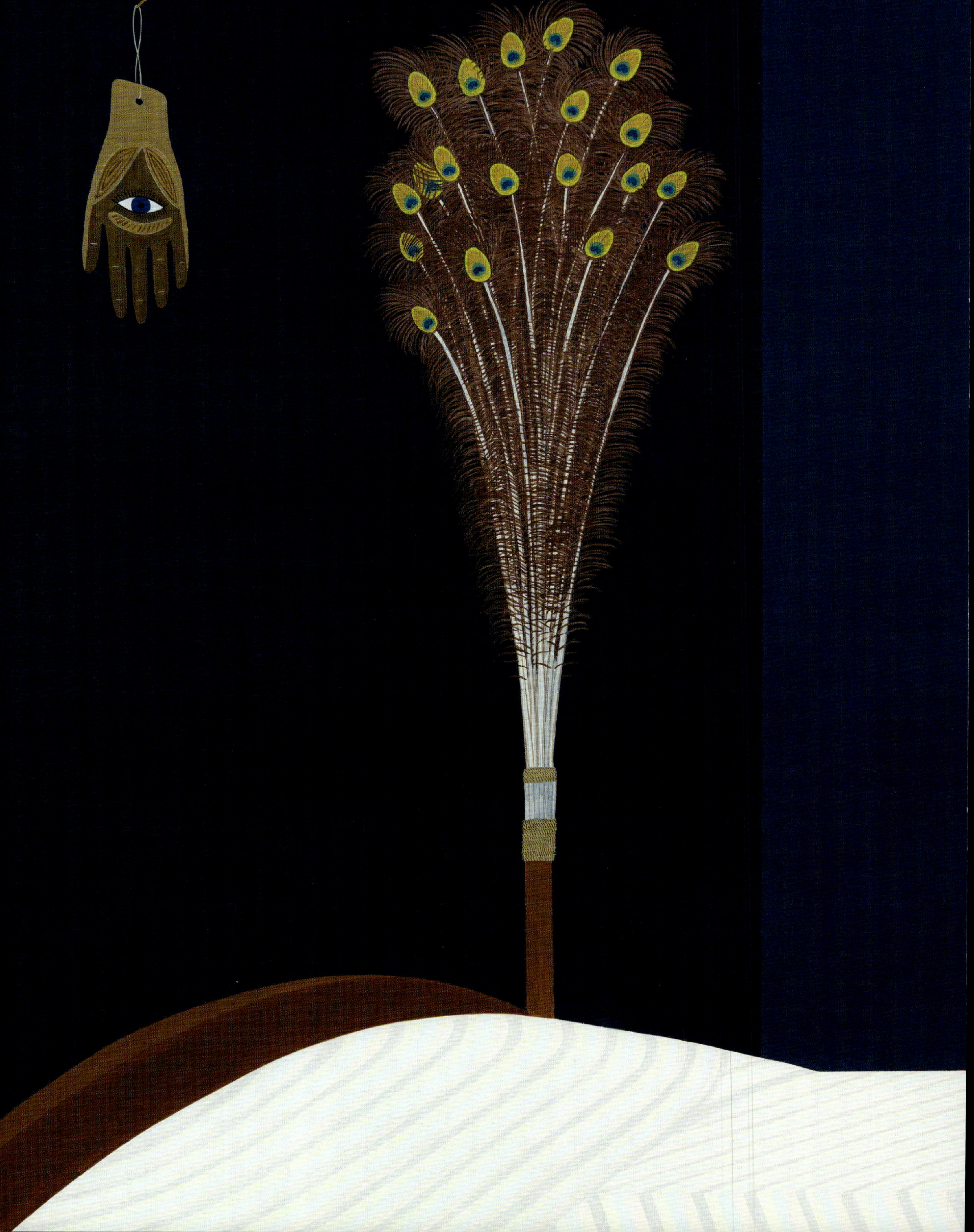

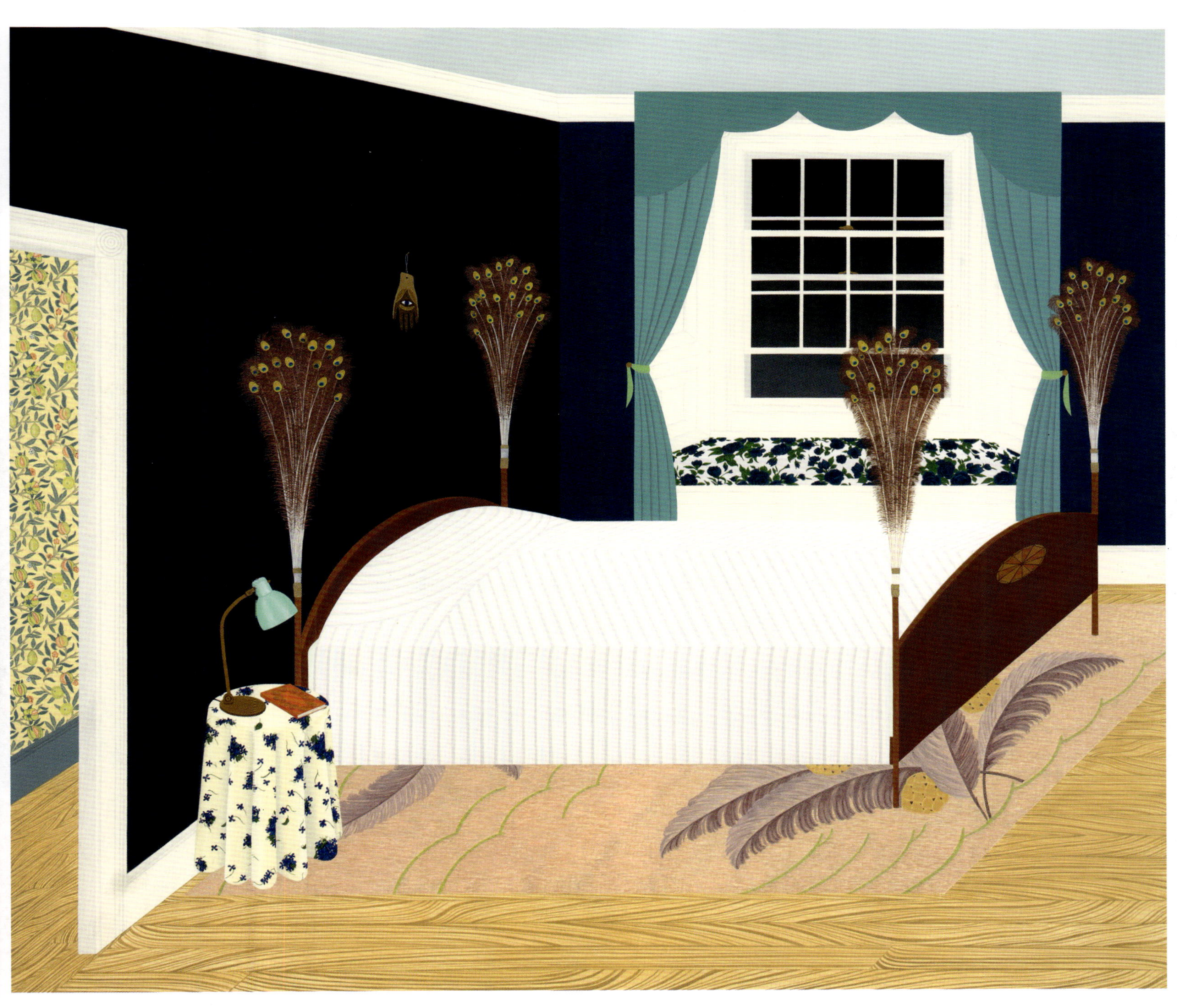

Bedroom with Peacock Feathers, 2017
oil on canvas
72 × 84 inches

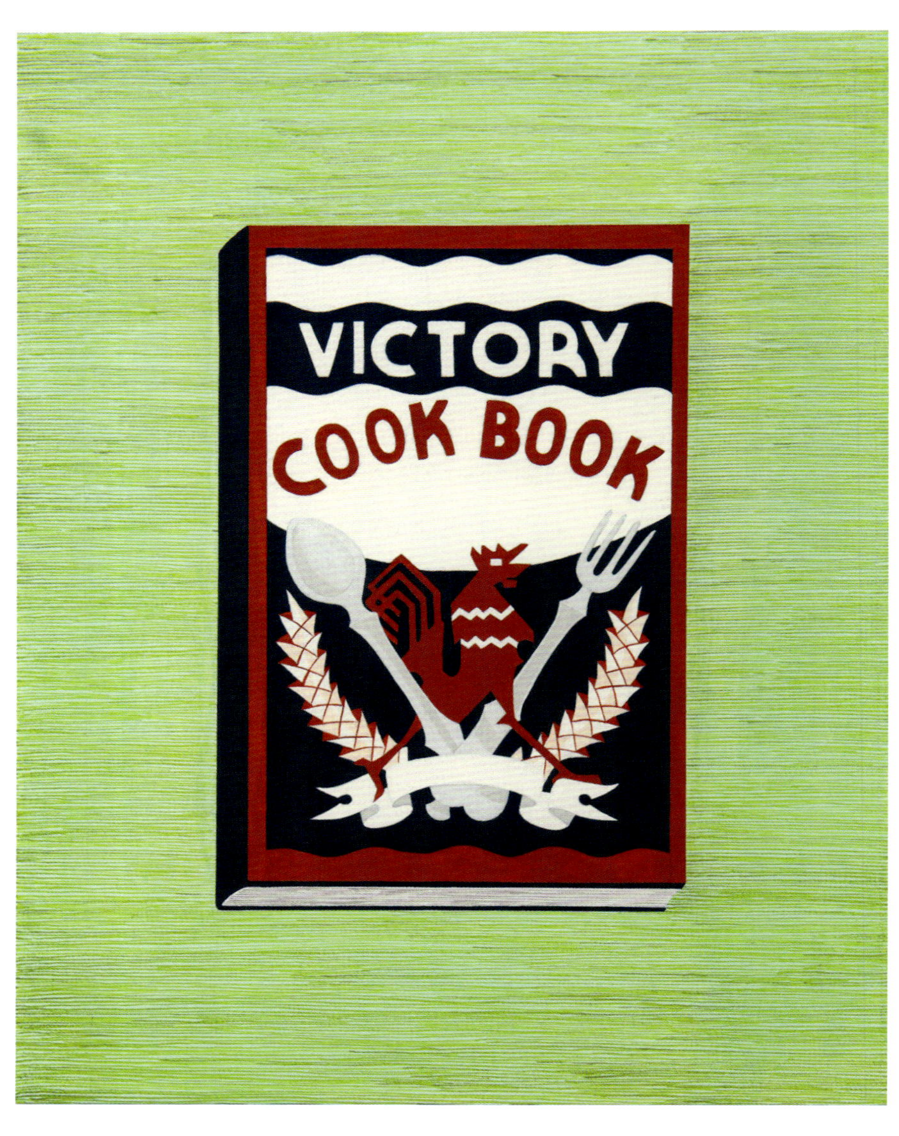

Victory Cookbook, 2017
oil on canvas
14 × 11 inches

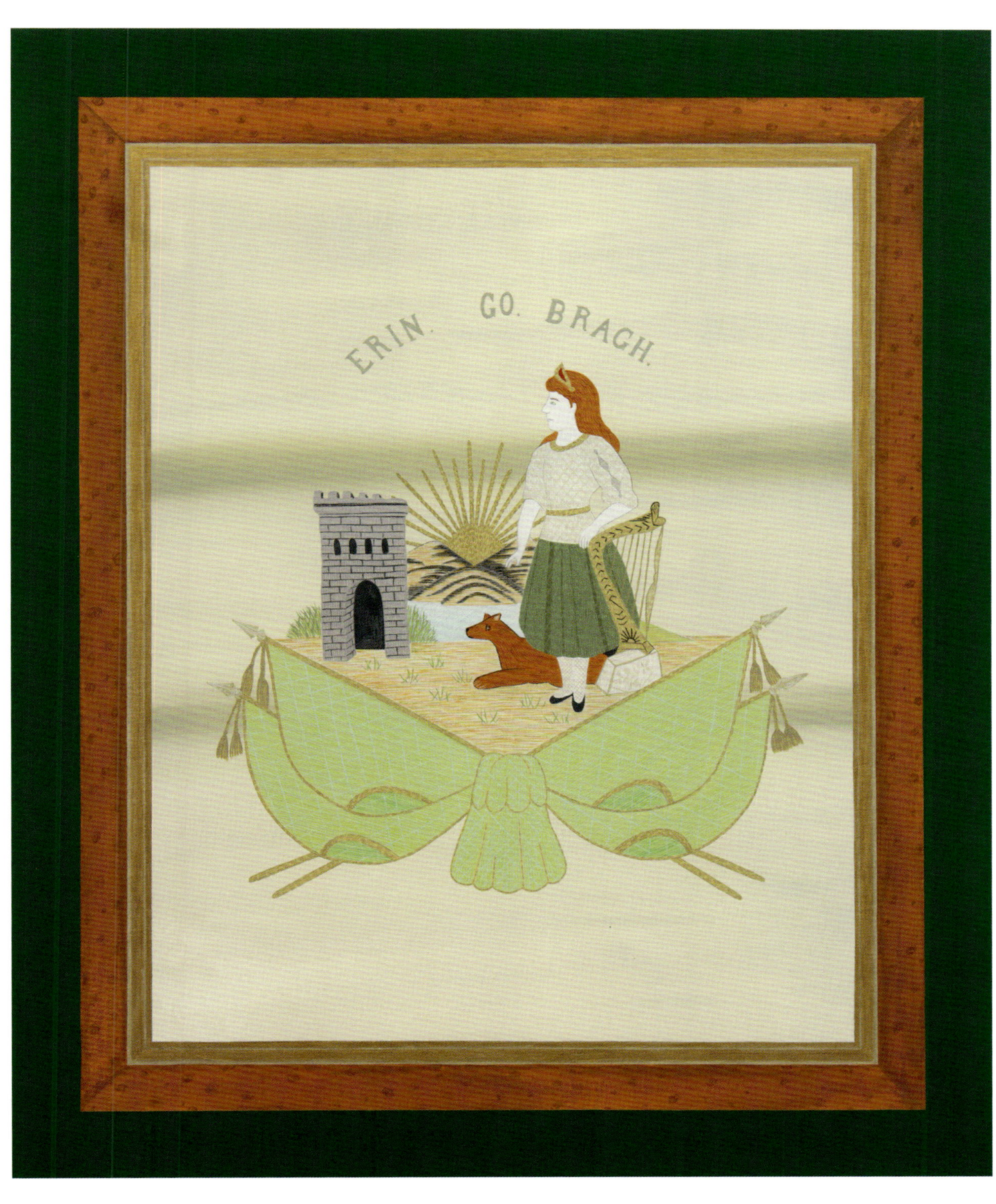

Erin Go Bragh, 2017
oil on canvas
24 × 20 inches

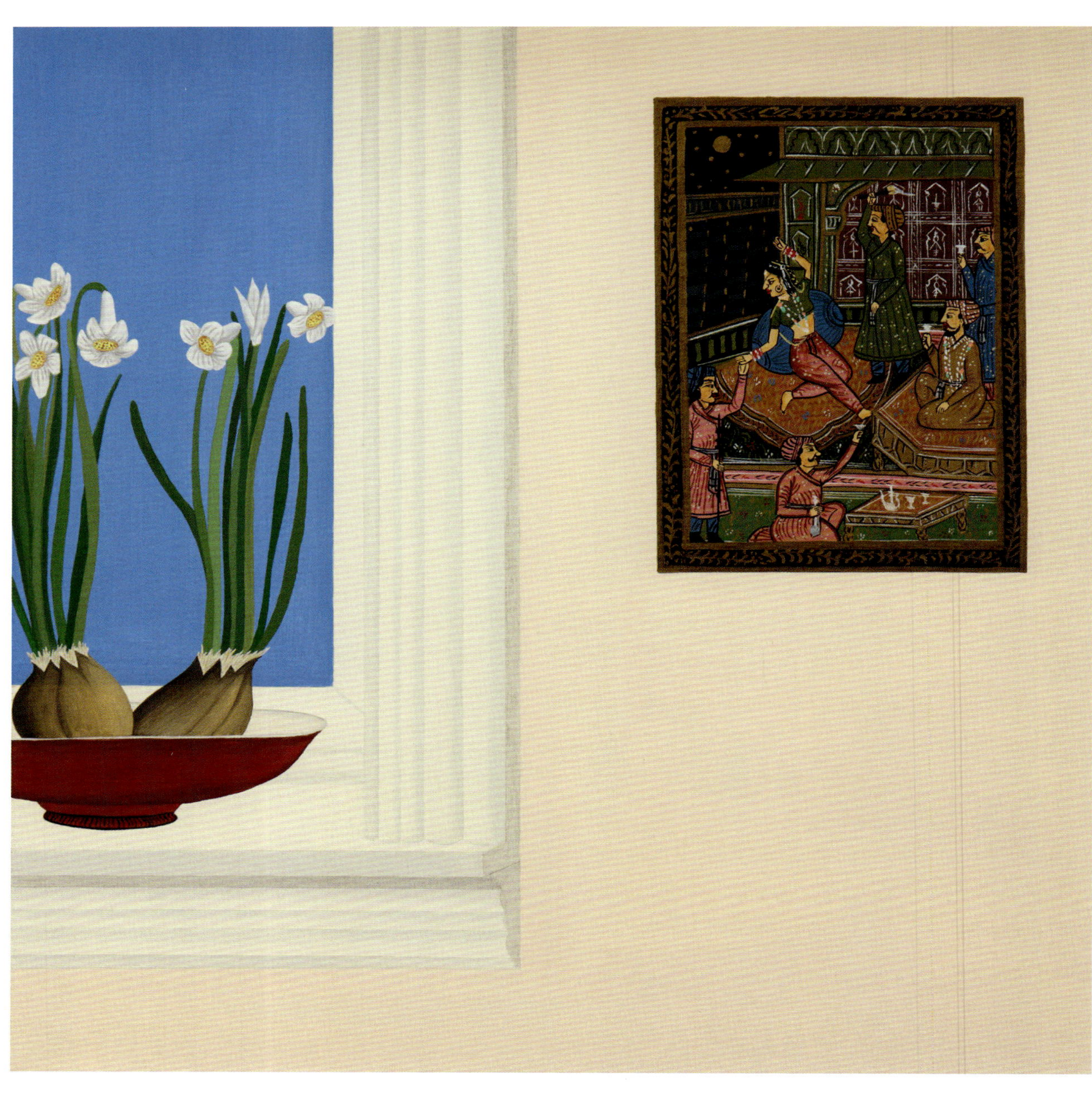

In Memoriam (for Emily), 2017
oil on canvas
14 × 14 inches

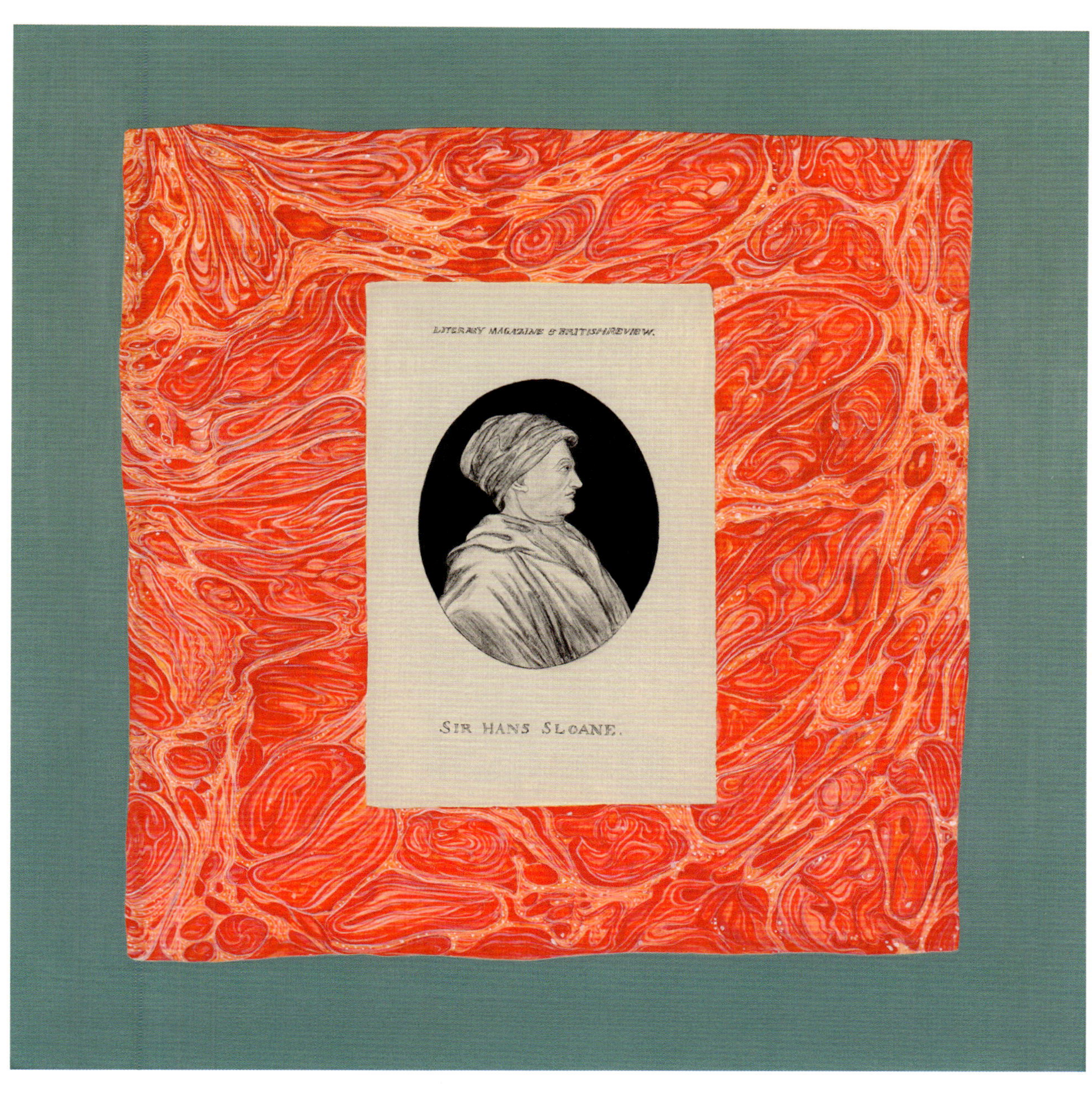

Sir Hans Sloane, 2017
oil on canvas
14 ¼ × 14 inches

Matamoe, 2017
oil on canvas
16 3/16 × 20 inches

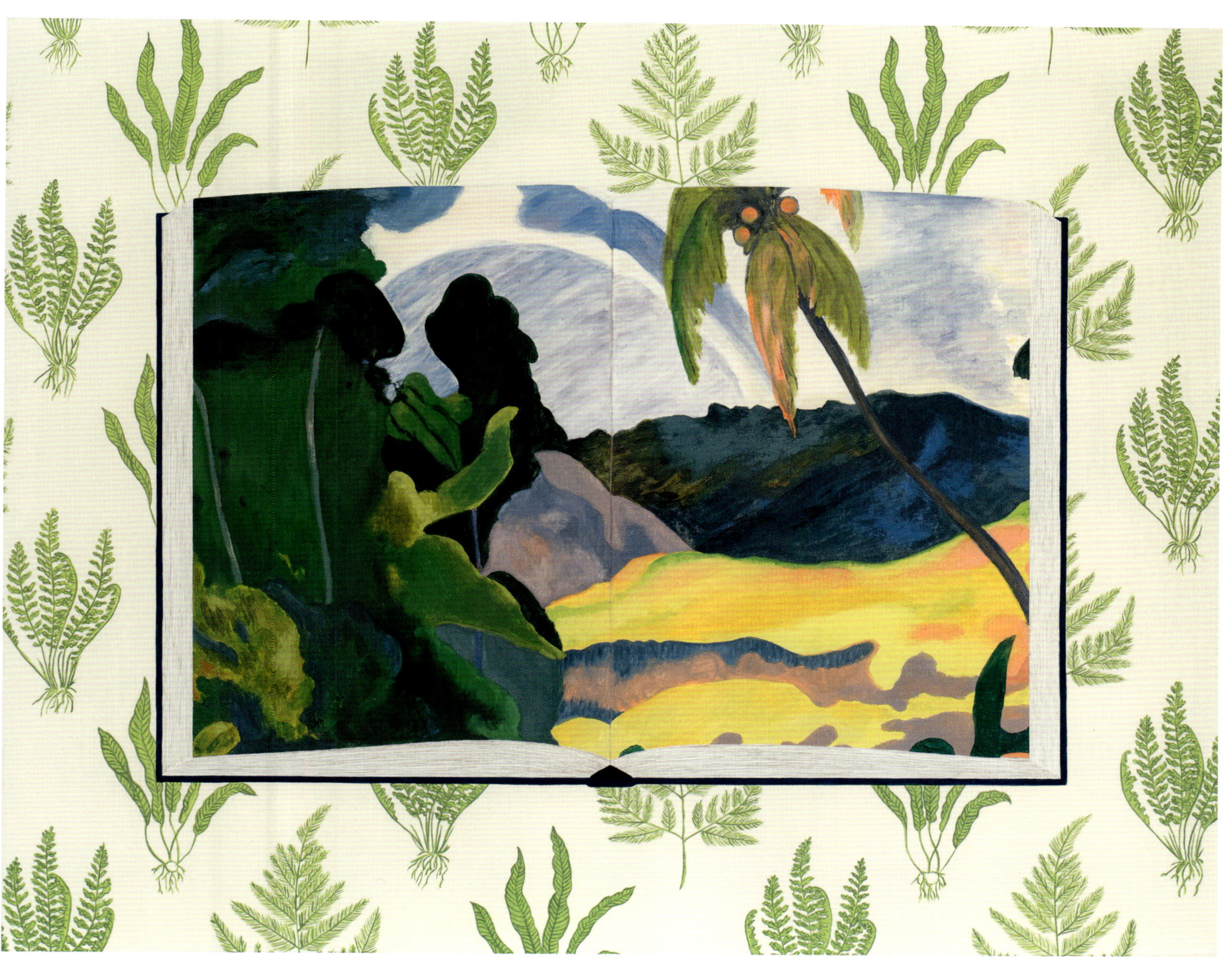

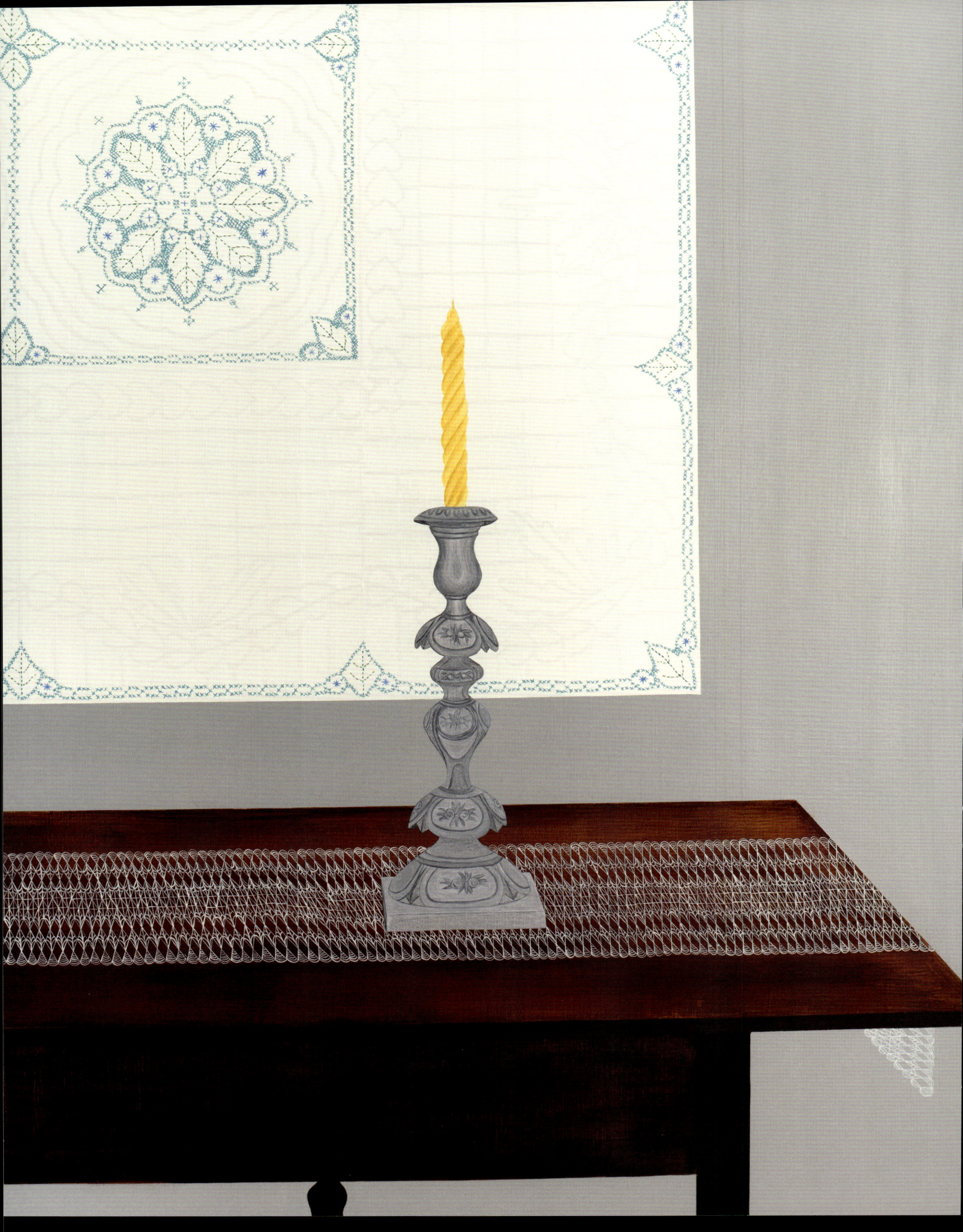

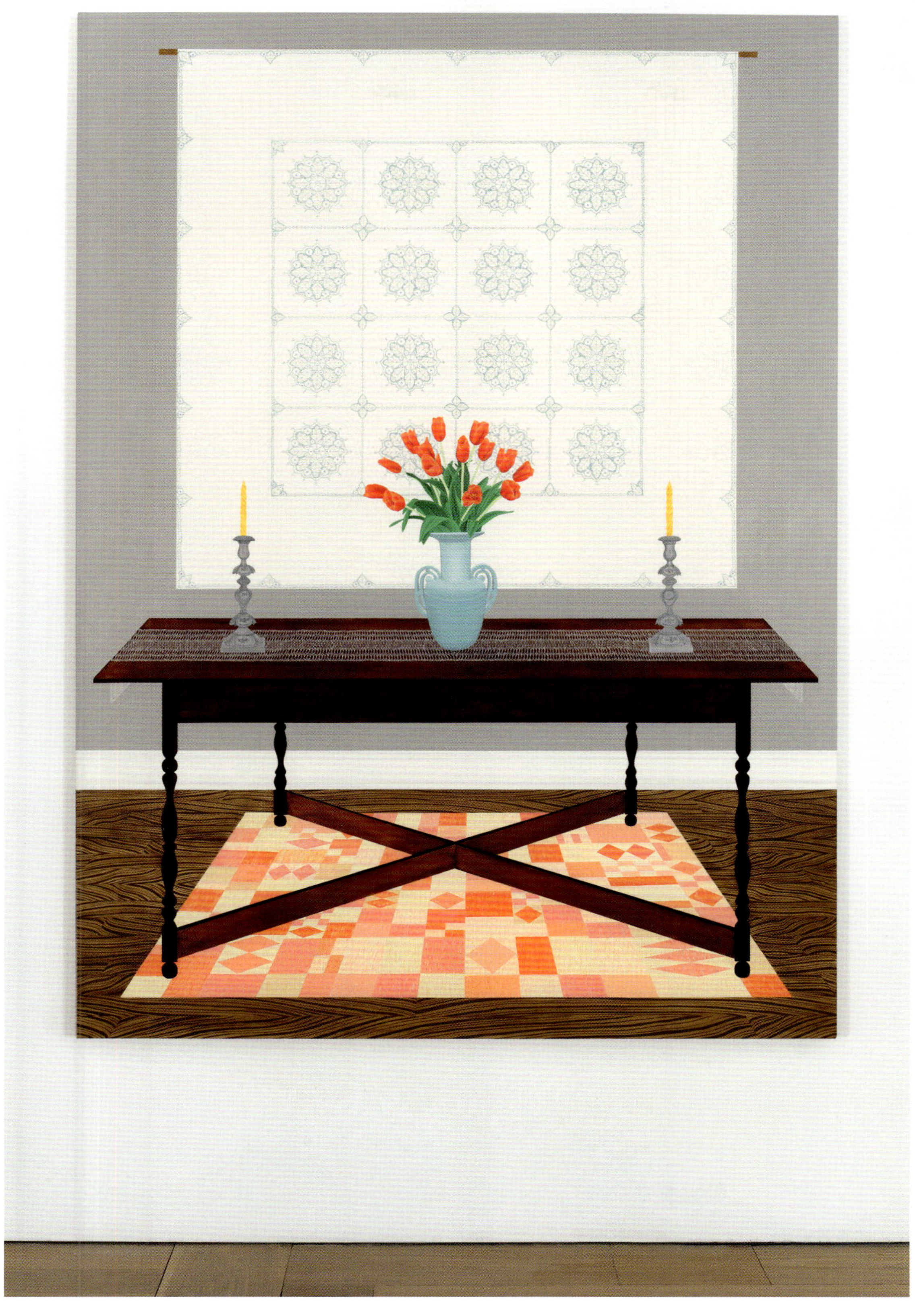

Foyer (Helen's Quilt), 2017
oil on canvas
84 × 60 inches
Davis Museum at Wellesley College,
Wellesley, MA, Museum purchase,
The Dorothy Johnston Towne
(Class of 1923) Fund 2018.160

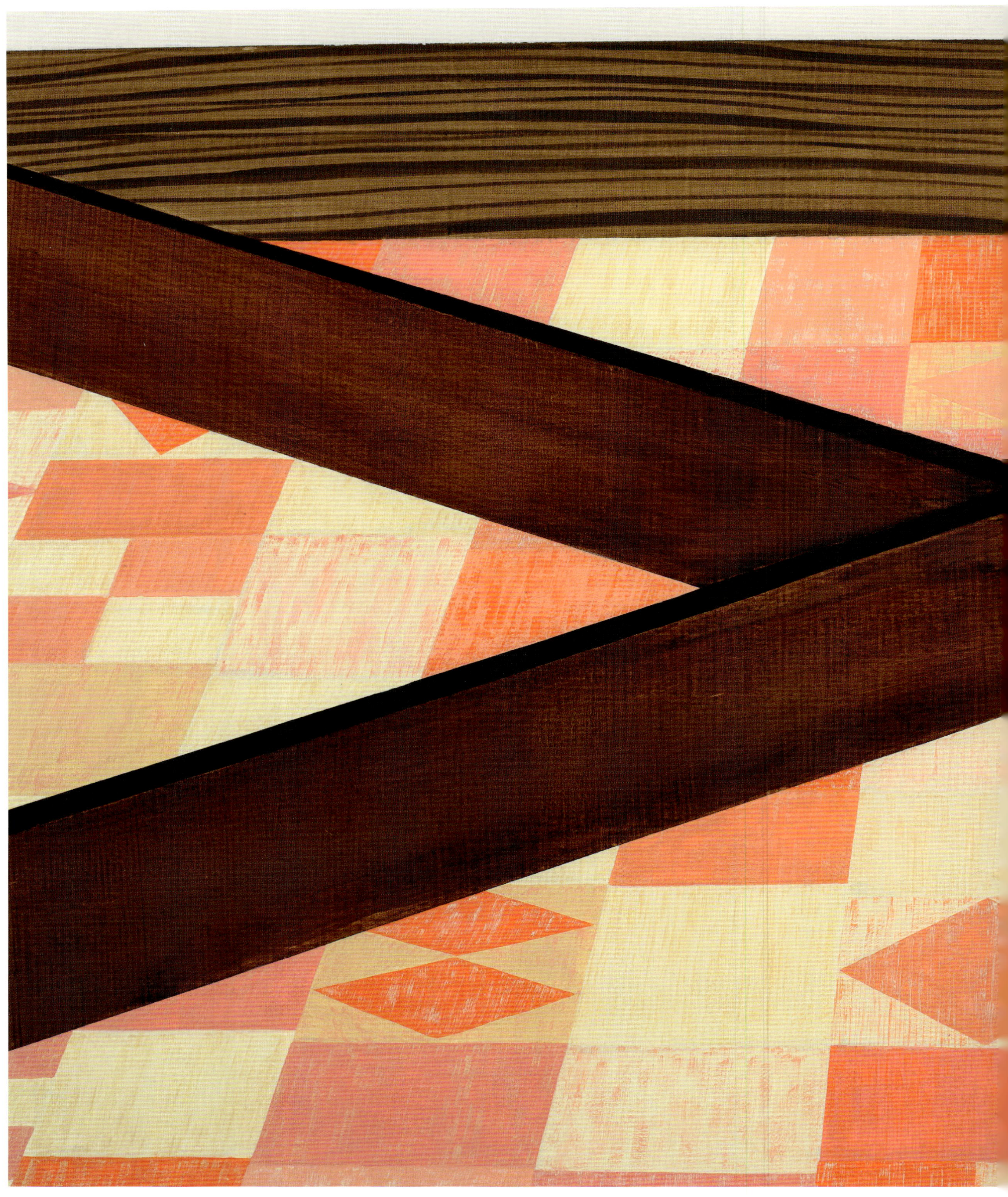

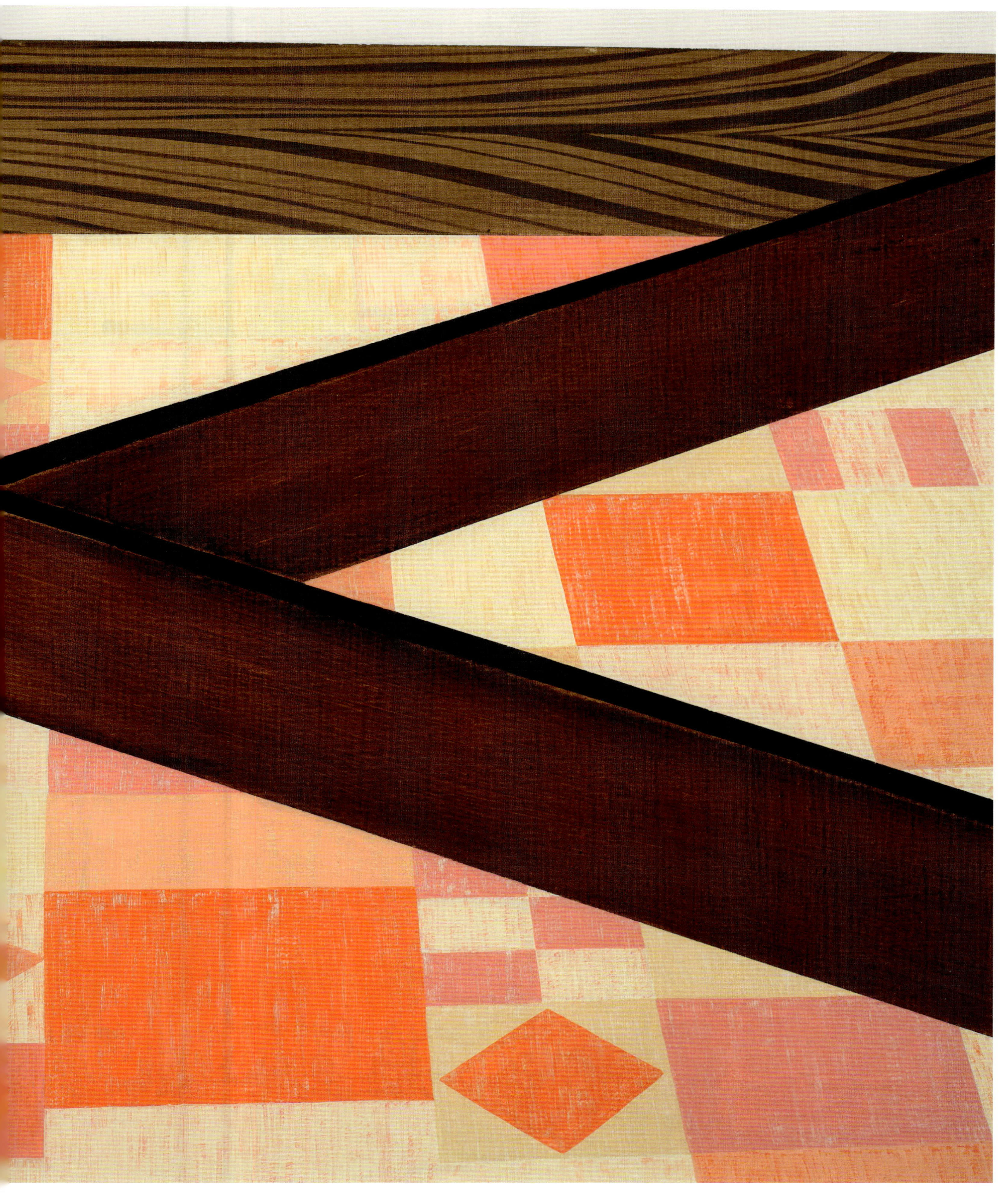

Variations par Benedictus, 2017
oil on canvas
16 × 20 inches

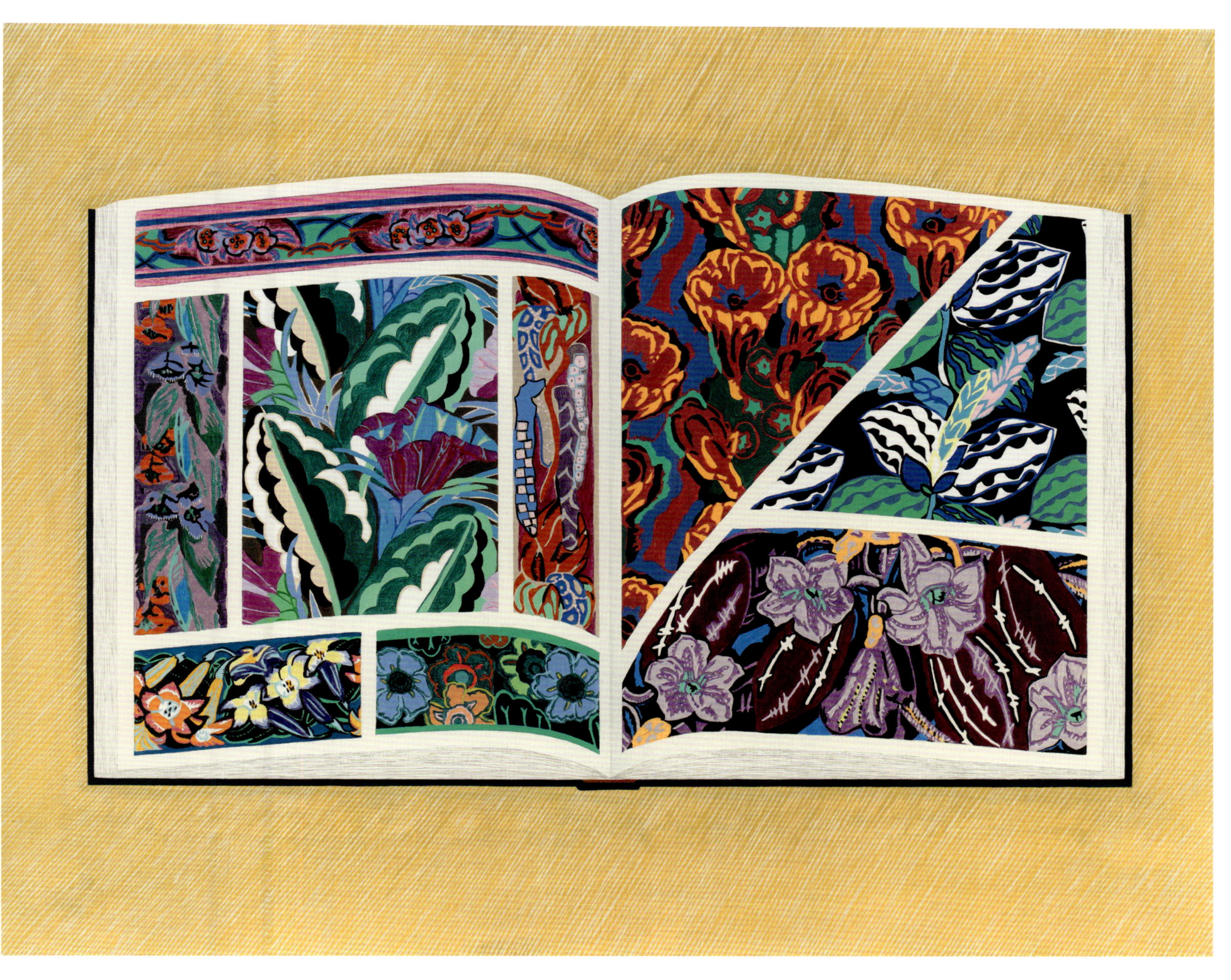

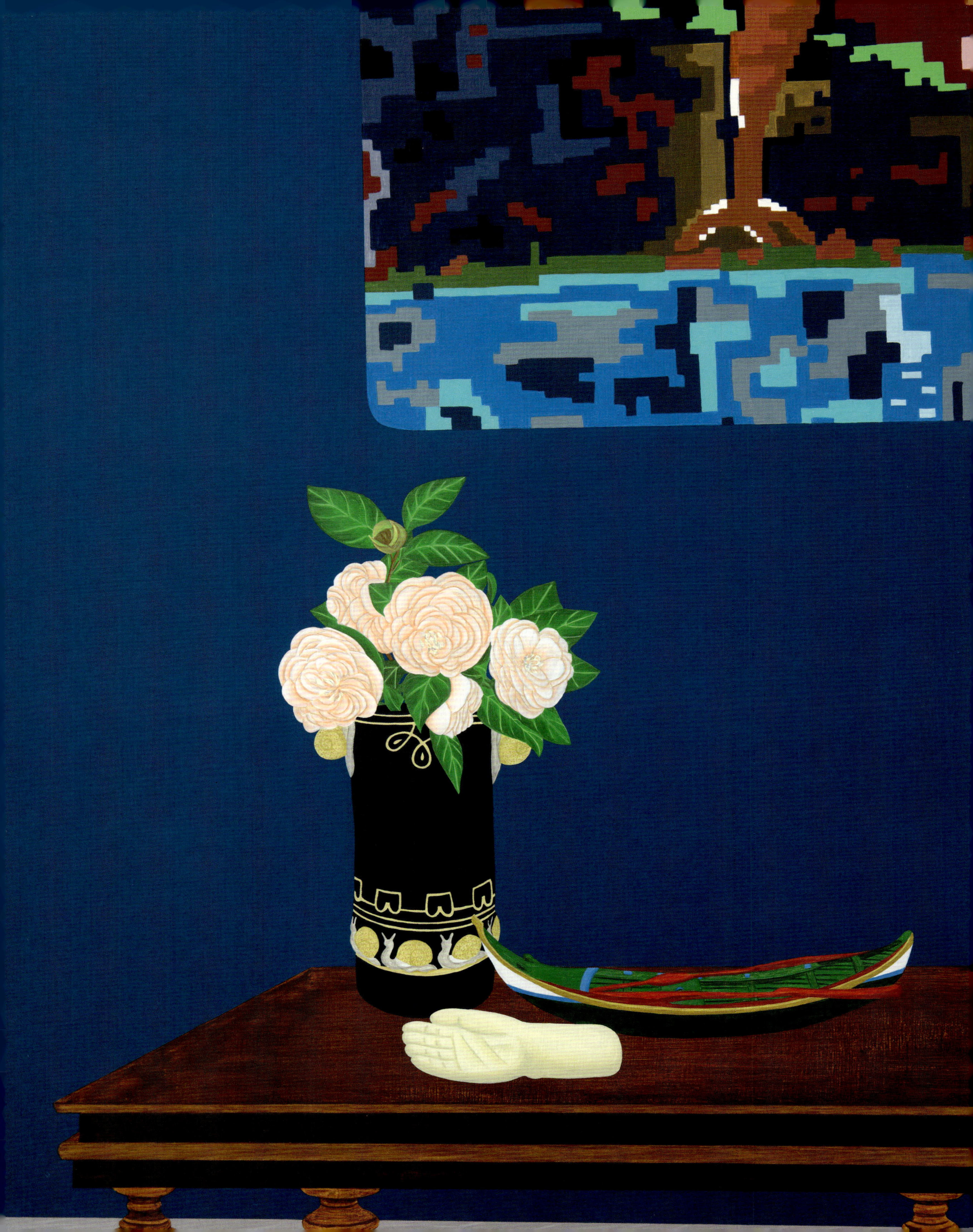

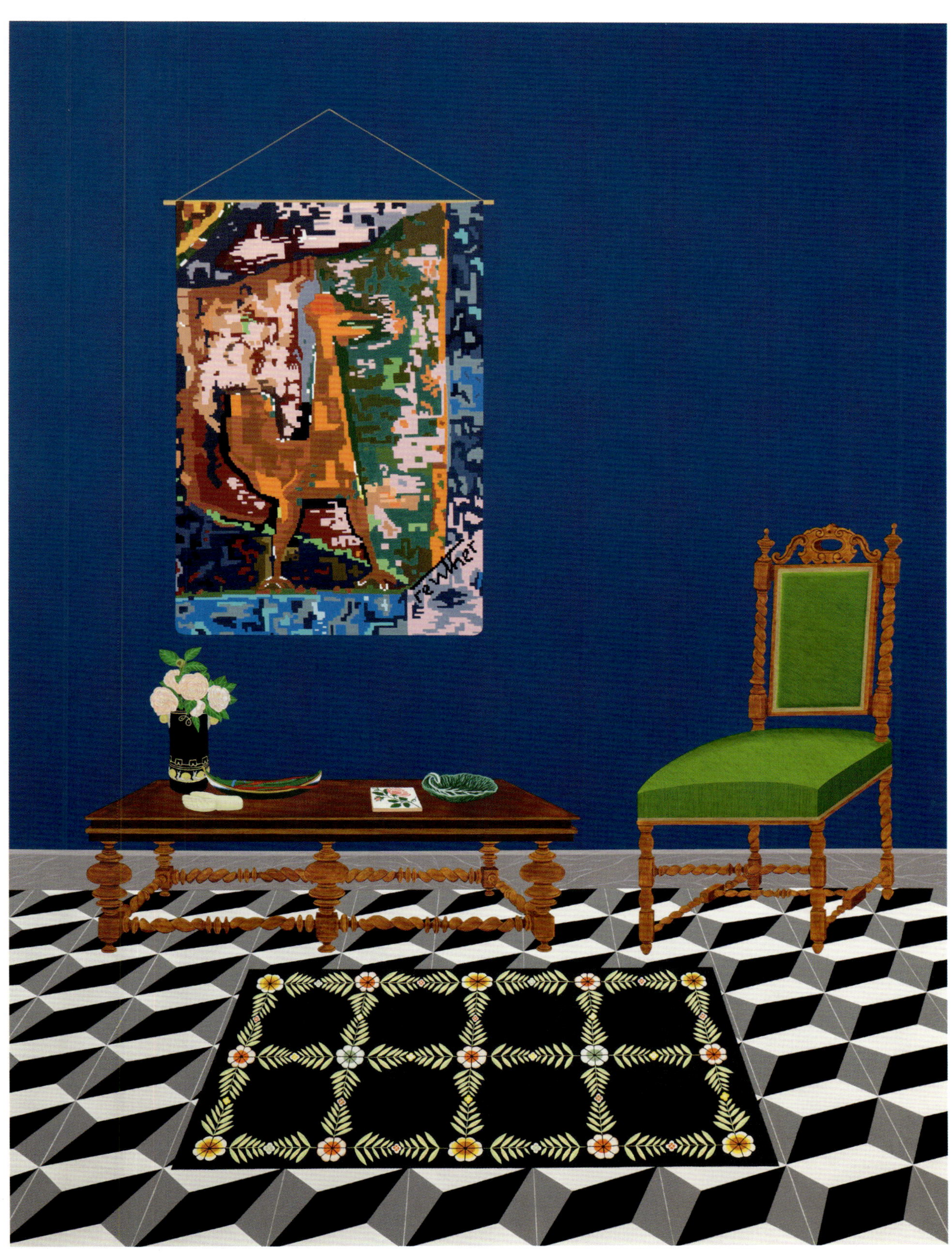

Untitled (Portugal), 2018
oil on canvas
84 × 60 inches

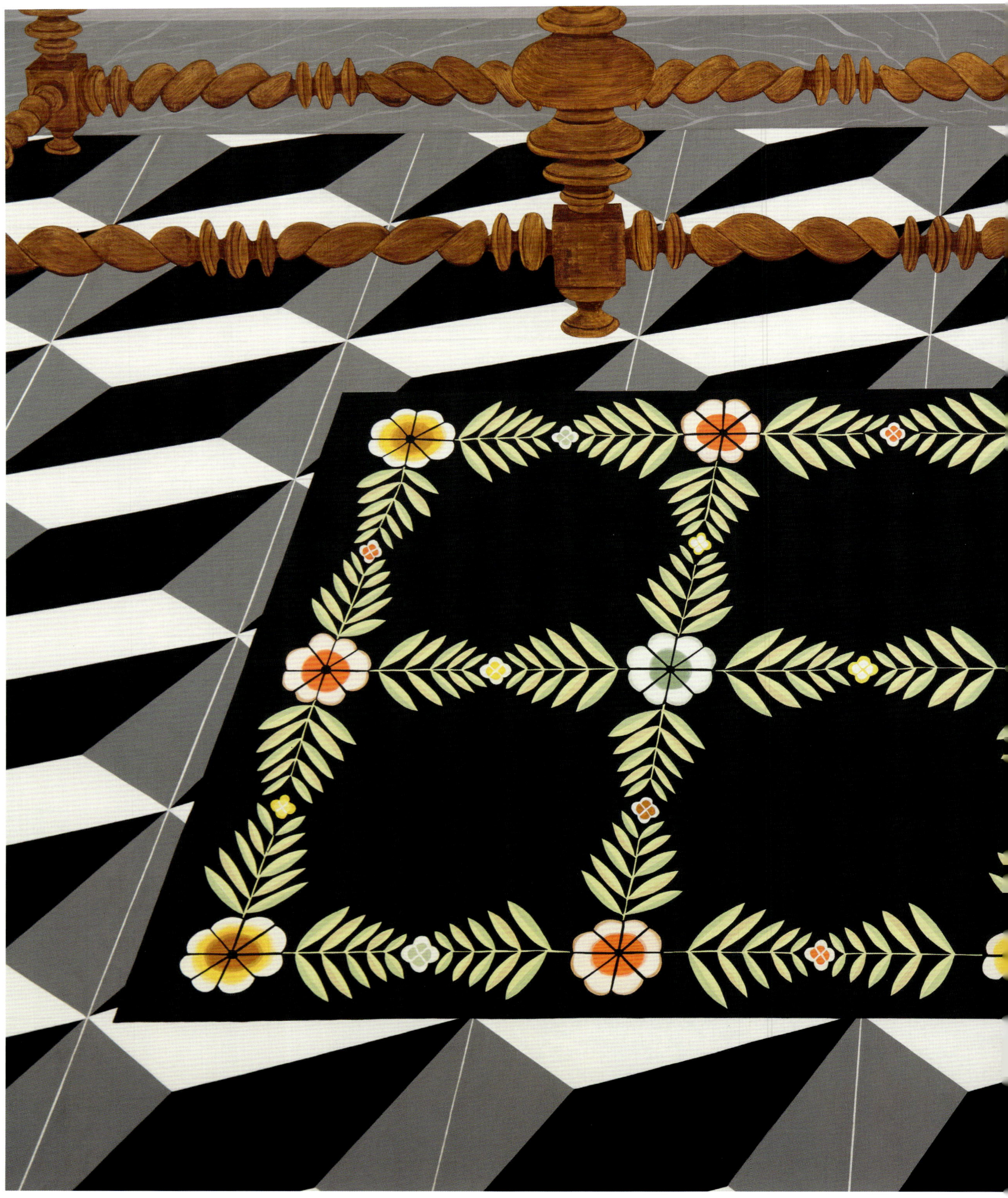

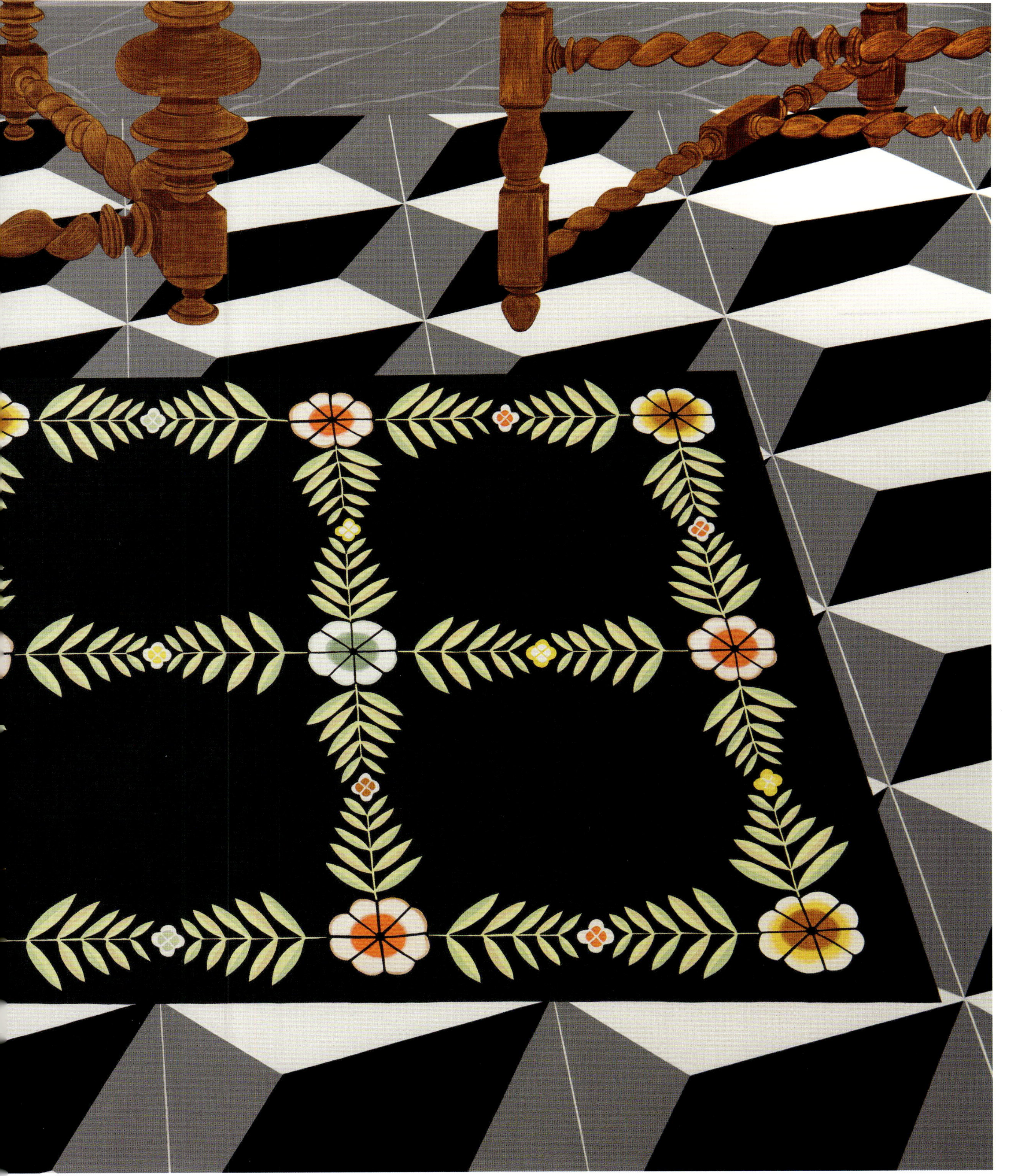

Wharton Esherick
2018

Drop Leaf Desk (Wharton Esherick), 2018
oil on canvas
84 × 60 inches

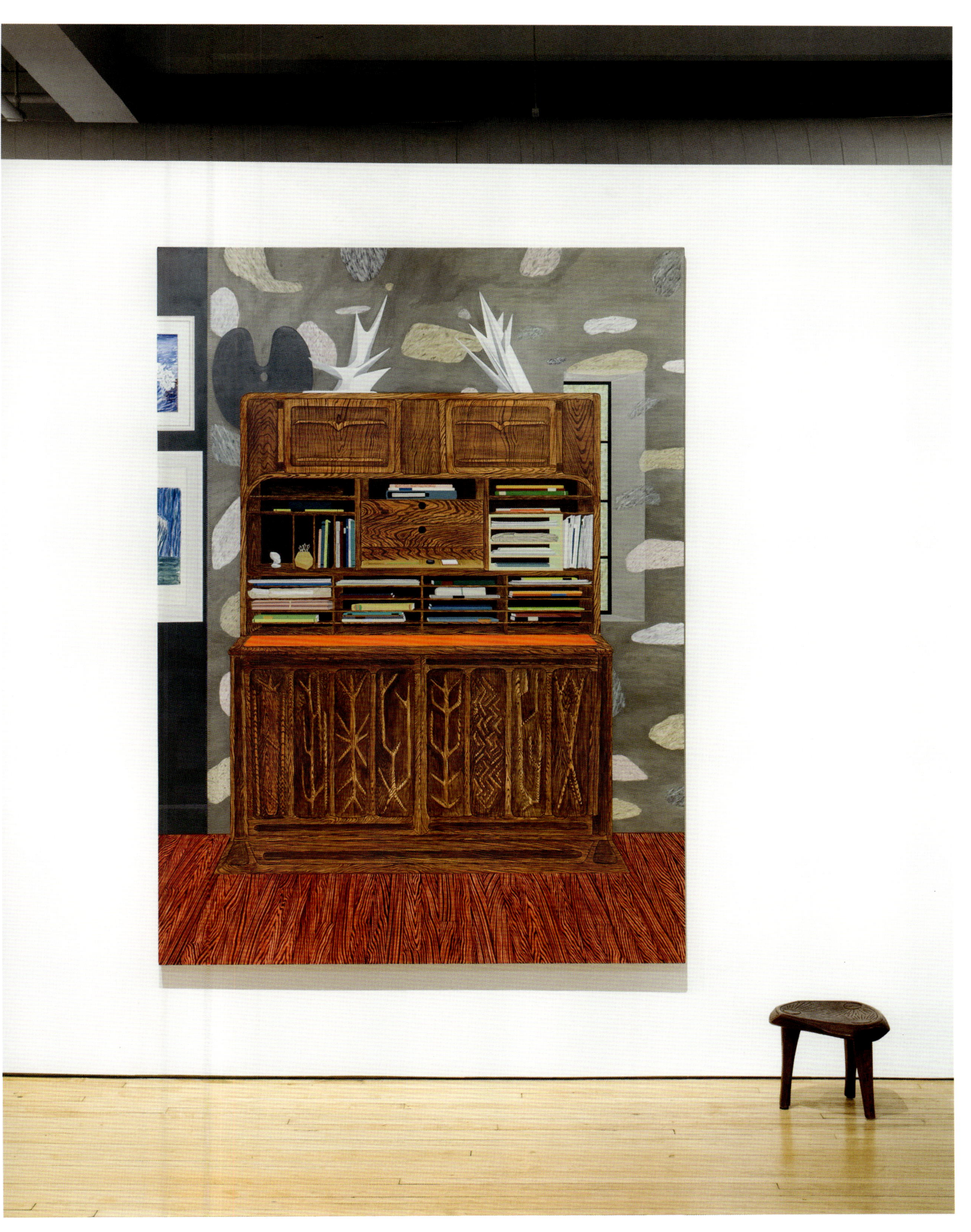

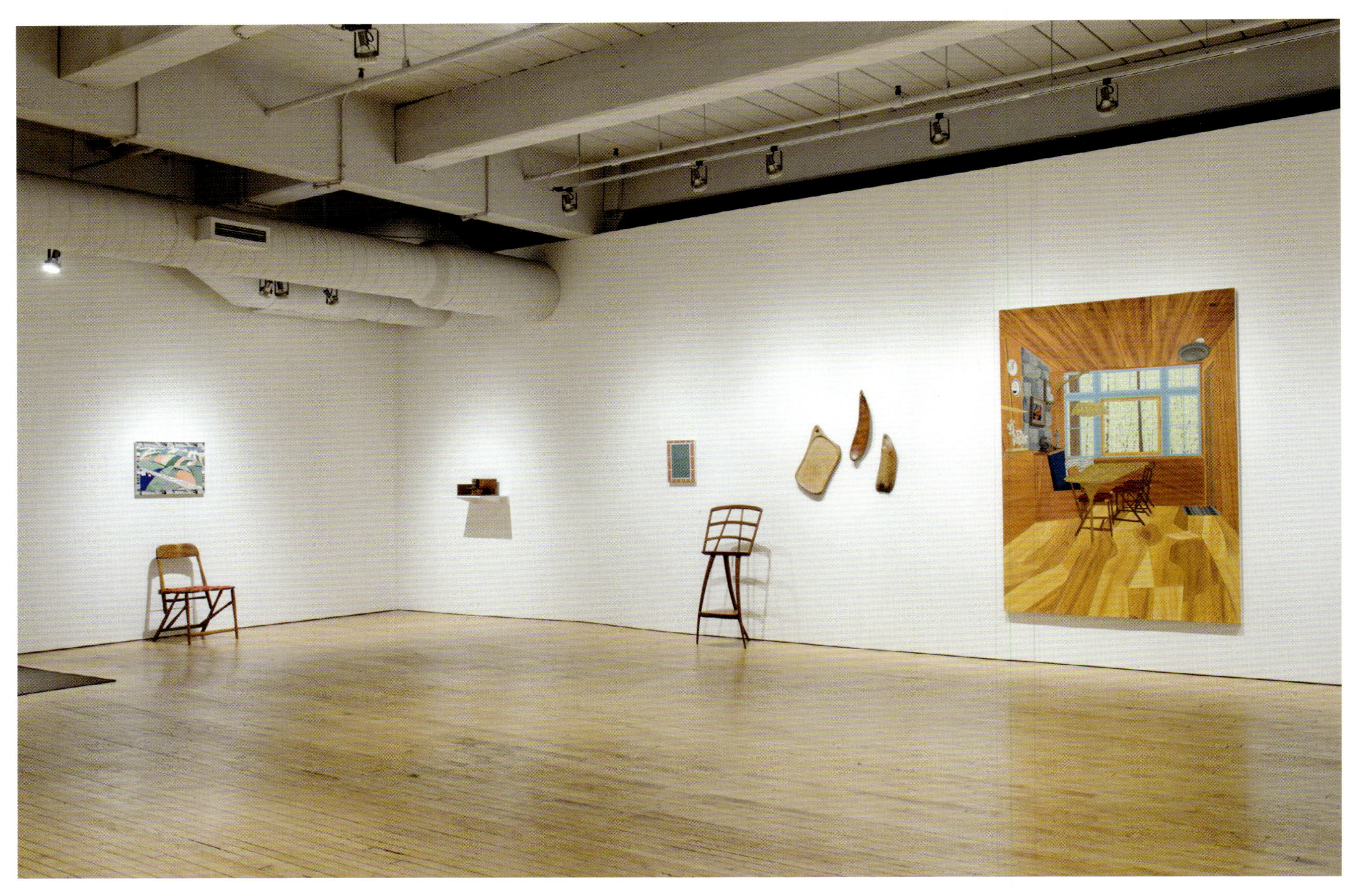

Installation view of *Becky Suss/Wharton Esherick*, Fleisher/Ollman Gallery, Philadelphia, 2018

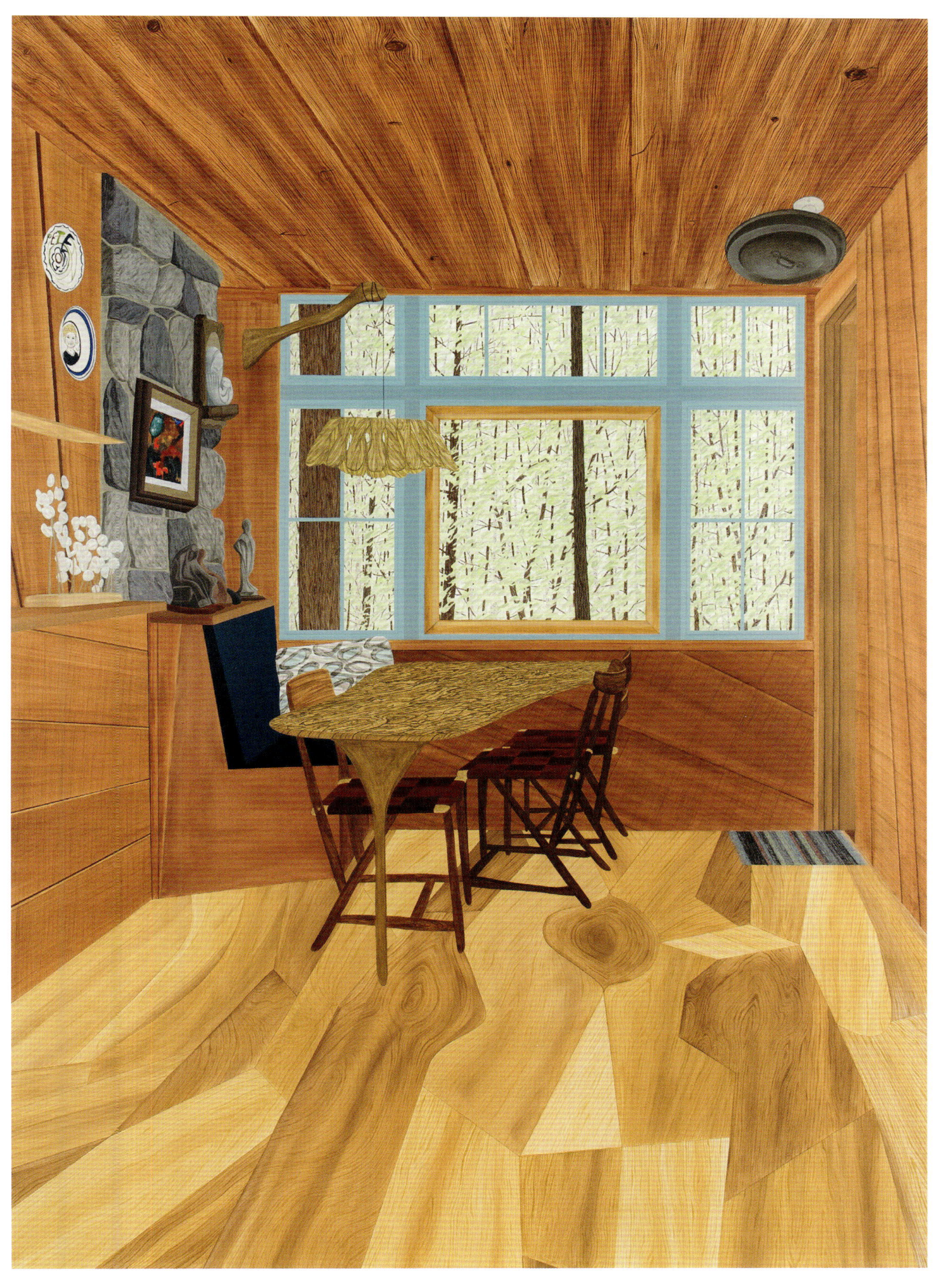

Dining Room (Wharton Esherick), 2018
oil on canvas
84 × 60 inches

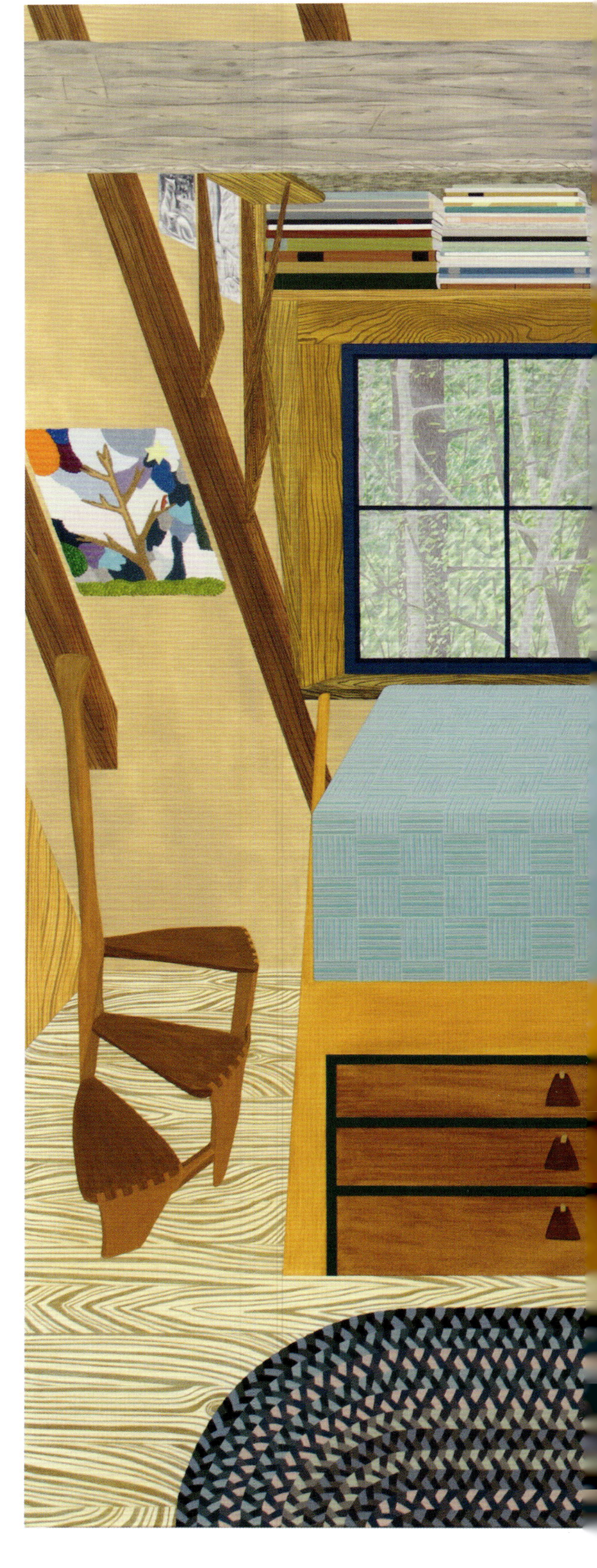

Wharton Esherick Bedroom, 2018
oil on canvas
72 × 84 inches

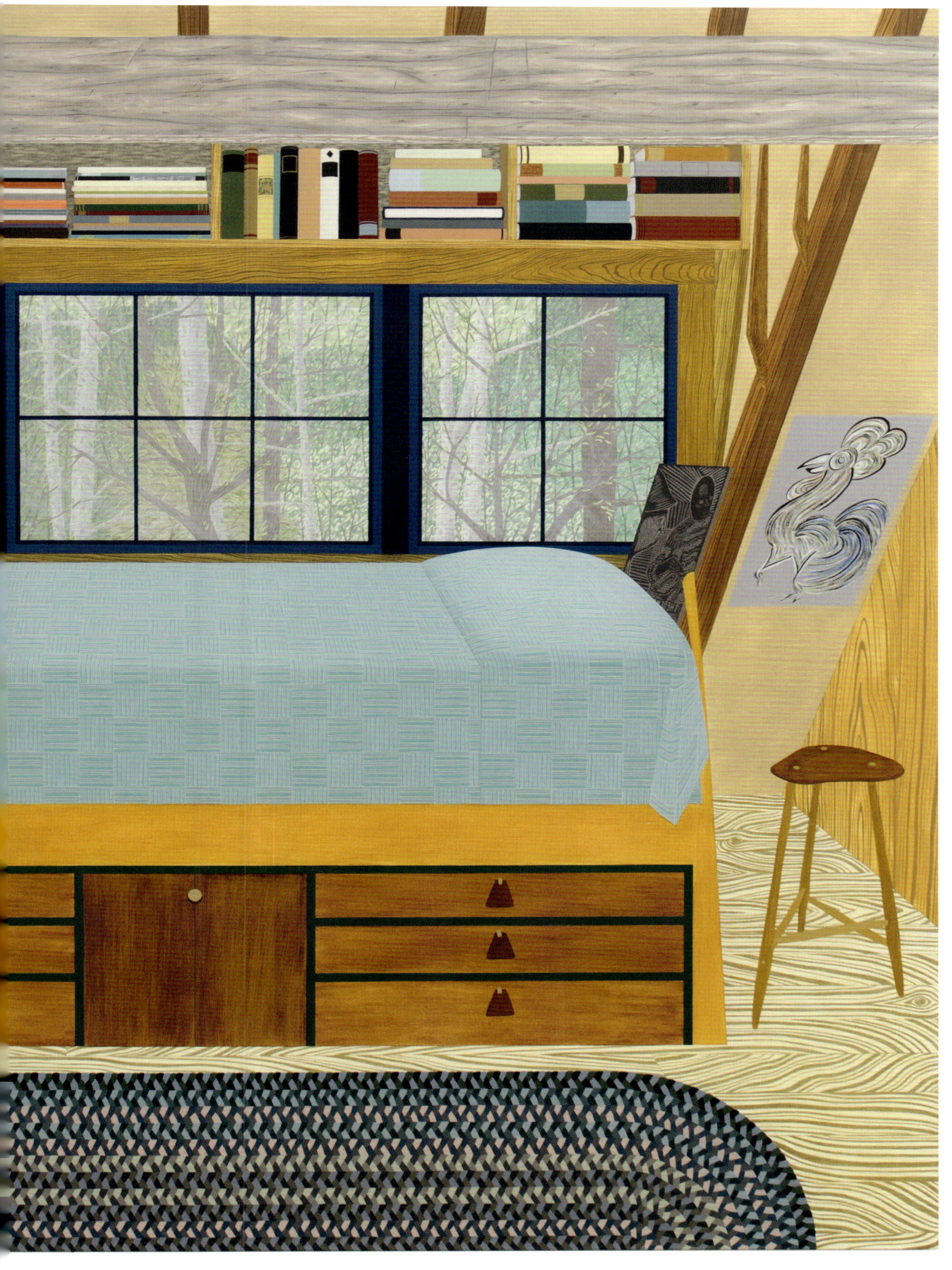

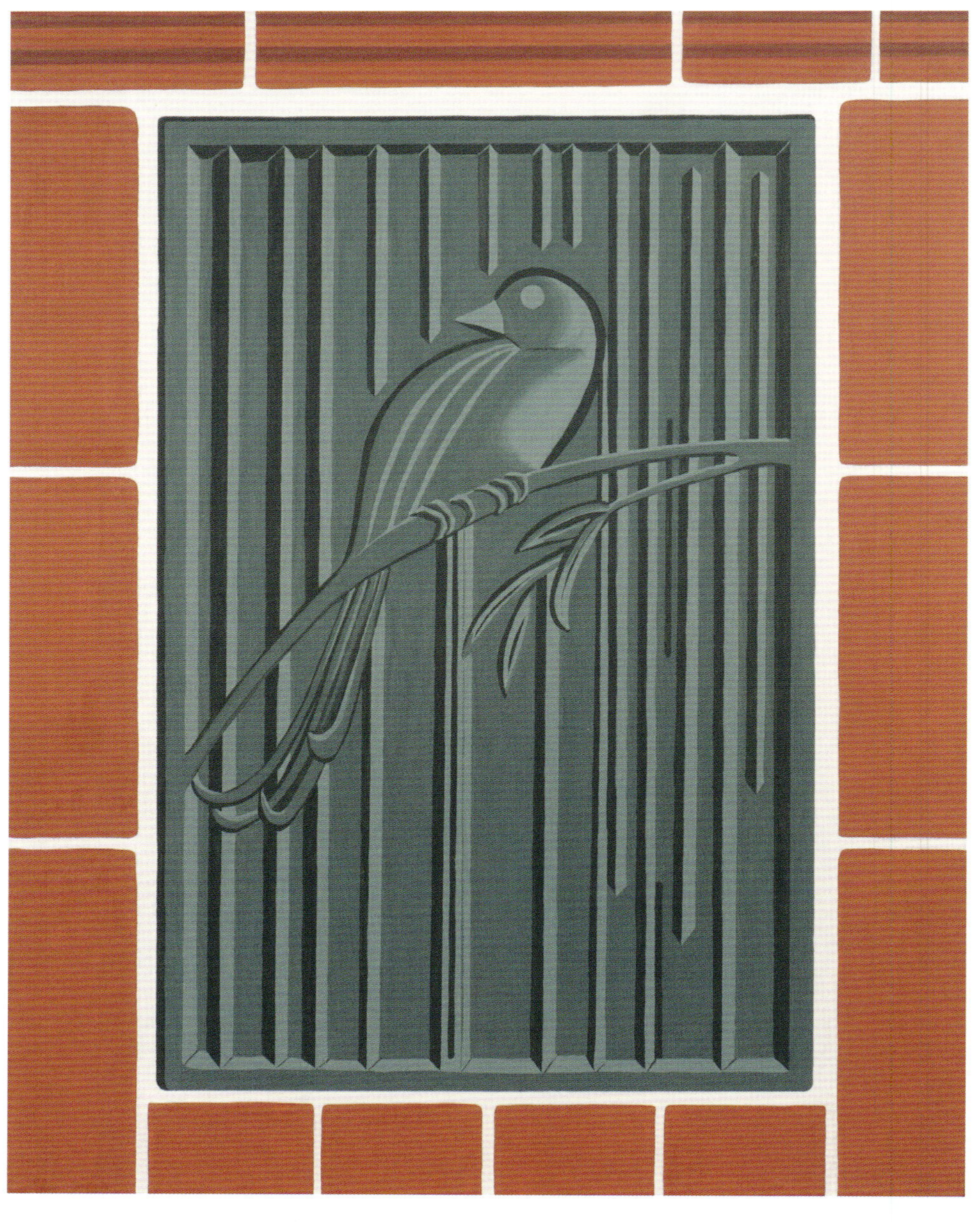

Bird in Rain (Wharton Esherick), 2018
oil on canvas over panel
14 × 11 inches

Installation view of *Becky Suss/Wharton Esherick*, Fleisher/Ollman Gallery, Philadelphia, 2018

Rhymes of Early Jungle Folk by Mary E. Marcy (Wharton Esherick), 2018
oil on canvas over panel
14 × 11 inches

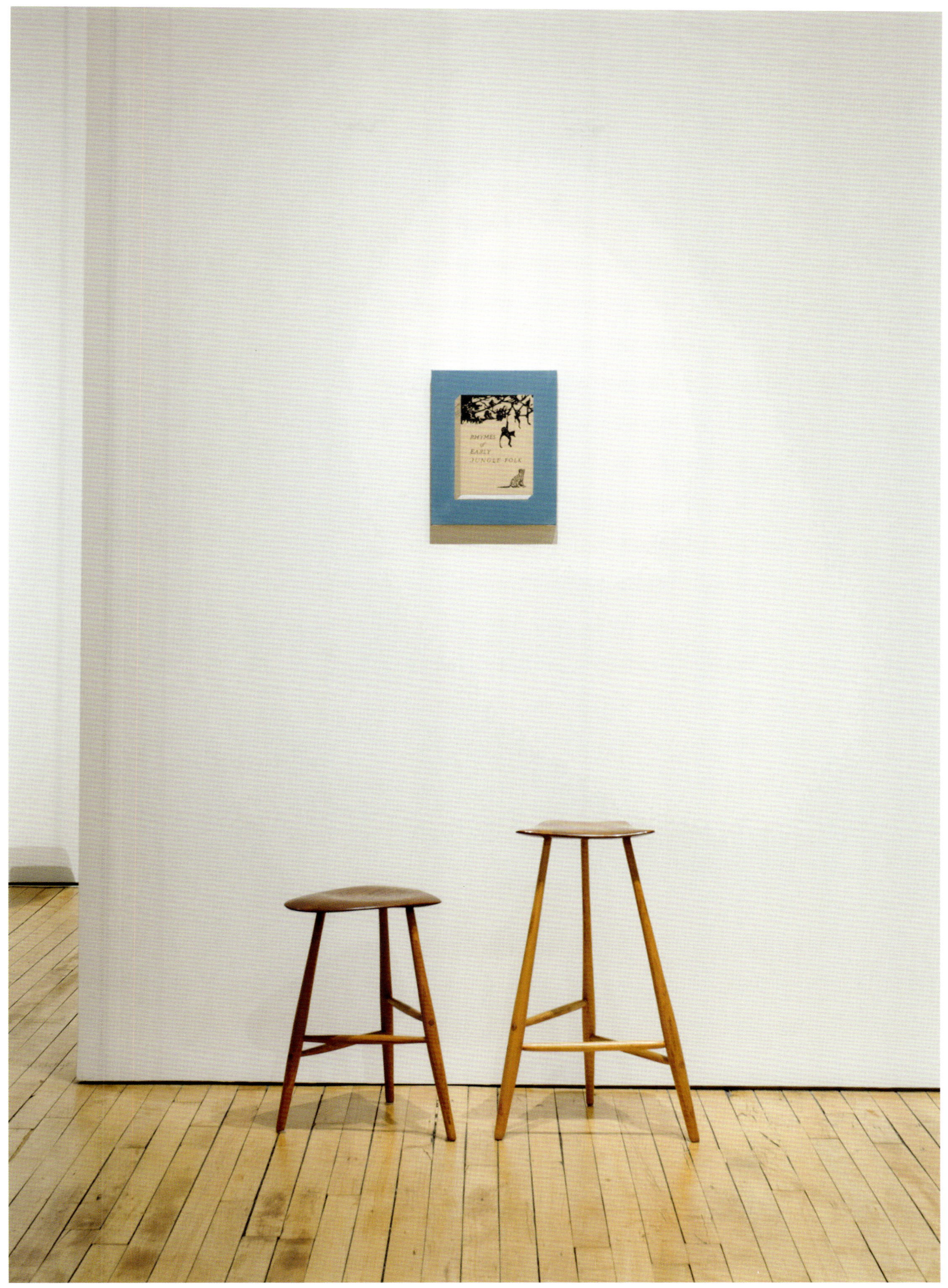
RHYMES
of
EARLY
JUNGLE FOLK

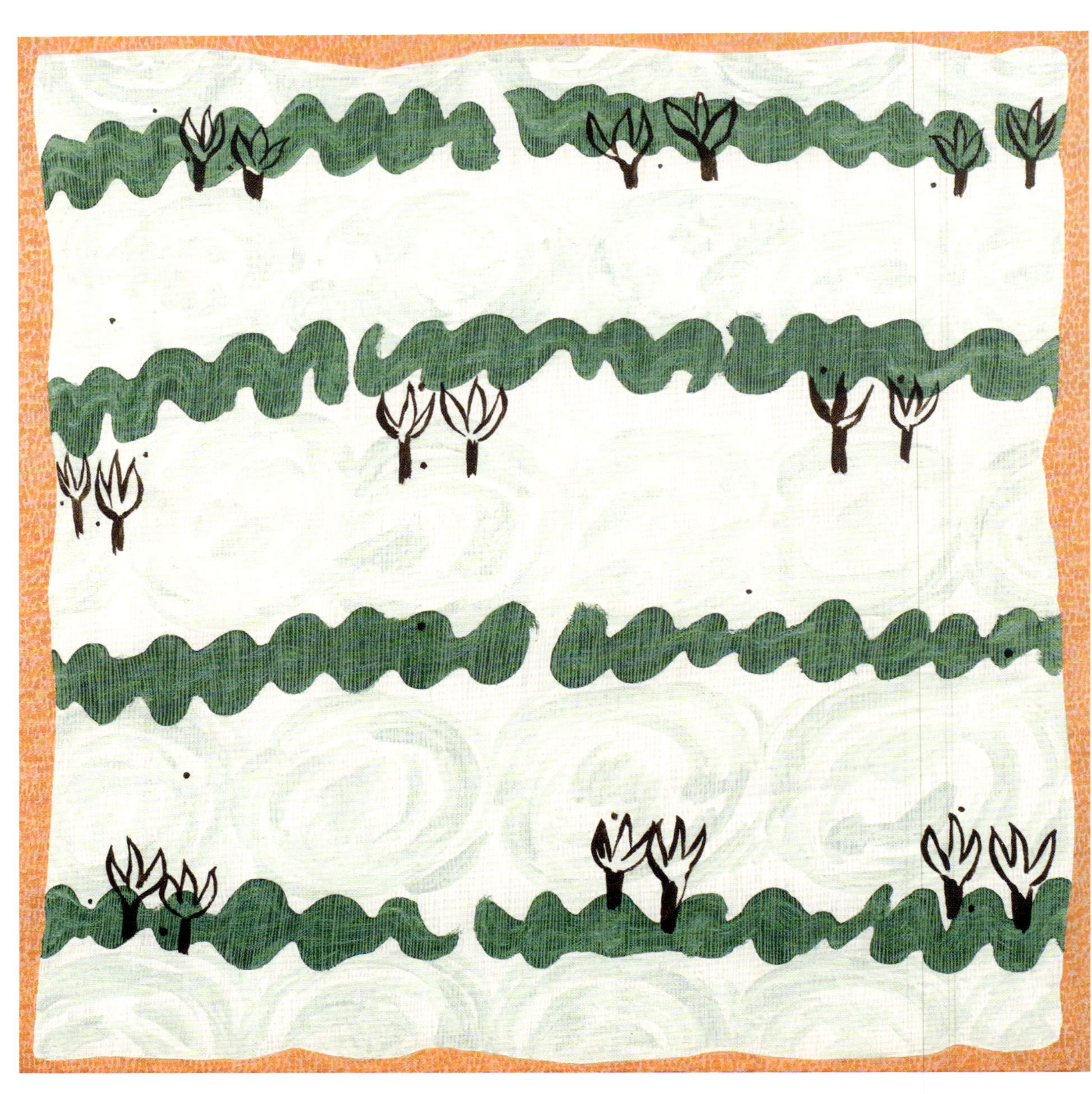

June Groff Pillow (Wharton Esherick), 2018
oil on canvas over panel
14 × 14 inches

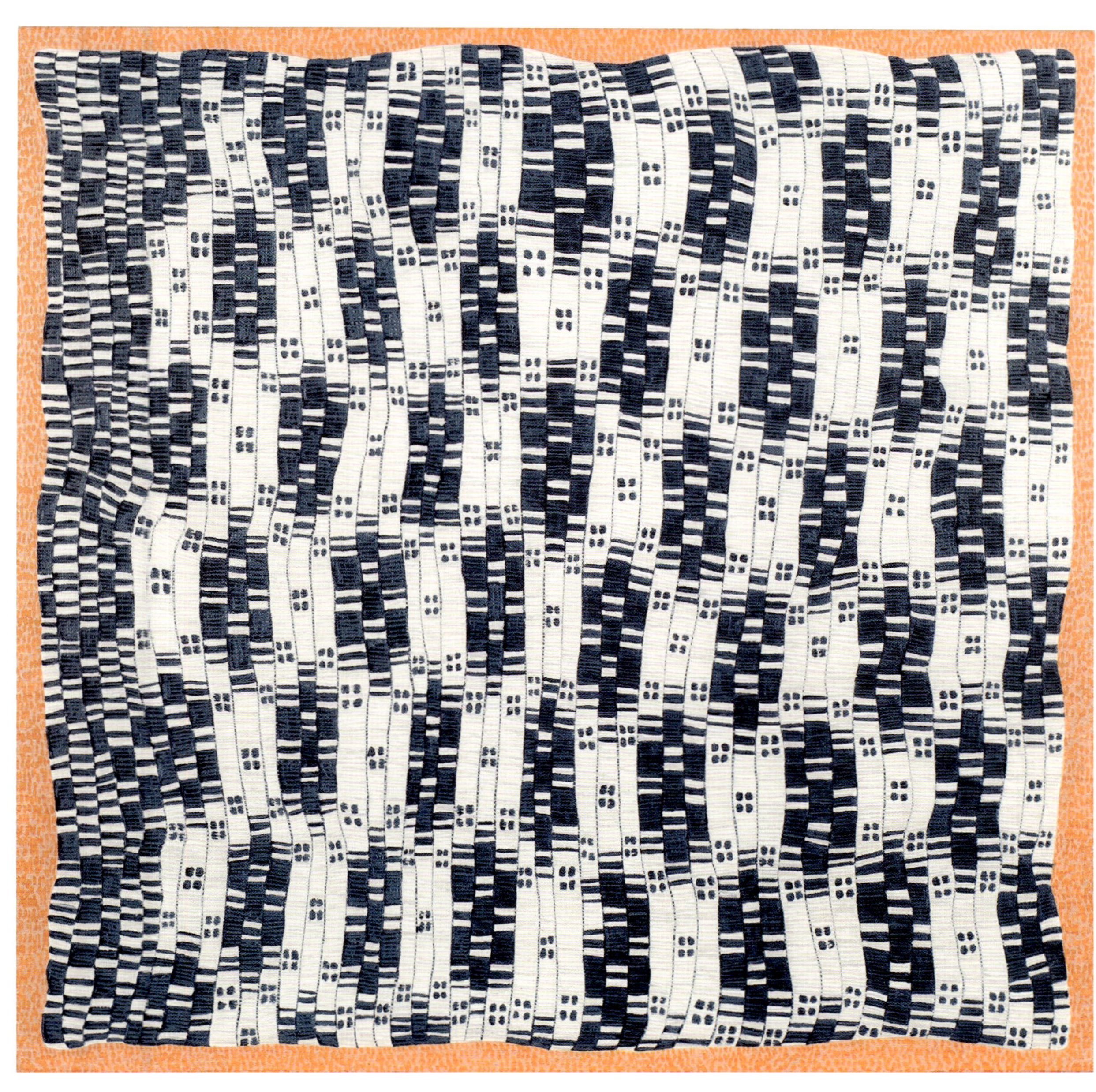

Letty Esherick Pillow (Wharton Esherick),
2018
oil on canvas over panel
14 × 14 inches

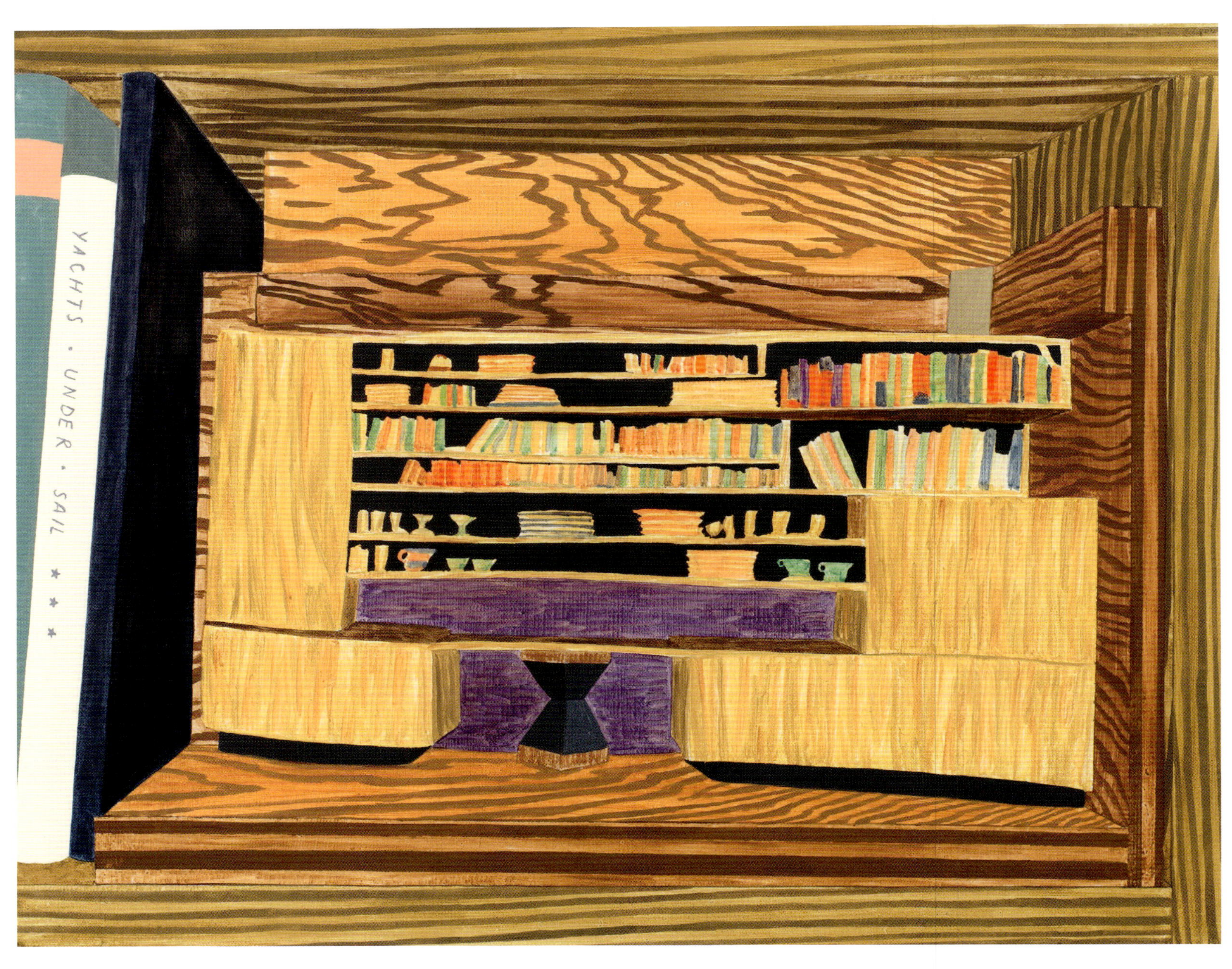

Maquette #2 (Wharton Esherick), 2018
oil on canvas over panel
11 × 14 inches

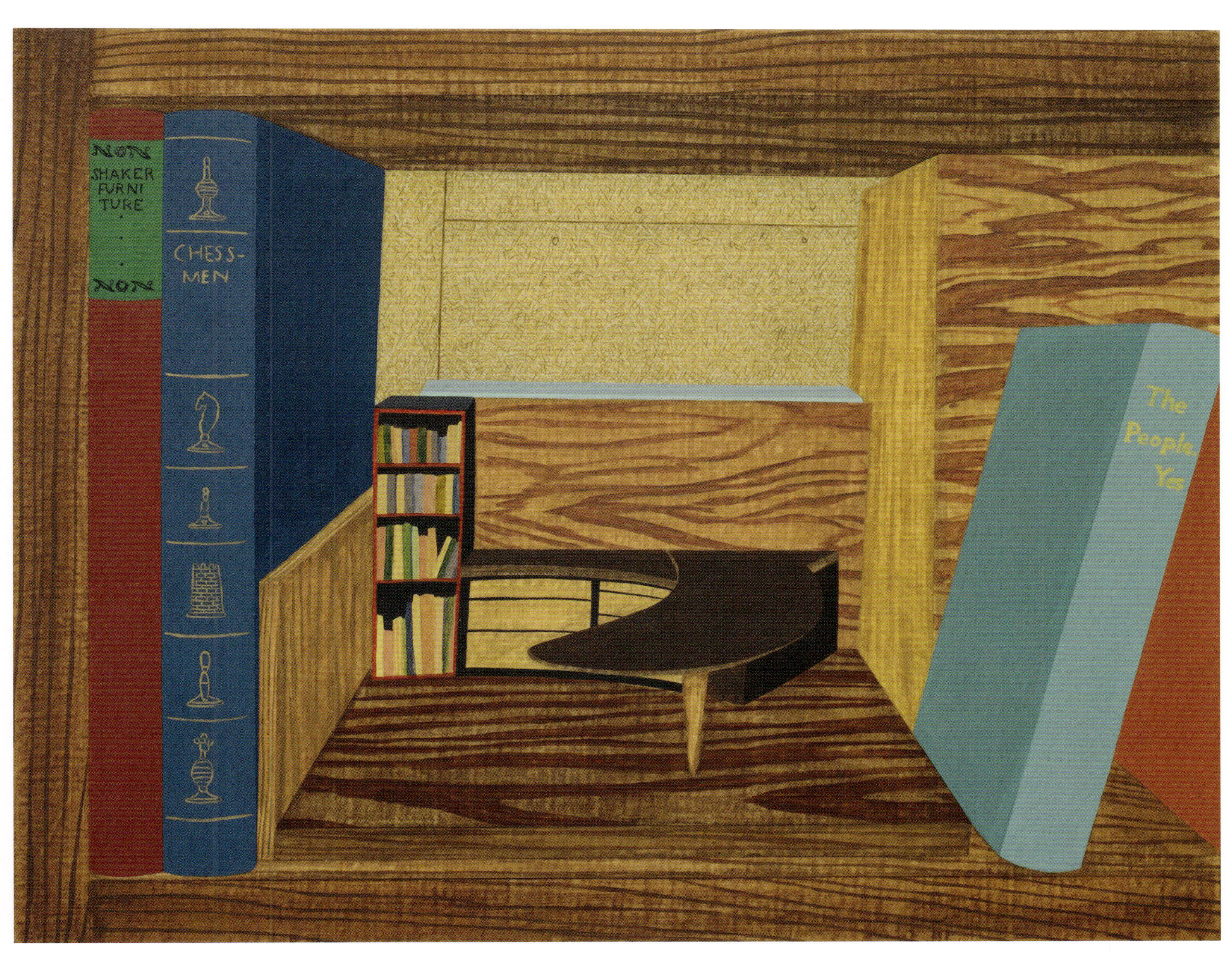

Maquette (Wharton Esherick), 2018
oil on canvas
11 × 14 inches

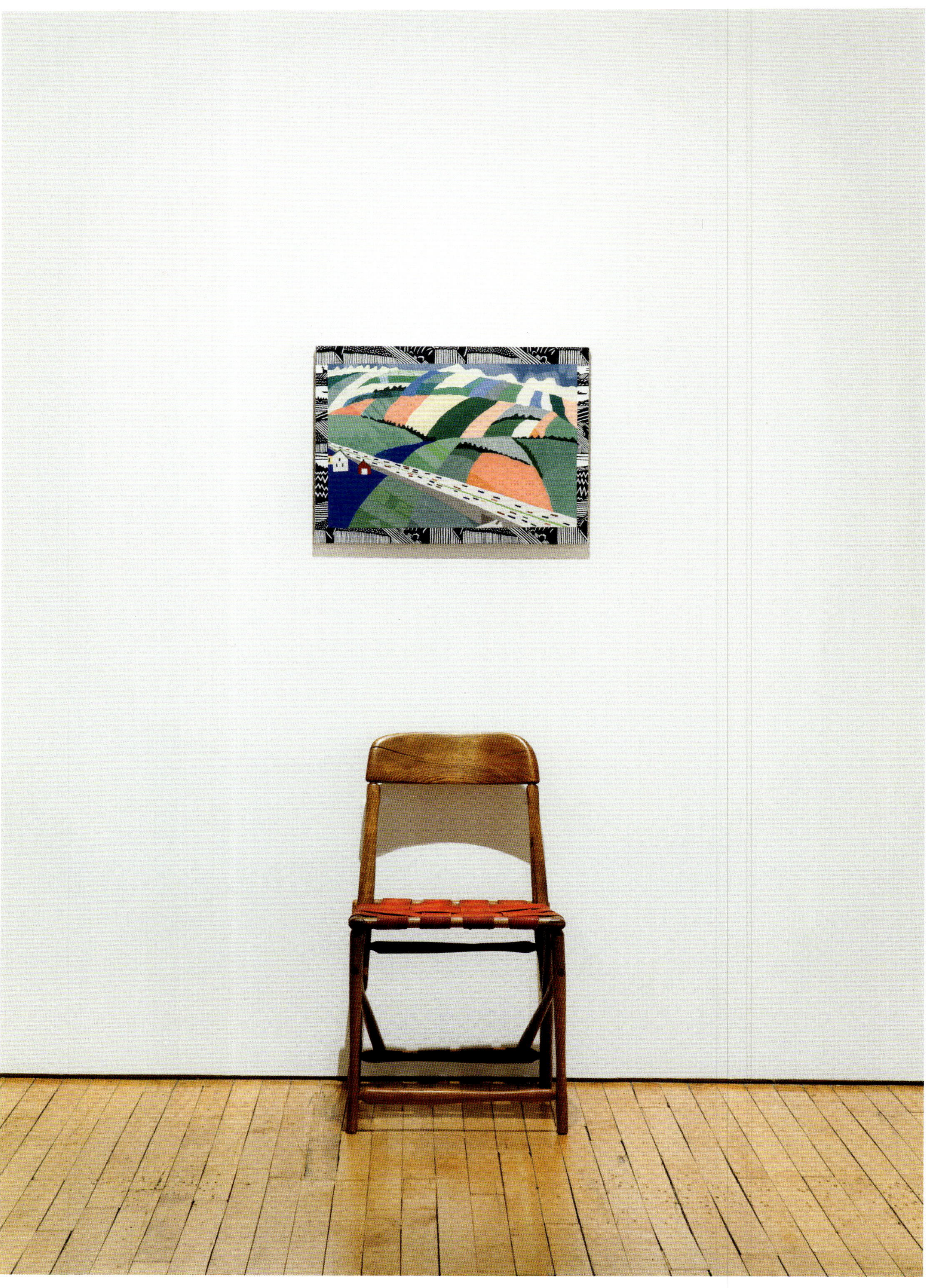

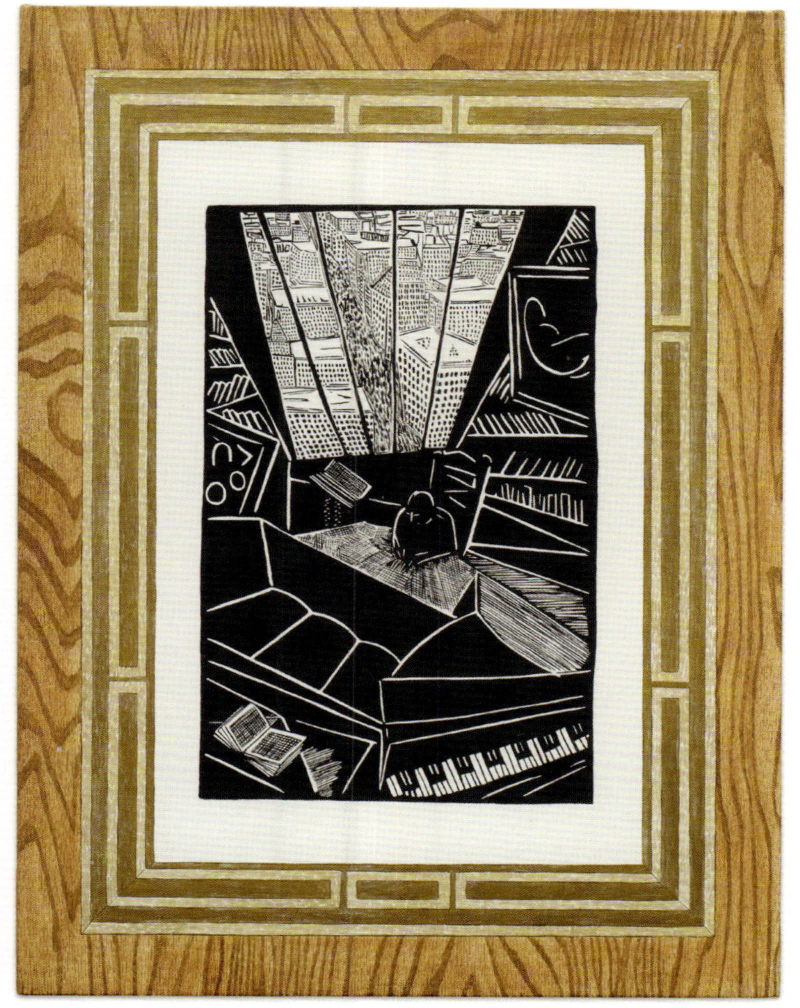

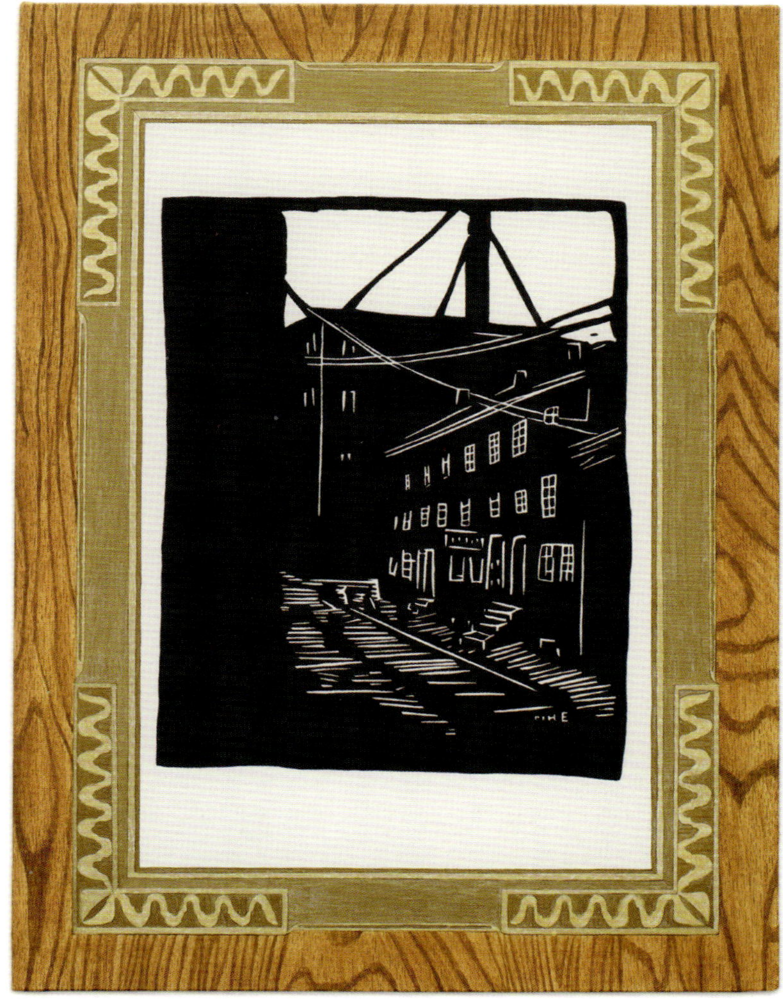

Installation view of *Becky Suss/Wharton Esherick*, Fleisher/Ollman Gallery, Philadelphia, 2018

Mrs. Thayer's 'Almy's Turnpike' Needlepoint on Holzhausen Wallpaper (Wharton Esherick), 2018
oil on canvas
18 × 24 inches

Theodore Dreiser, of a Great City/ Philadelphia Centaur Shop (Wharton Esherick), 2018
oil on canvas over panel
diptych, 24 × 18 inches each

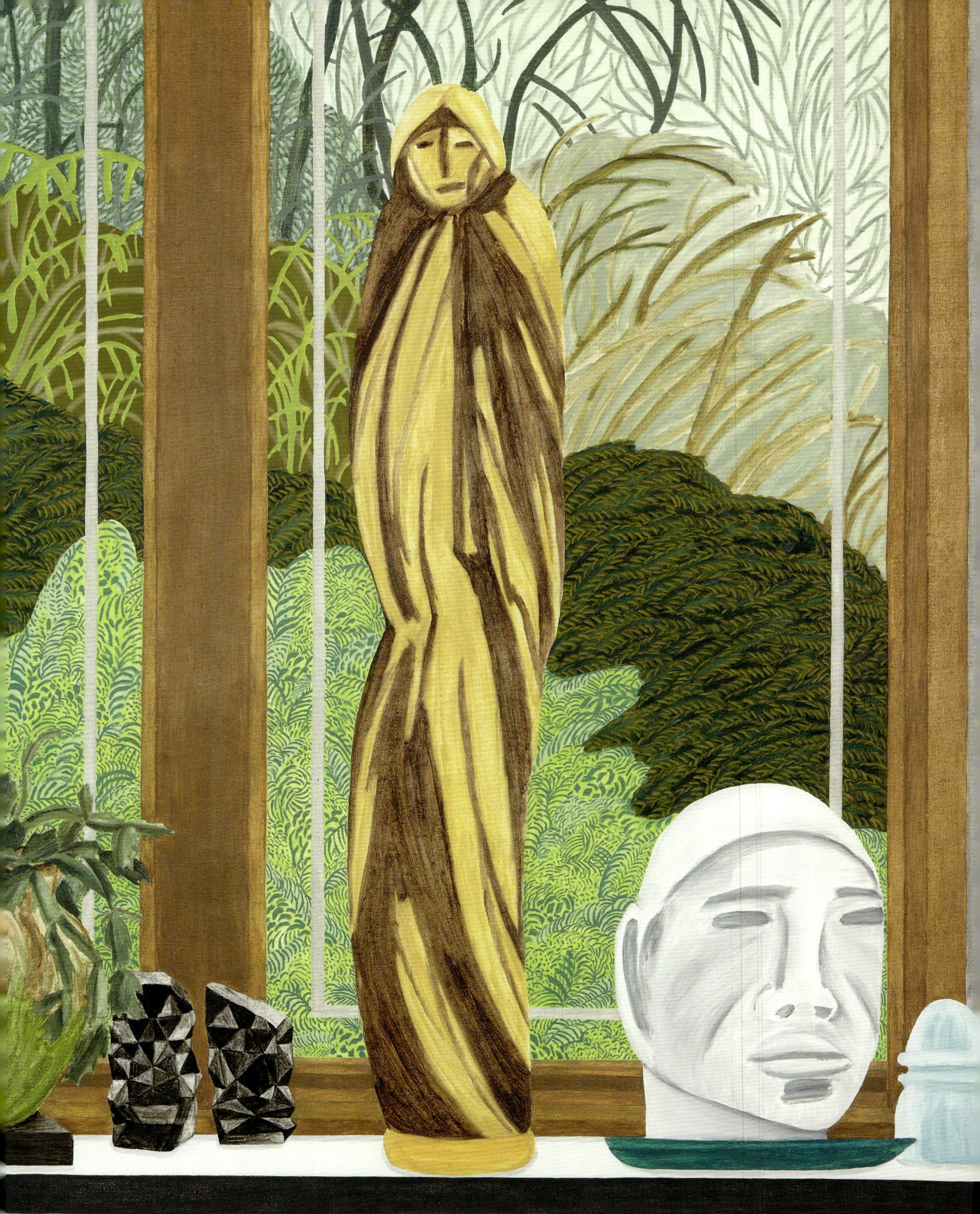

In Conversation with Becky Suss

Helen Molesworth

Helen Molesworth: A question I've been asking artists lately is a version of a question that the radio program host Krista Tippett asks her guests. She asks, "What was the spiritual backdrop of your childhood?," which is a remarkably revealing question. I've tweaked it a bit and am asking "What was the cultural backdrop of your childhood?" Were you a library kid? Did you go to museums? Did you look at comic books? How would you describe the cultural landscape of your childhood?
Becky Suss: It's funny because I feel like the two questions overlap. Her question is interesting to me because it was really relevant to the first body of work I did with interiors. I grew up Jewish—my dad is Jewish, his whole family was Jewish, but they were the kind of Jews that had lobster on Saturdays, you know? So not particularly religious, but culturally Jewish. My dad thought Lincoln and Roosevelt were Jewish. He just assumed that all the good guys were Jewish. My mom was Irish Catholic, and also not very religious. They raised me and my siblings as Jews, we were bat mitzvahed, and there was this sort of "there's a little girl named Rebecca and she lives in the USSR and she's not allowed to have a Bat Mitzvah, so your gonna have one." This cultural, secular Judaism was an interesting backdrop for my first body of work about my grandparents. They had a house on Long Island that was demolished after they died which I made all these paintings about, and their taste was so specific that older Jewish people from the Northeast who came to the show knew that space. They knew the art on the walls—Jack Levine or William Gropper—they recognized the objects because they were so specific. It was an American Jewish story and they all shared that same story. They were children of Russian immigrants who were either working class or poor. They lived in the same parts of Brooklyn, grew up to fight in World War II, moved from Brooklyn to Queens to Long Island, and then they "made it." It was interesting to me that you could tell that story to someone by putting these objects in a room, you could make a painting of a domestic room, and these people recognized everything.
Art was always very important in our house. My mom volunteered with a program called Art Goes to School. It wasn't exactly about art history, but they would bring big posters of different artworks into the classroom and the idea was to talk about composition and color and all those kinds of things. It was designed to give kids a basic understanding of how to look at art: "Hey! What do you see?" "That's right! that is what you see! What does this remind you of?" It let the kids know that they did understand art, that it wasn't some out-of-reach thing meant for rich people and grown-ups. She was always dragging us to museums, and I say dragging because even though I was a kid who loved art, I think when you're a kid it still feels like a drag . . .

HM: What museums was she dragging you to?
BS: The PMA in Philadelphia. Also, my grandparents lived on Long Island but in the early '80s they bought an apartment in the city, so we would spend a lot of time in New York. We'd go every two or three months and then we went to MoMA and The Met.

76 Meadow Woods Road, detail, 2012

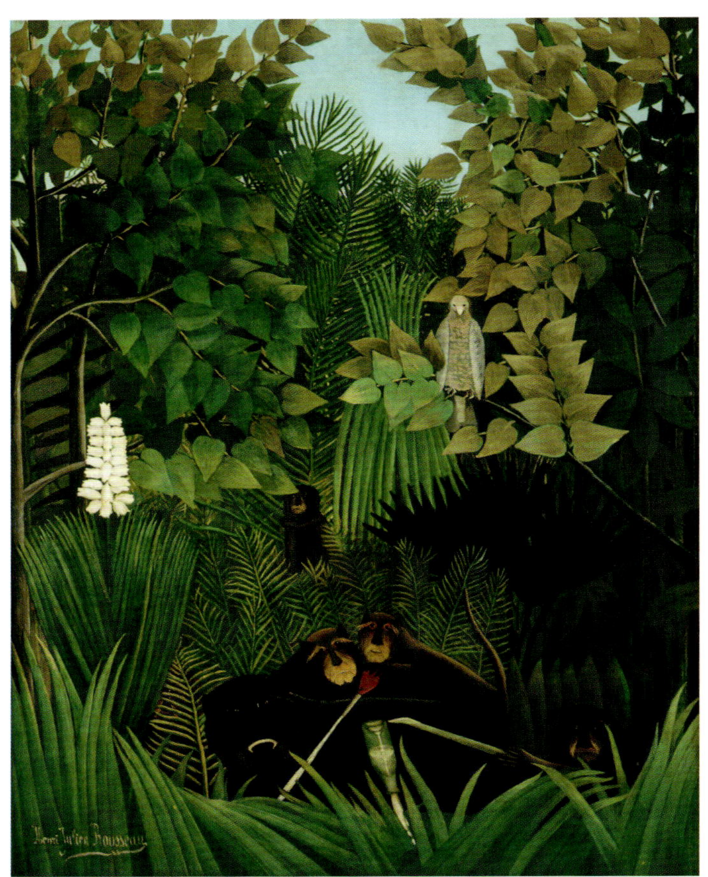

Henri Julien Félix Rousseau
The Merry Jesters, 1906
oil on canvas, 57 ⅜ × 44 ⅝ inches
Philadelphia Museum of Art: The Louise and Walter Arensberg Collection, 1950, inv. 1950-134-176. Courtesy of the Philadelphia Museum of Art

HM: Did you have favorite things in the Philadelphia Museum as a child?
BS: I wrote my college essay about a Rousseau painting there. I had a poster of *The Merry Jesters* in my room. I think that poster is gonna make it into a painting that I'm doing in a new series. I loved Rousseau, I loved Horace Pippin. I liked a lot of self-taught artists, without knowing that I liked the self-taught artists.

HM: That's interesting. I've never thought about Pippin in relation to your work, but it's a very lively association for me—all those interiors and the intensity of the mark making—it's interesting to think about you being drawn to that as a younger person.
BS: I think there's something really direct about them, almost like a diorama. You can imagine he was painting from a little diorama versus an actual room. They are composed, self-contained, and compact, so frontal. It's a very direct approach to space.

HM: You're so right about that frontal, diorama-like view into a space, which is almost anthropological in its gaze. They are so different than Rousseau. Pippin feels like a poet of the quotidian, whereas Rousseau is all about the space of fantasy.
BS: Rousseau's are almost all outside, they were landscapes, and for the first ten years of making art I loved landscapes. It is so hard to make a green painting, because it will always compete with what you see out the window. But man did Rousseau succeed! Those paintings are total magic!

HM: There's also something in both Pippin and Rousseau that is key to thinking about your work: the mark making is extremely meticulous rather than expressive. I wonder—given that you can clearly make any kind of mark you want—how you feel about painting in the wake of abstract expressionism . . .
BS: It's interesting because those were childhood favorites. As I got older, it was Philip Guston and De Kooning and all of the things that you're taught about what a painting is supposed to be. Even in the '90s and early 2000s when I was in school, there were still ideas like, "oh, you can't paint from a photograph" and "you wanna use a big brush" and "don't worry about how much paint your using" and all these things that aren't the way I work.

HM: Did you go to a liberal arts college or an art school?
BS: I went to a liberal arts college. I knew I wanted to make art. Another part my childhood background is my Great Uncle Sid, who my son is named after, and who lived in Philadelphia his whole life. He was a WPA-era artist, and I saw him all the time. He died at 100 when I was in my

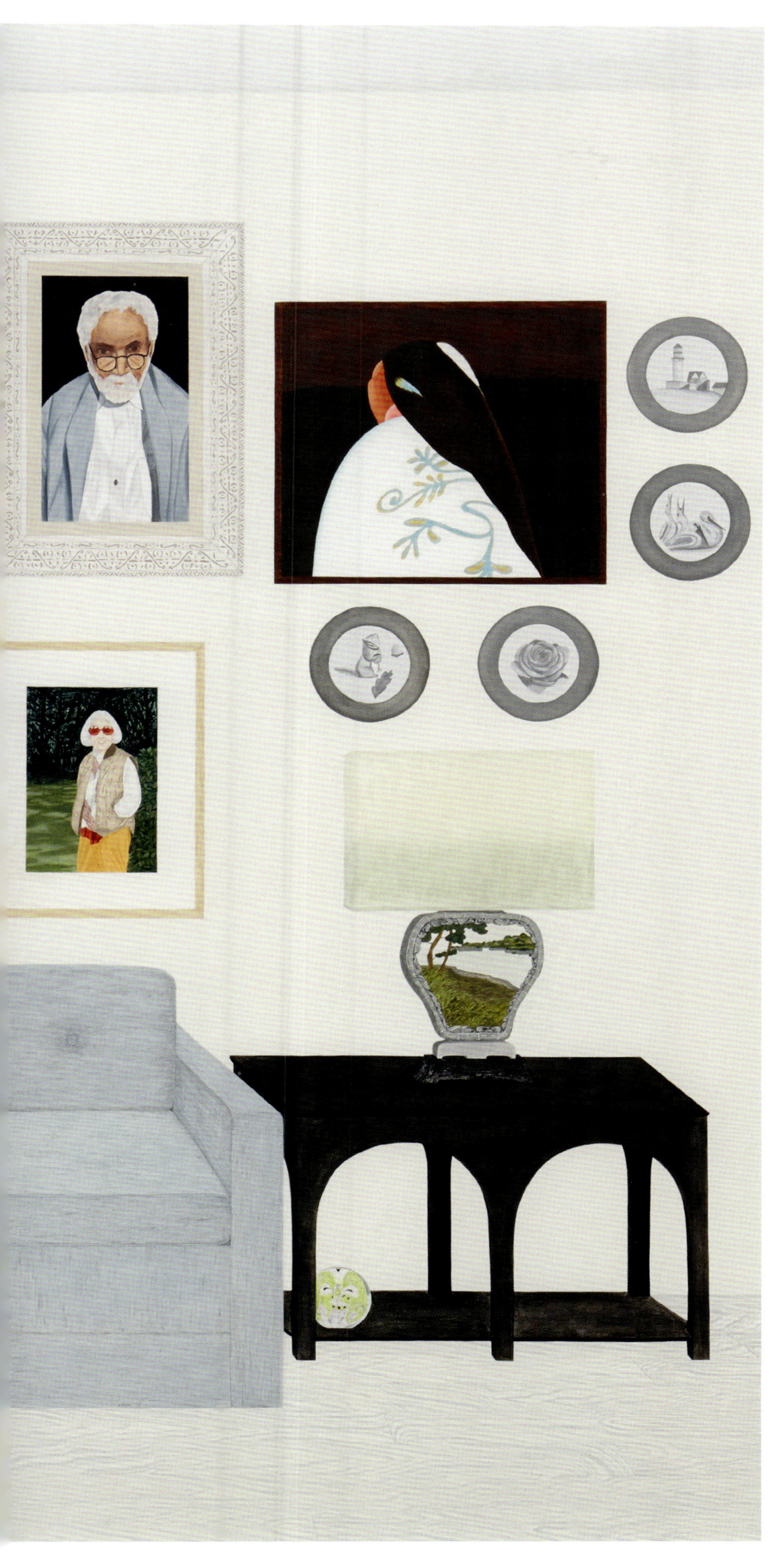

Living Room (Six Paintings, Four Plates), 2015
oil on linen
84 × 108 inches
The Heckscher Museum of Art, Huntington, NY; Gift from the Collection of Ninah and Michael Lynne, 2022.1

saw things and processed them and put them down in two dimensions. I remember Frank—Frank Bramblett—talking about how the sensibility of space had a lot more to do with Eastern painting than Western painting in terms of the stacking and the patterning and flattening. I don't think that was deliberate. I think it was instinct. But I feel like it's not a coincidence. The instinct fed the content and then the content fed the instinct.

HM: I wonder if we could pivot a bit. You're clearly interested in the decorative—carpet patterns, wood grain, fabric details—these things are all very alive in your works. How do you think about the decorative? What does the decorative mean to you? Do you think about it as similar to, or different from, décor, meaning, the arranging of space, which is something your paintings do, in a major way?
BS: I feel like this is another one of those things that people tell you is bad, you know?

HM: Exactly!
BS: The decorative was bad and you didn't want to make anything that had to do with that, and it also got close to illustration, which was also bad. These were the things that you didn't want to do, and I always had the inclination to love them. Even as a kid, I had very visceral reactions to other kids in the class if they came in and were wearing something that I thought was really cool. I remember that feeling. The feeling of opening my closet and looking at the patterns and loving the way that it felt to see that stuff. When I started to make work that included pattern, it was part of letting go of the idea that it was a bad thing, because I always thought the decorative was rich and beautiful and interesting.

HM: I think many of us who are interested in this kind of work all have this narrative of "It's really bad," and there's some internal moment when you're just like, "Fuck it! This is what interests me." And then you have to come up with a narrative about why and how it's interesting to you . . .
BS: When I started making these paintings, I thought to myself, "This is going to be part set painting." It's going to be a way of recreating a place where people's lives can play out, in the same way my family's lives played out in front of that original space this is depicting. The other part of it was archival. I wanted a place to collect all these things. Because if I make them when they're gone, and I don't have them, or I do have them but they're very precious and I'm afraid to use them, I can have a sense of ownership over them once I've painted them. There's a way that these decorative elements tell you so much. You can see something and know the decade it was designed, and you make your own personal attachments to it, or you can have a historical attachment to it, like "That's a pretty quintessential mid-1950s chair that was in every house in America." I think of décor as something that can really help tell a story. I'll build a story and think about the person that might have lived in this space, the woman that made all these decisions to put this home together. I think that opportunity for story telling is interesting.

HM: That's slightly counterintuitive, art historically speaking, the decorative and the narrative have often been held apart from one another. Narrative is the realm of stories, whereas the decorative

Kashmir, 1967
Courtesy of Warren Suss

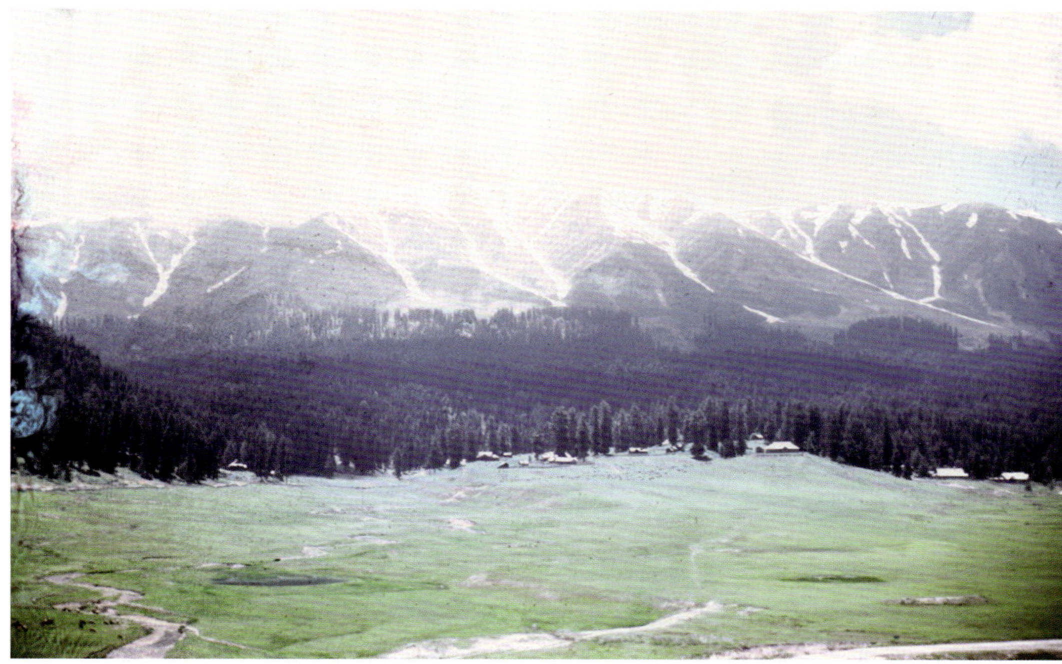

resists narrative because pattern is infinite and has a relationship to abstraction. Your paintings play with that a little; there are moments where they seem so representational, but I can find myself lost in the pattern of the wood grain, which is abstract. Or I get lost in the bookshelves and they become a stripe painting.
BS: Sometimes I talk about these paintings as my way of being greedy. I've come to the conclusion that I make these interiors because I'm selfish. I want to be able to do everything. I want to make a painting that is an interior and is large scale and relates to abstract expressionism. I can make a landscape either by making a painting within the painting or by painting a view out of a window. I can make a still life because the room can contain it. I used to love Gerhard Richter so much because he gets to do everything, you know, and people accept it because he's Gerhard Richter. [*laughs*] He got to do everything because he made his own conceptual framework. I can do all these different types of painting within the framework of a domestic interior.

HM: I have one last question. So, you have this memory space that you're working with, real and actual spaces, and you fill them up with the ubiquitous and the specific. Recently, there's been a shift in the work in which you're actively inventing rooms that you've read about in novels and children's books. You make a picture of a room that someone else has described in a literary way. I'm curious if you could talk about the difference, for you, in painting invented rooms rather than remembered rooms? It feels like a big conceptual shift.
BS: The first book painting I made was from Salman Rushdie's *Haroun and the Sea of Stories*. I read it with my father when I was a kid, and I think part of how I remember that book and its imagery is related to my father having gone to Kashmir in 1967 and the little papier-mâché boxes he brought back with him to our house. He told stories about the houseboat he stayed on and the

politics in Kashmir then. I was thinking about my dad in the '60s and the way Rushdie made a fictionalized version of Kashmir. I love the way the stories are totally separate, and also how they're not, because we live our lives through storytelling and books and narratives and art, and they will always intersect and overlap.

I think in some ways it's liberating to make work that is removed from direct autobiography because you get to pick whatever you want, your choices become sort of limitless. I remember having a conversation with Matthew Brannon, a great artist and a friend. He was teaching at Skowhegan when I was there and he said, "What are you gonna do next? No one's gonna want to see pictures of your grandma's house forever." [*laughs*] It was sort of a joke, but it stuck in my head, and I was like, "Shit, what *am* I gonna do?"

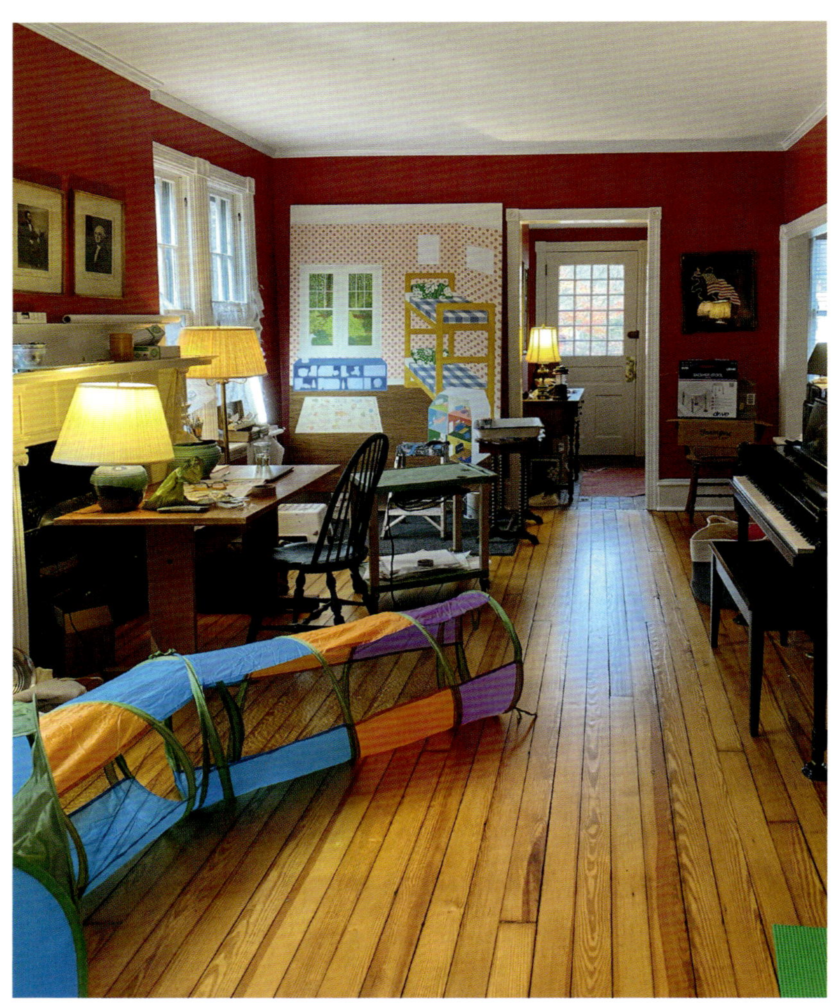

8 Greenwood Place (my bedroom), in progress in the home of the artist's parents, 2021
Courtesy of Becky Suss

HM: Do you think you're going to stay in these fictional, literary spaces, or are you already coming up with new ideas, shifting toward something else?
BS: I'm onto the next thing. It takes me a long time to make stuff, so I'll have a couple of things floating around, and I'll do one and then I'll think, "Okay, this is what I'm gonna do for the next like six or seven paintings," and most of the time it's great, because, like I said earlier, they all end up folding in on themselves. During Covid we lost our child-care, and my mom said, "I'll watch Sid for you." But it was a bit of a commute, so I decided to bring a painting to their house where she was watching him. I was thinking, "Man, I'm gonna go back to this house and I'm going to watch my three-year-old son play out his days in front of the same walls that I played my three-year-old days in front of, with the same caretaker, my mom . . ."

HM: That's kind of incredible.
BS: So I thought, "I'm going to make a painting of my childhood room." But from what era? My room looks different because it's a guest room now. I started to think about all the iterations of this room, and how rooms and homes are palimpsests. There are bits of architecture from different times; wallpaper coming through that has been painted over; what was once a closet is turned into a duct and then there's a new closet built next to it. Rooms are these amazing examples of how one place or object can contain all these traces that tell the story of decades, generations. So I think I'm going to make a series of paintings of the same room. It makes so much sense right now. I'm in this house, in its current iteration, and I'm also incorporating its other iterations.

I'm going to try and make at least five paintings for a show next spring that will be the same room in different eras and there will be moments you can track from painting to painting.

HM: That's great! And it rhymes so beautifully with many of the things that we've talked about, especially the process of psychoanalysis and the constant re-evaluation and re-narration of one's own life. It seems like what you're developing is the skill to understand why you might be summoning certain things at certain times; why certain things remain intractable and can't change, while others are available for change.
BS: Part of me was also thinking now that I am comfortable with making paintings of stories and spaces that are not my own. I can make this painting about this room that was my bedroom and turn the story on its end a little bit. I can reimagine the room through a lens of storytelling. I'm thinking about little moments where you can twist something towards a story or a song or something remembered. One of the paintings will be like a bookshelf painting, on it I will paint a record player (that I picked out the trash) and I stole records from my dad, and I don't know how I'm going to gesture towards that Grateful Dead album in the painting, but I gotta do it somehow! Part of it is the magic of something like *The White Album* by The Beatles—I mean the storytelling in *The White Album* is insane . . .

HM: Epic . . .
BS: I feel like if you could go back to that time in life—age twelve, thirteen, fourteen—and conflate all the stories in *The White Album* with how life feels like an adventure at that age, that moment when your parents let you do whatever you want, you know? I've been thinking about incense holders, candles, color combinations, little things that I feel I can use to embed the fictional storytelling in the paintings. I'm interested to see how, instead of pushing the autobiographical, I can fictionalize the paintings just a little bit.

HM: I'm so excited for you. Can't wait to see those paintings!

Where They Are
2019-2020

Henrik's House (Great Aunt Birte's Funeral), 2020
oil on canvas
60 × 72 inches

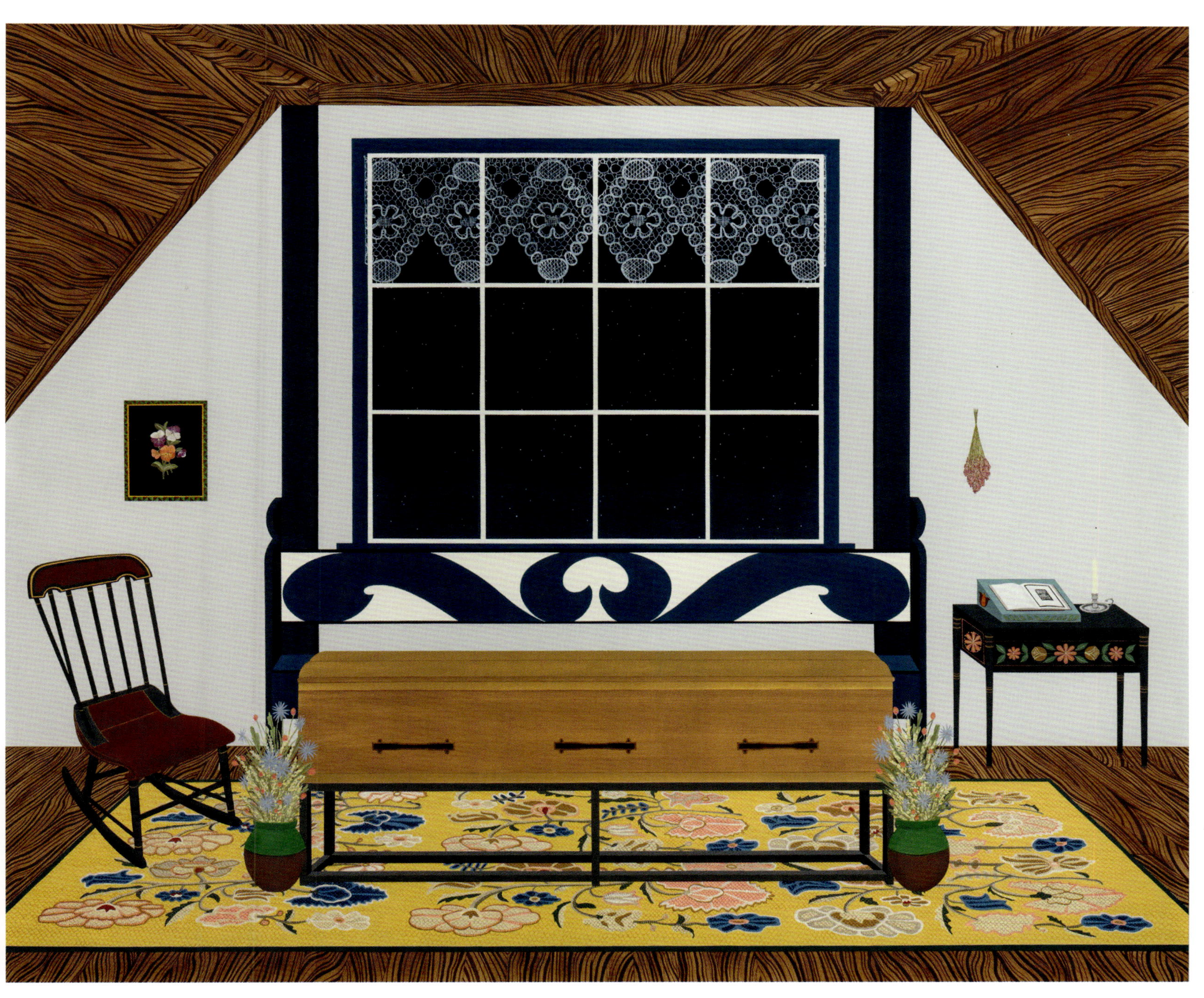

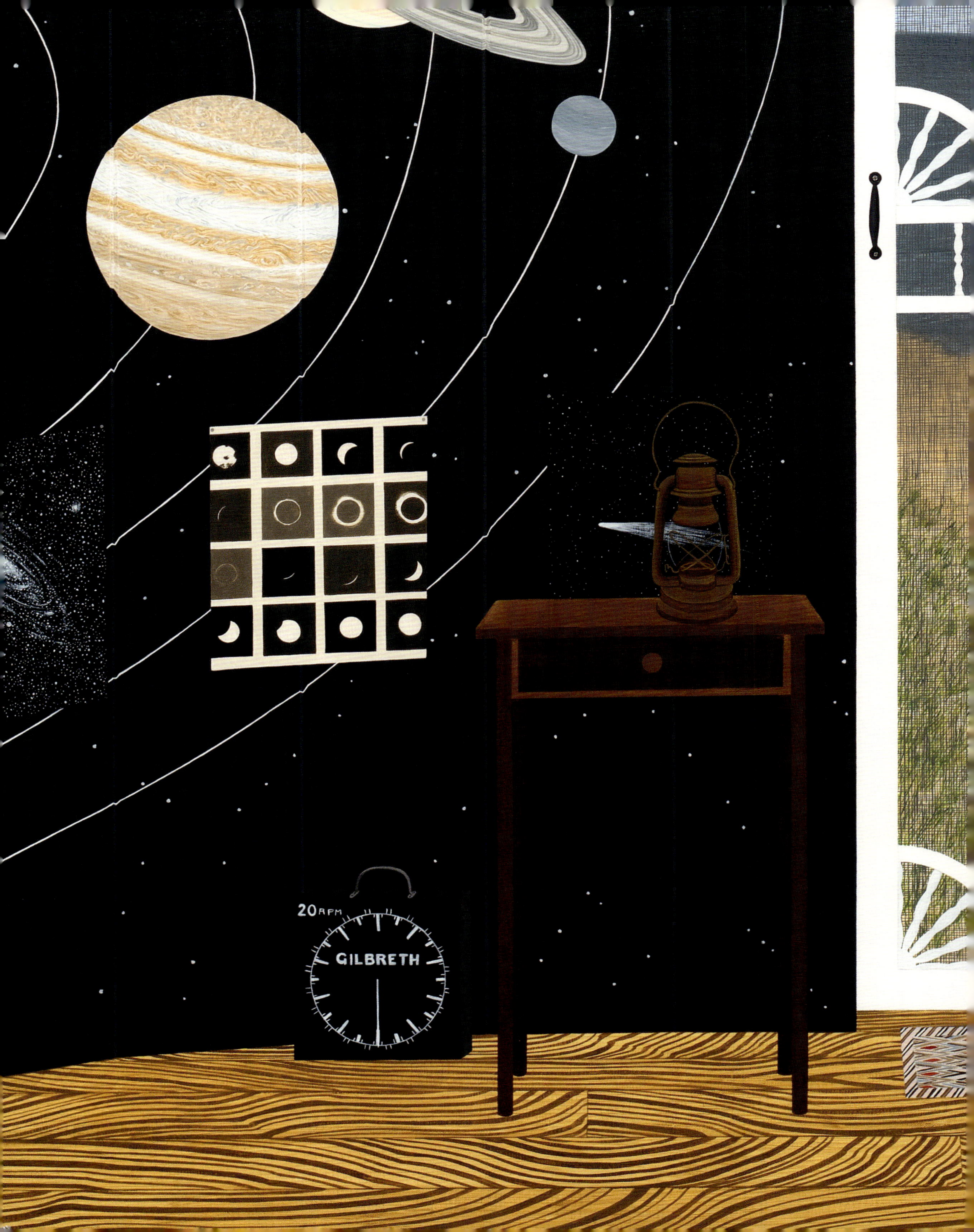
20RPM
GILBRETH

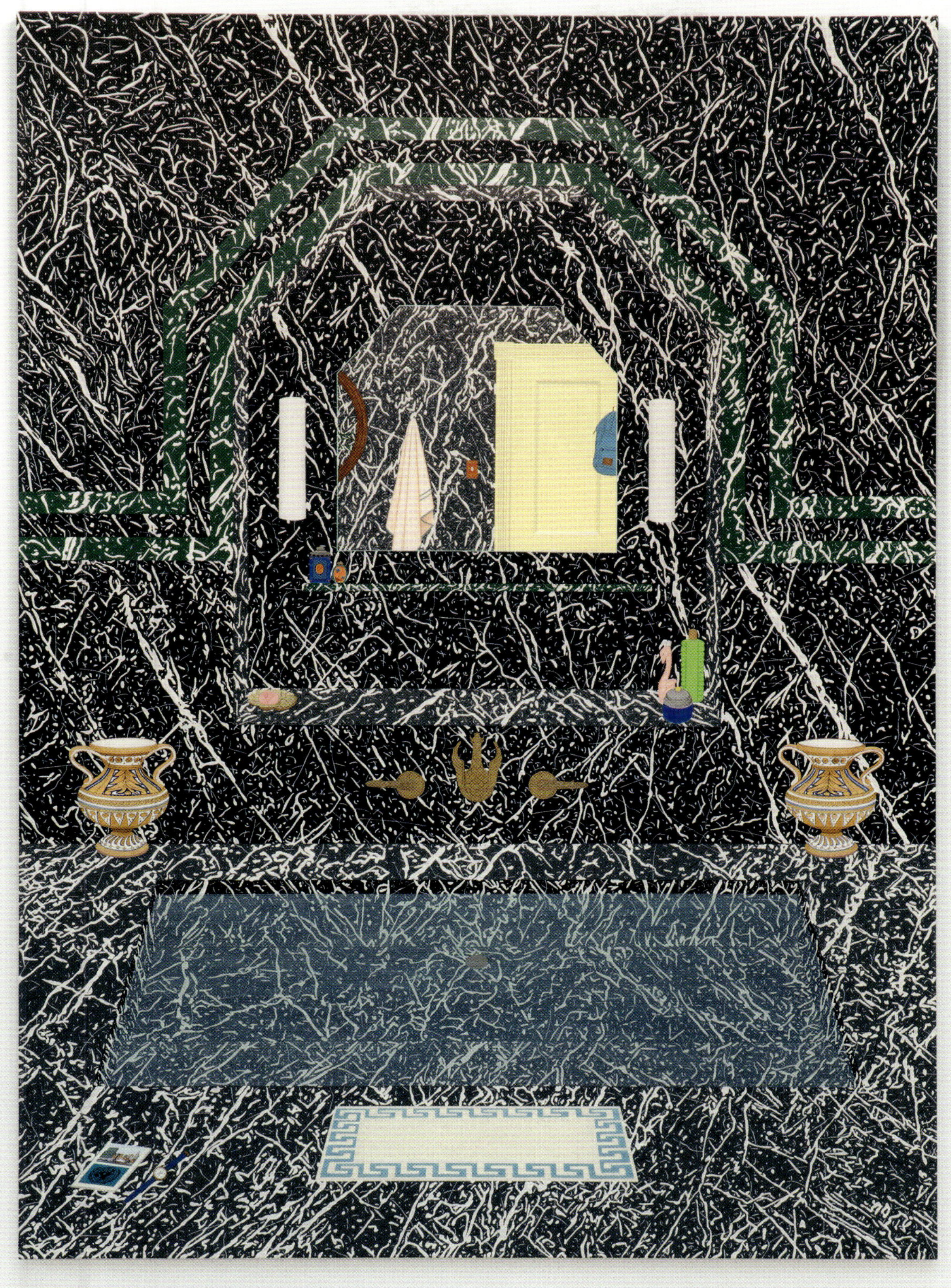

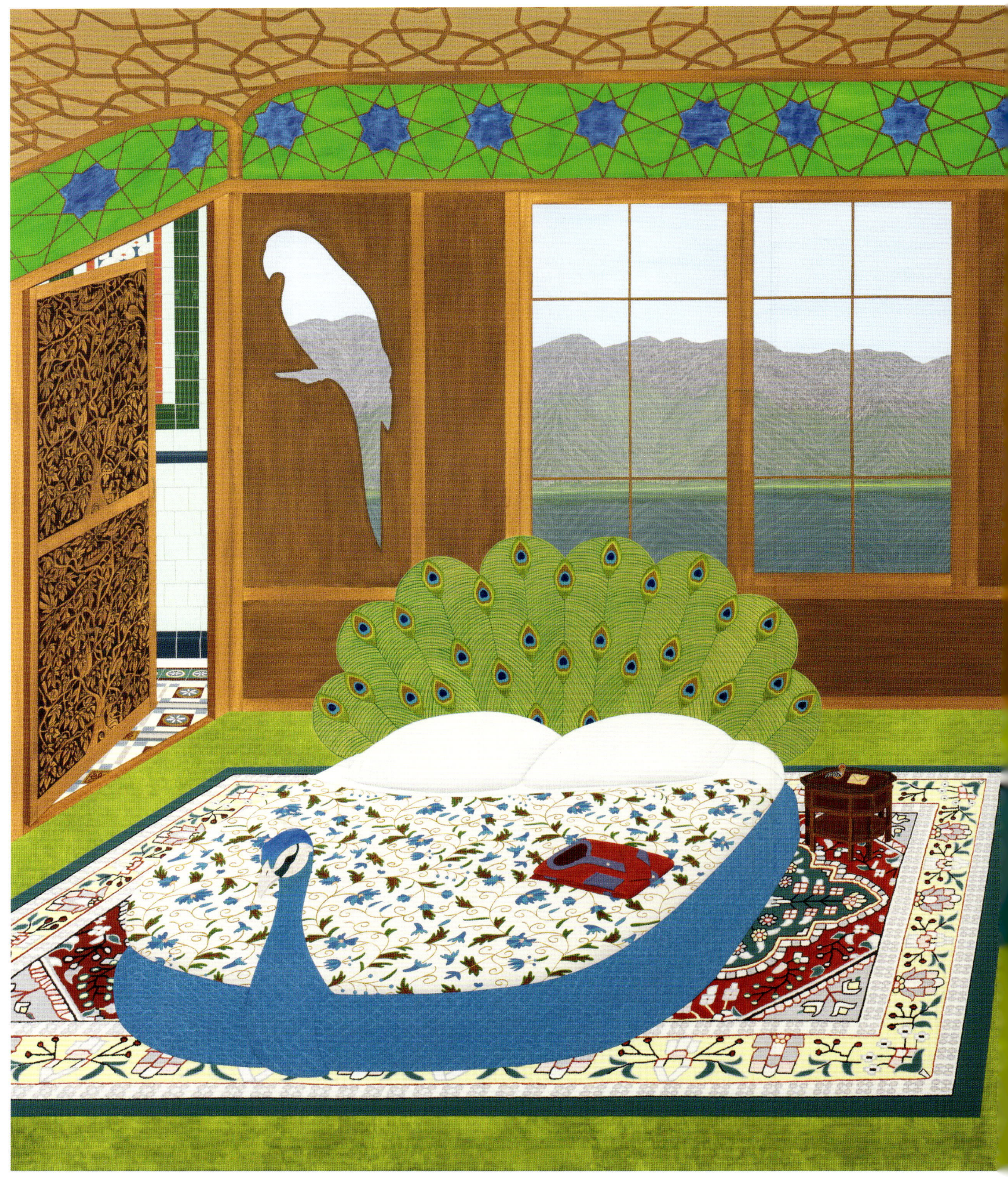

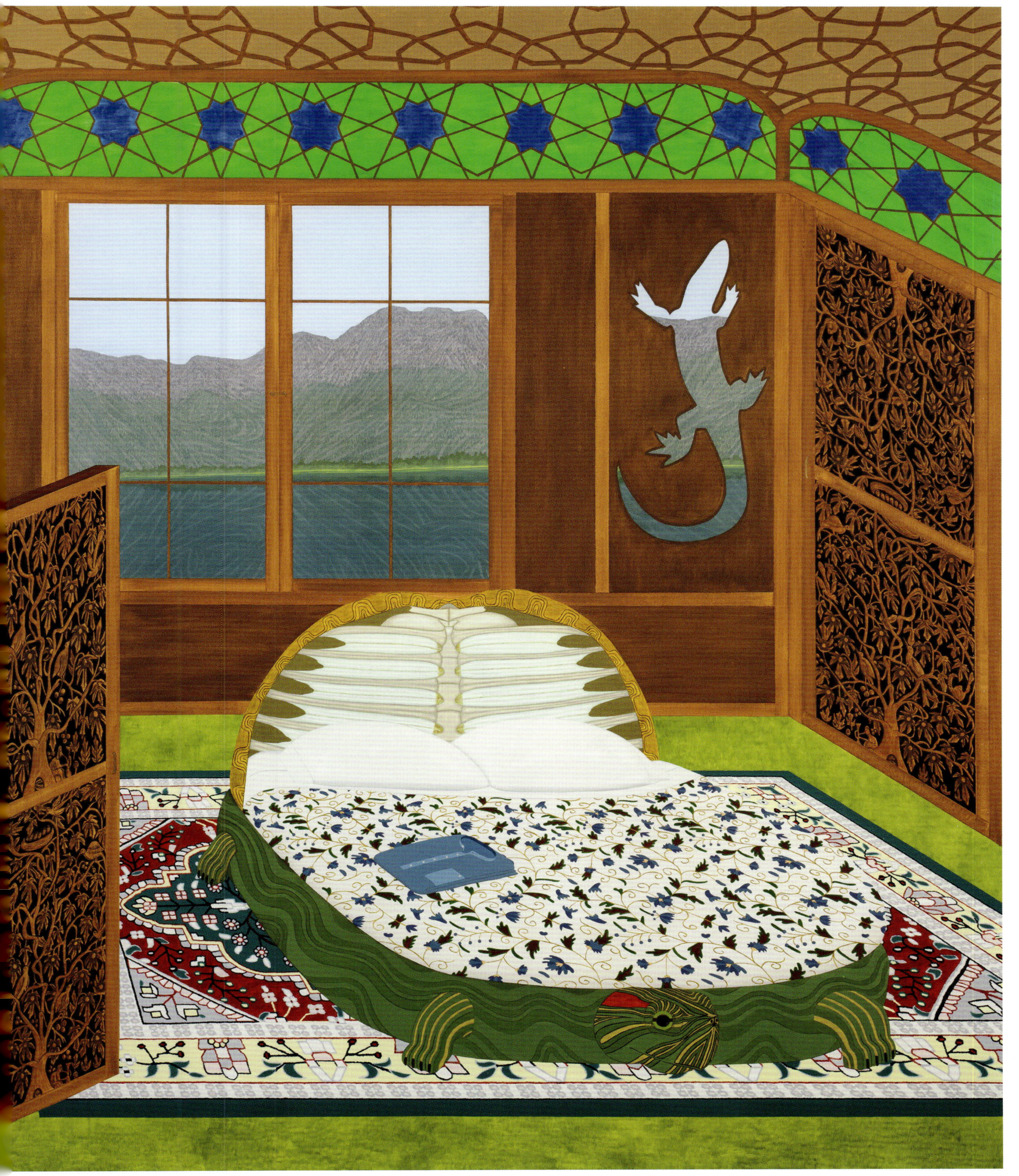

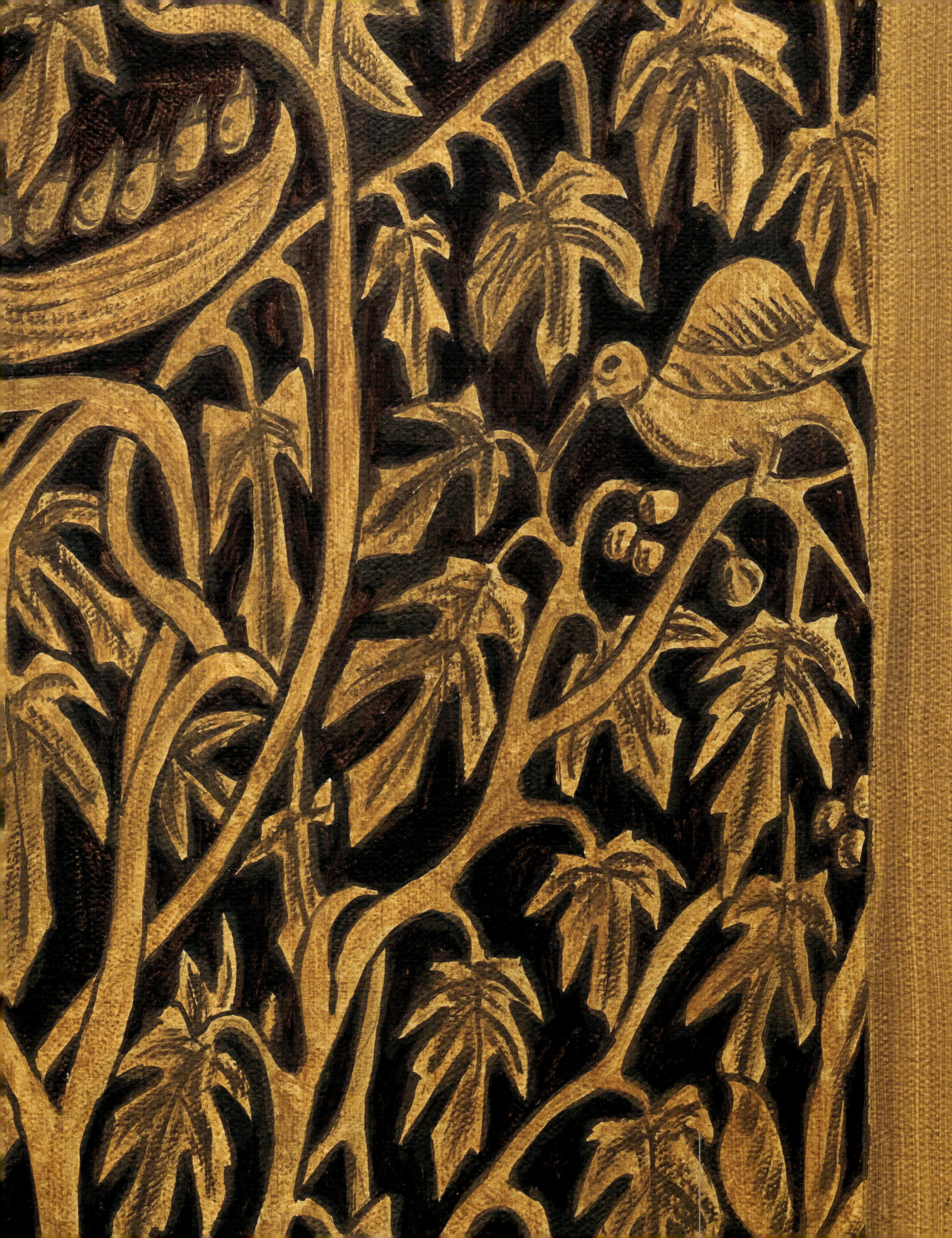

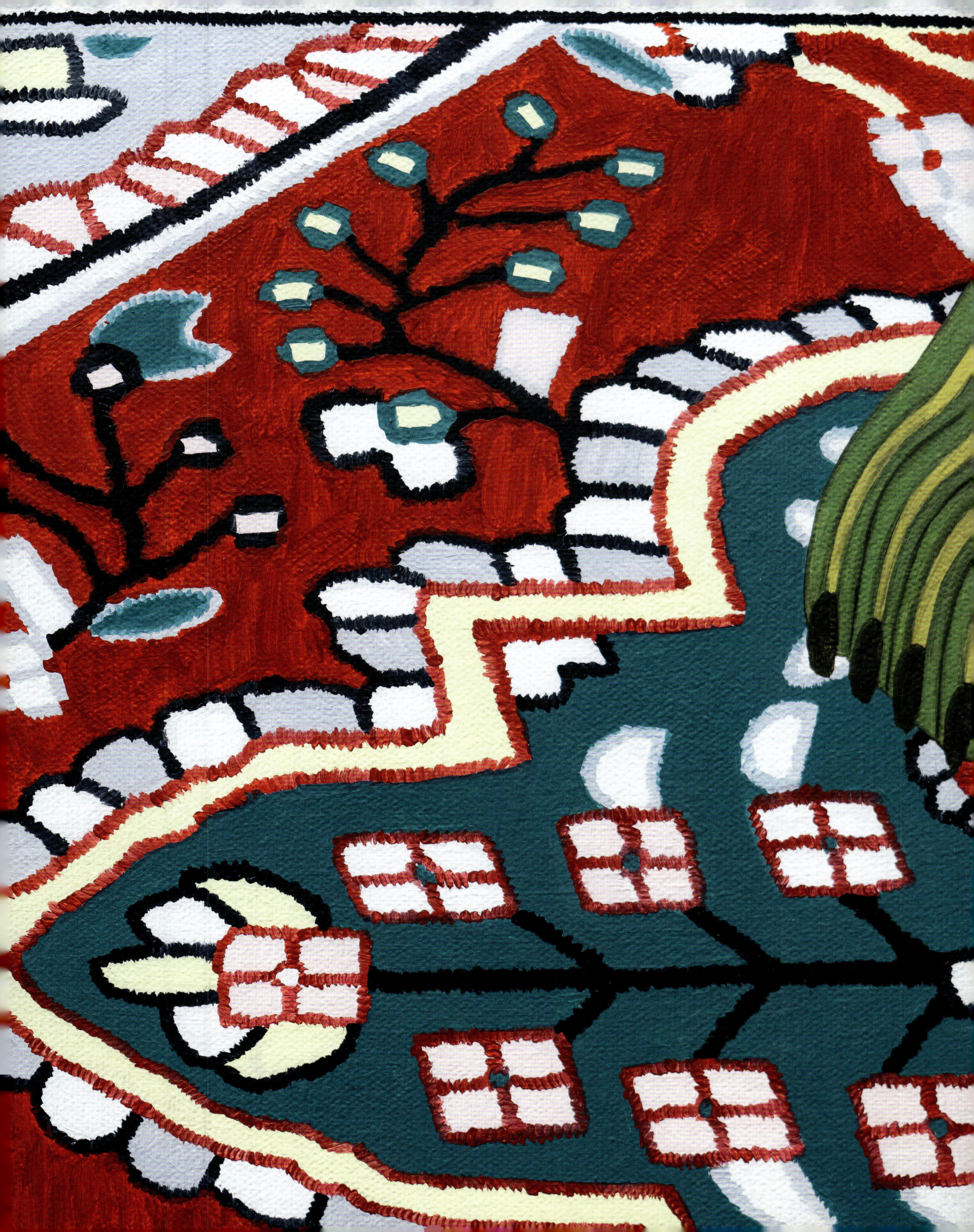

Behind the A-Z (Set vs Isis/Nefertiti), 2020
oil on canvas
84 × 60 inches

following pages
Installation view of *Where They Are*,
Jack Shainman Gallery, New York, 2020

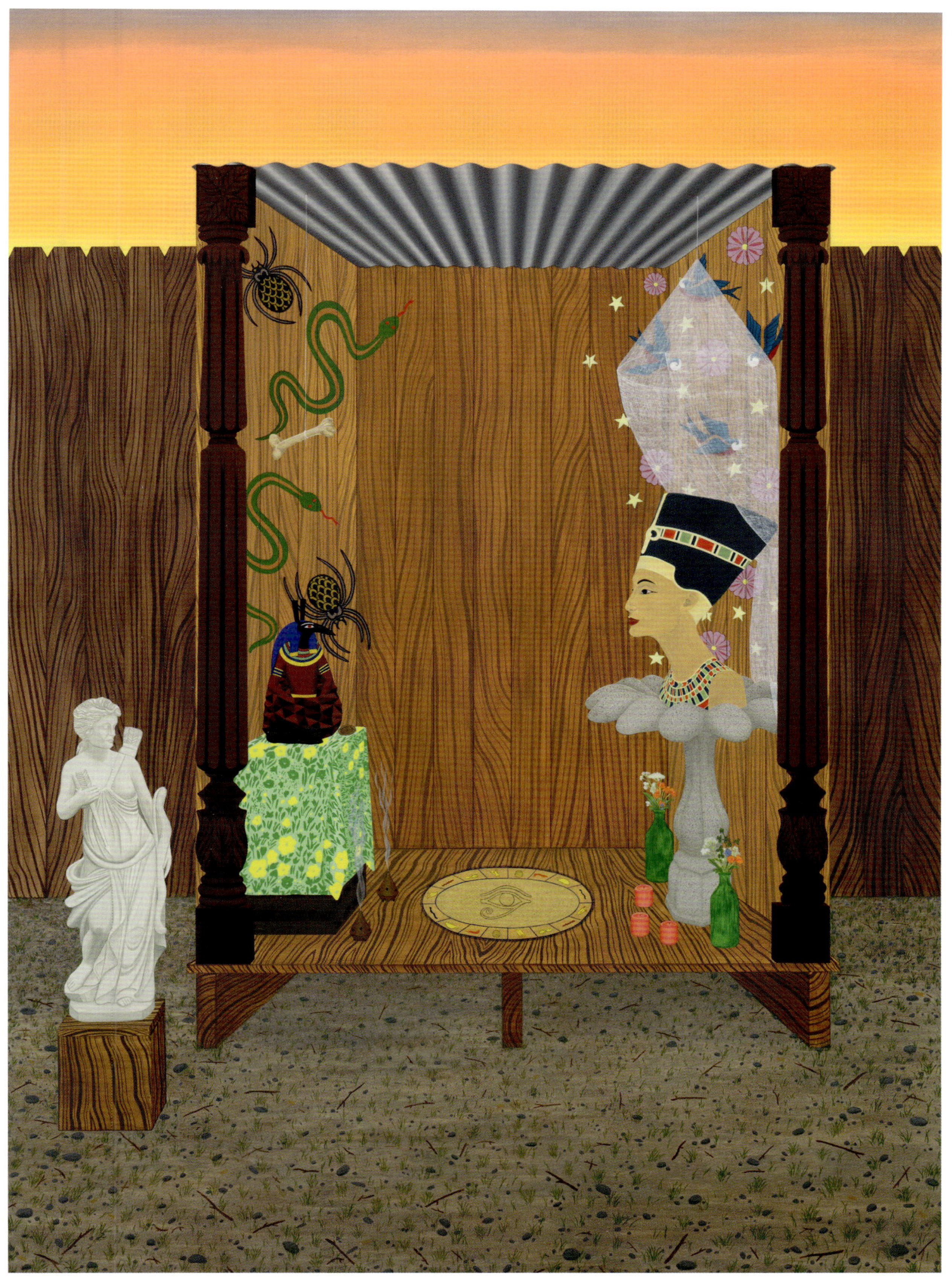

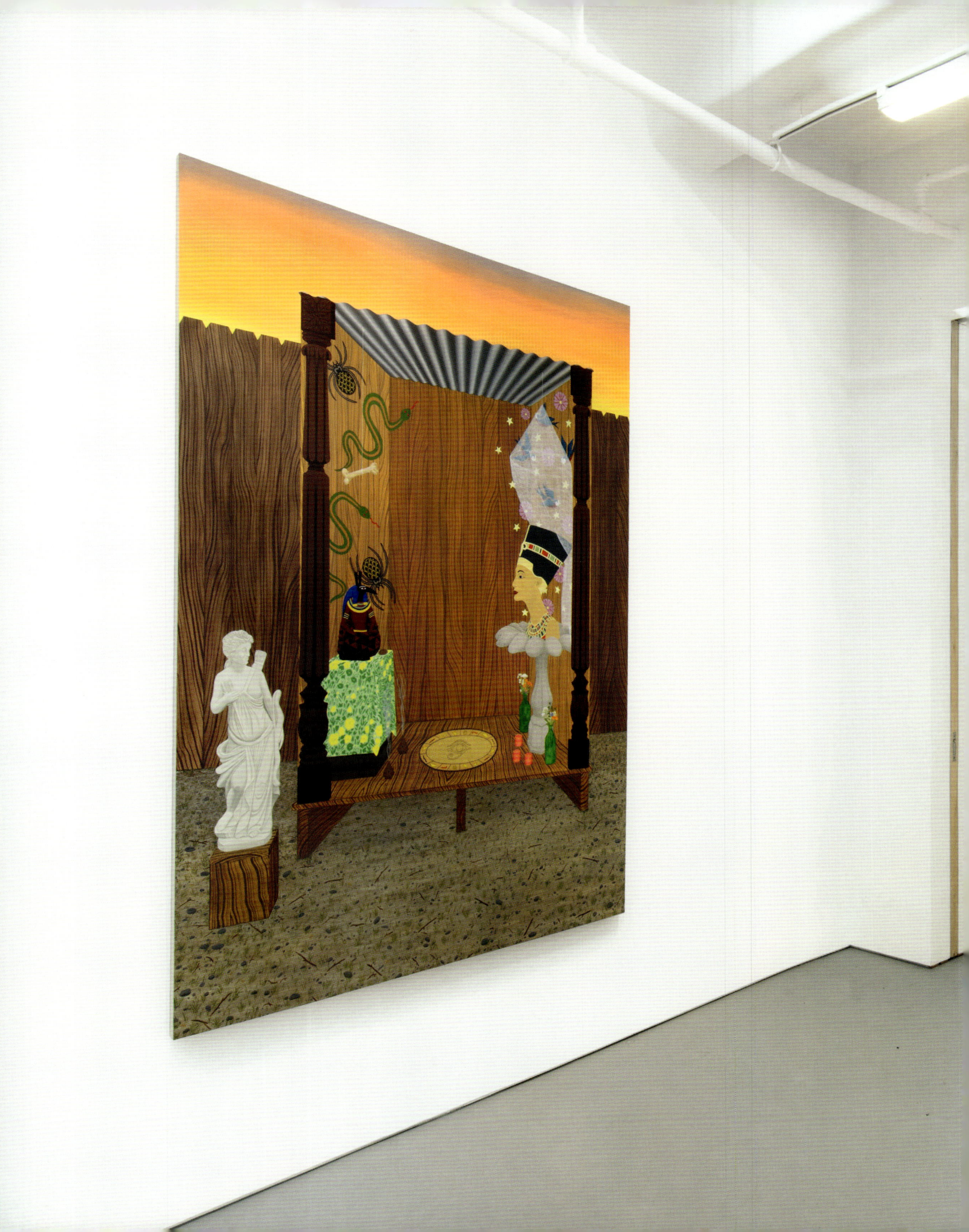

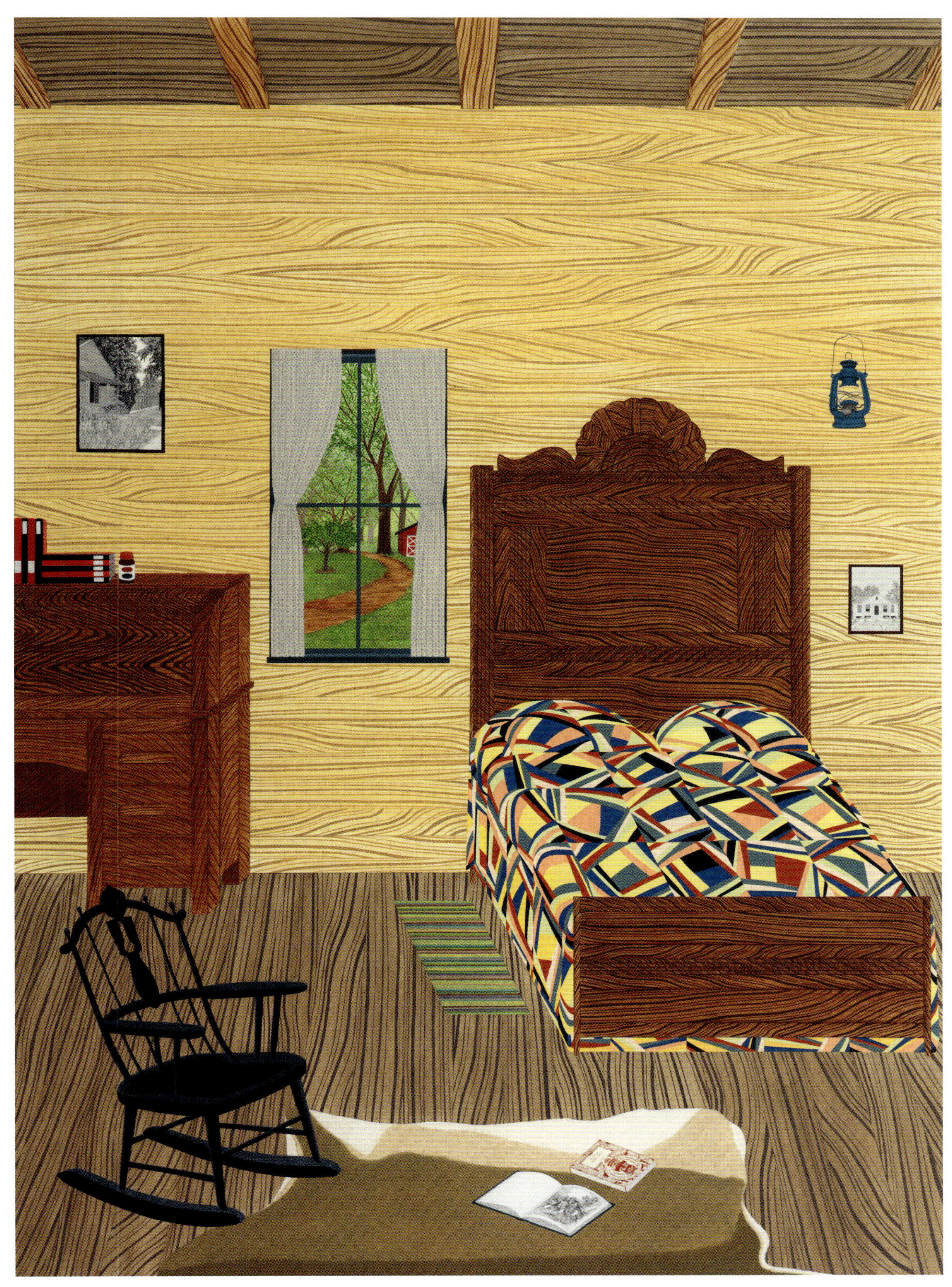

Logan Family Home (1933), 2020
oil on canvas
84 × 60 inches
The Museum of Contemporary Art,
Los Angeles. Purchase with funds
provided by Walker and Amanda Guffey

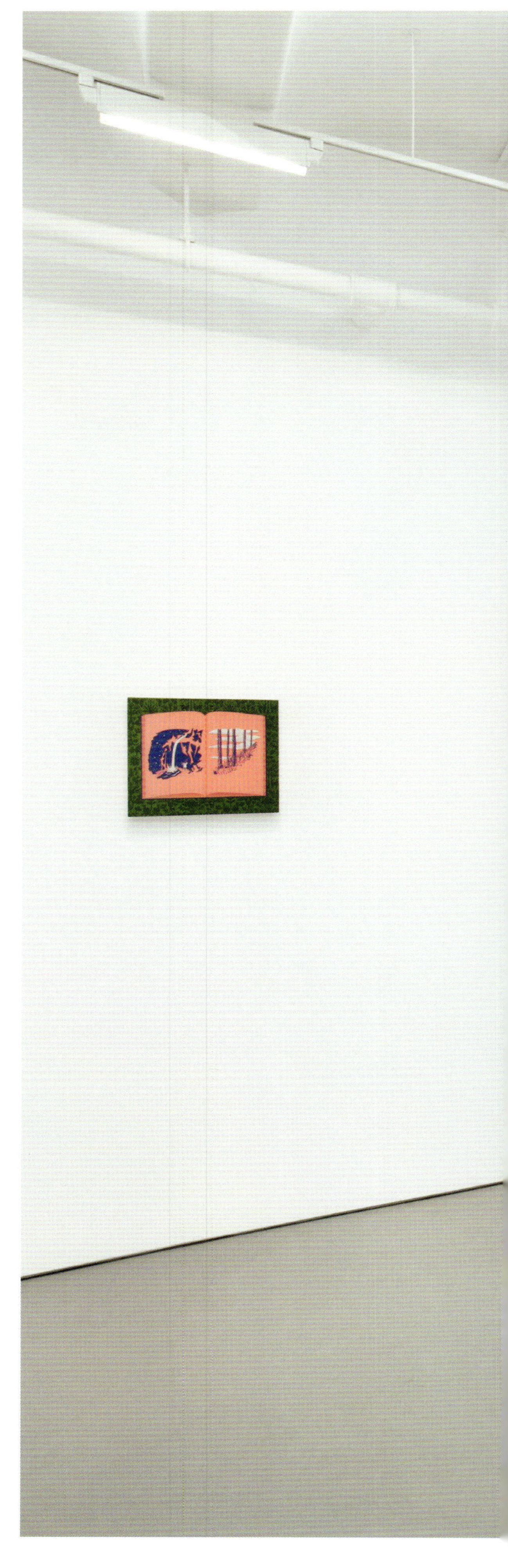

Installation view of *Where They Are*,
Jack Shainman Gallery, New York, 2020

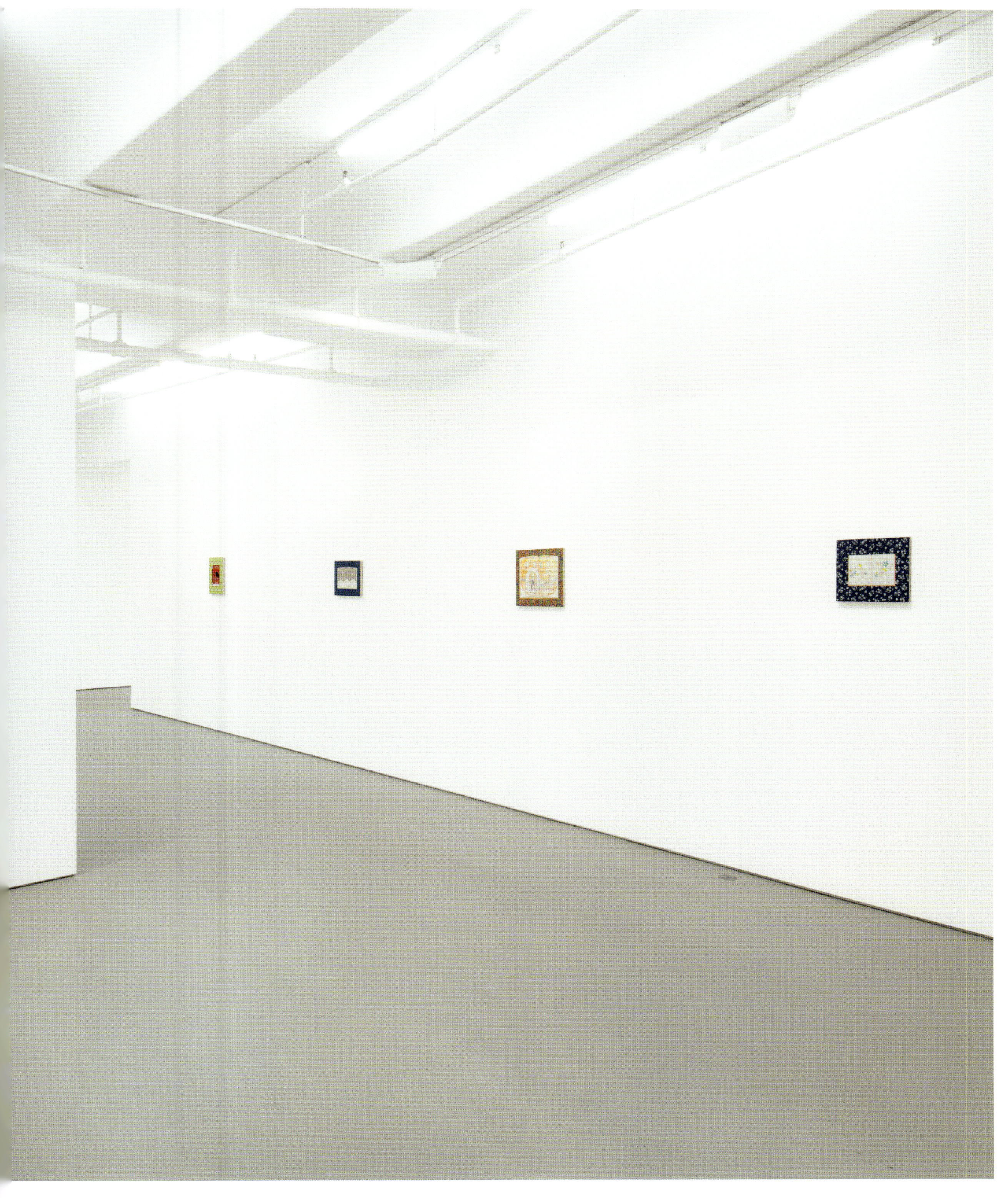

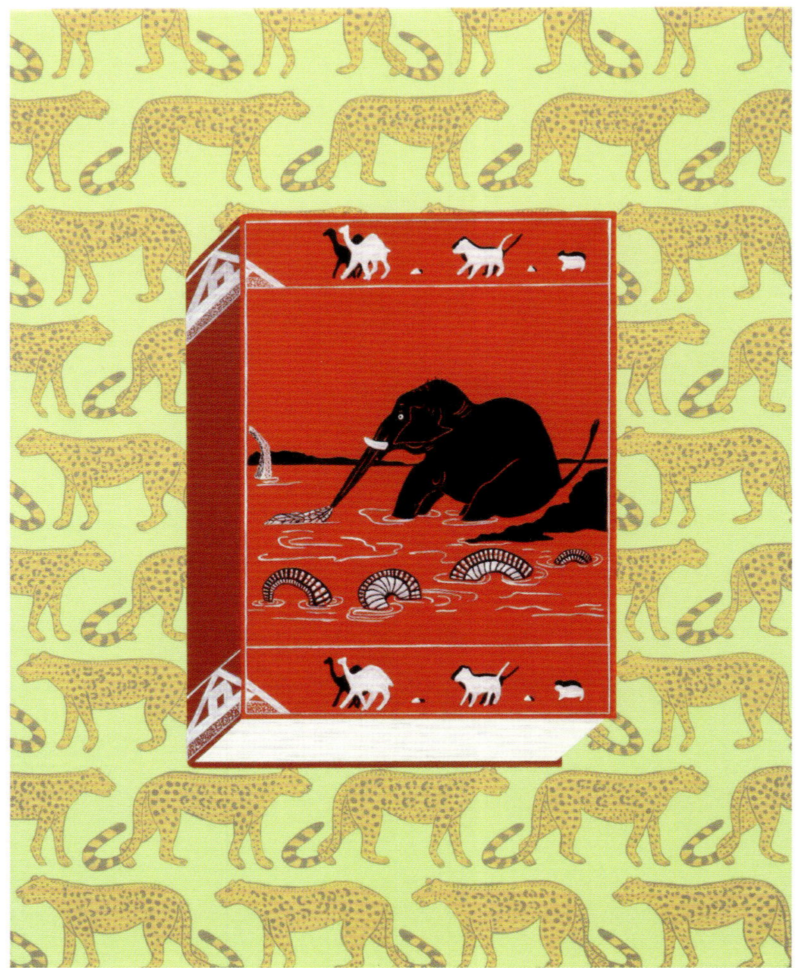

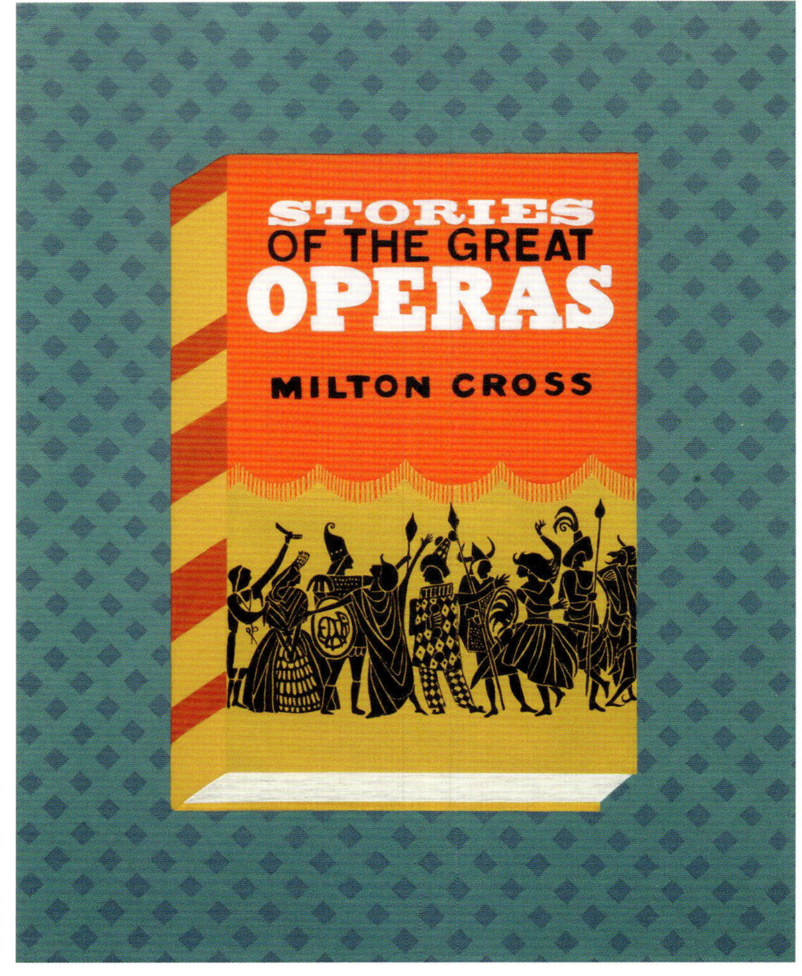

Just So Stories, 2020
oil on canvas
14 × 11 inches

Milton Cross, 2020
oil on canvas
14 ⅛ × 11 ⅛ inches

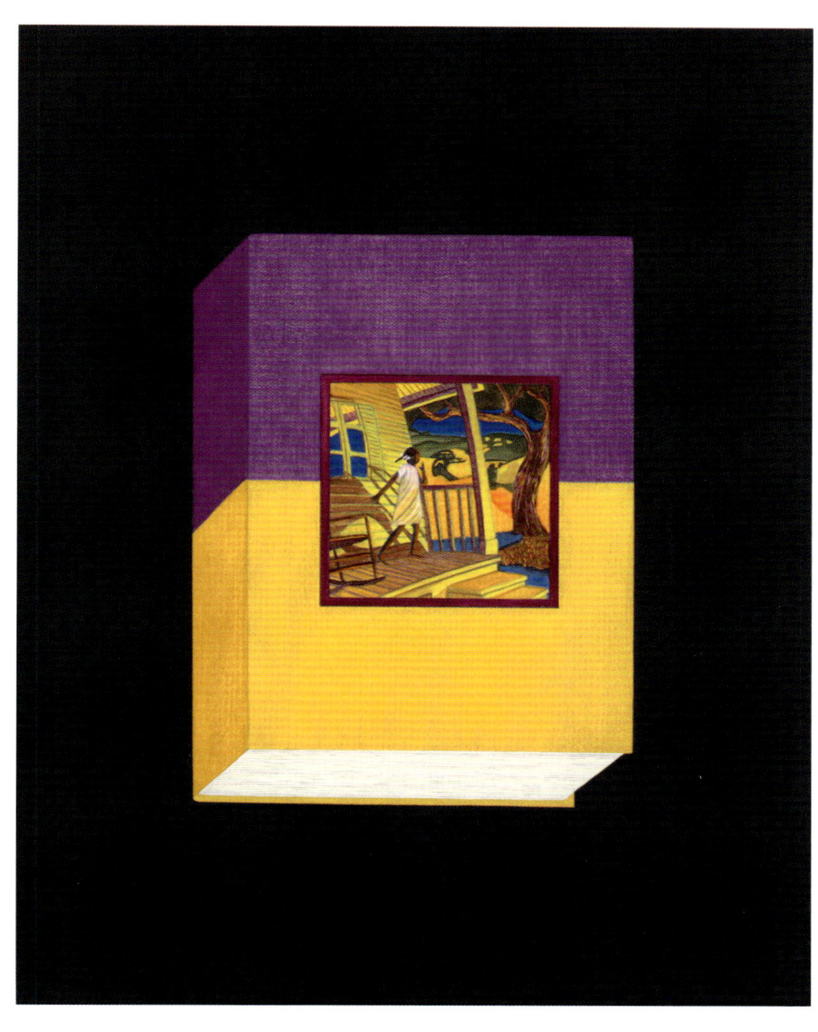

Roll of Thunder, 2020
oil on canvas
14 × 11 inches

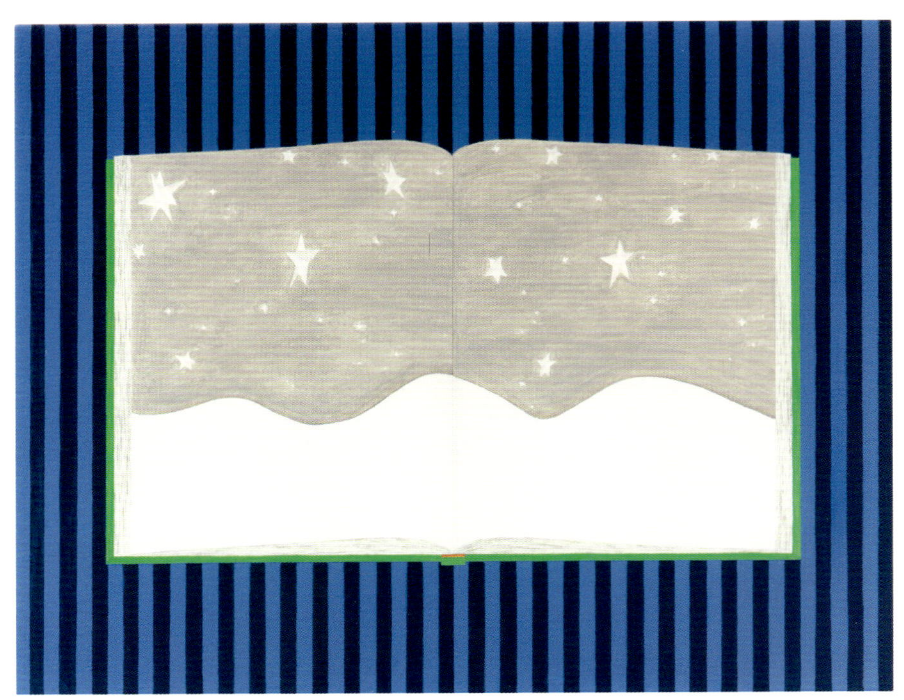

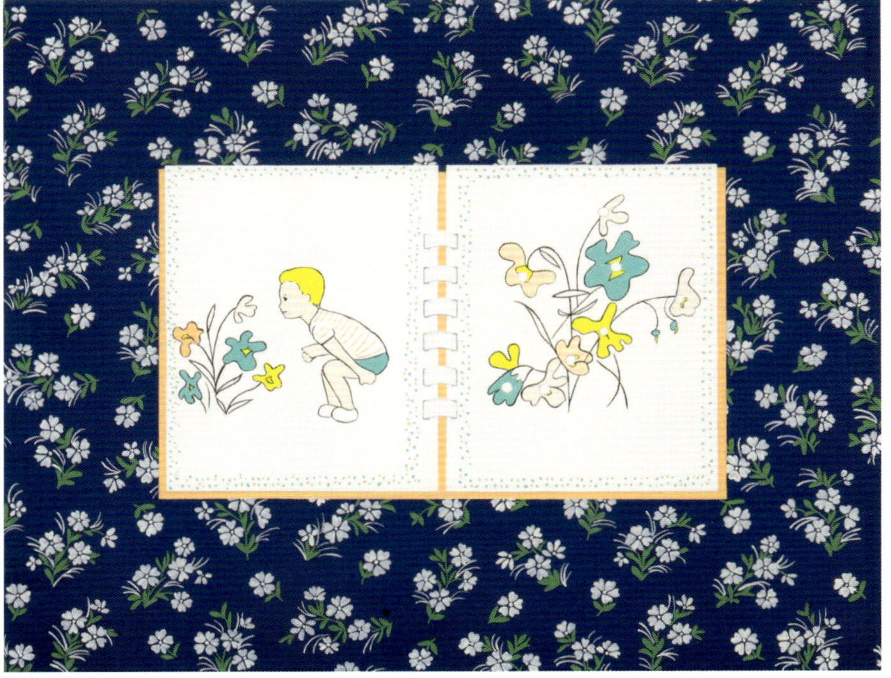

Goodnight Stars, Goodnight Air, 2020
oil on canvas
11 ⅛ × 14 inches

Now You Smell the Flowers, 2020
oil on canvas
11 ⅛ × 14 inches

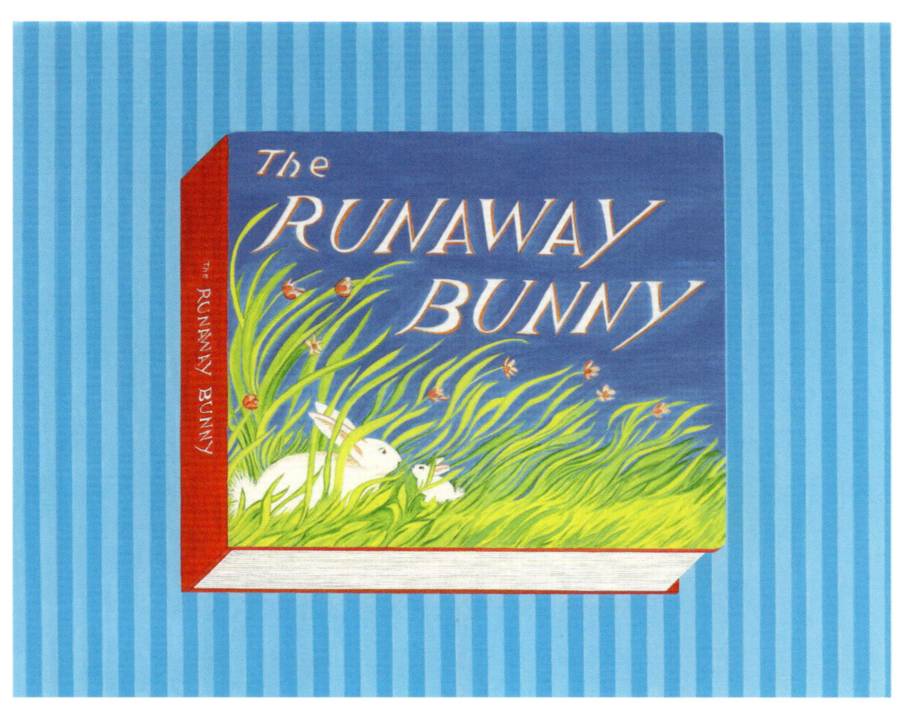

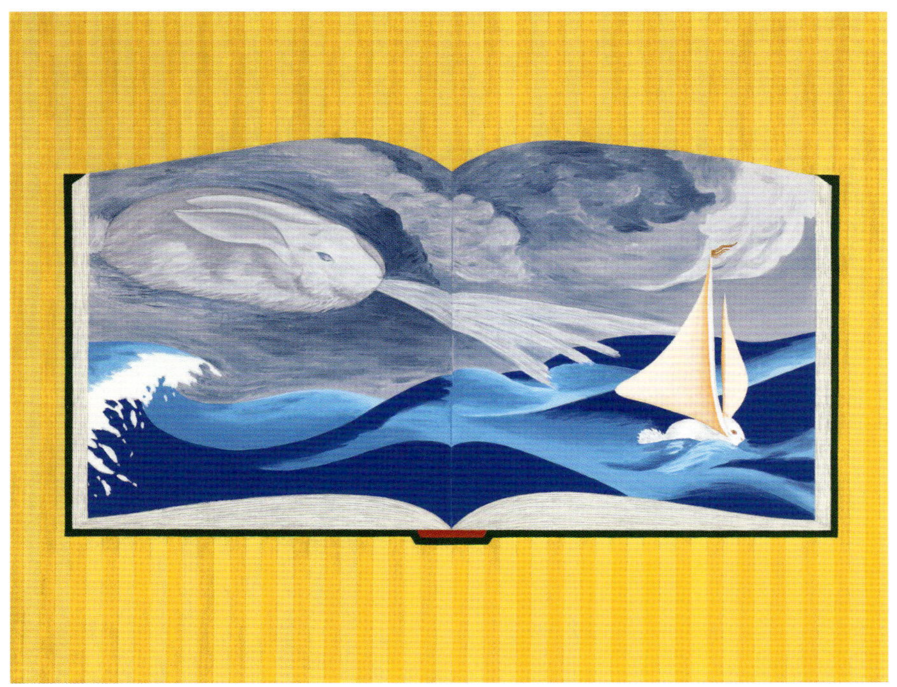

The Runaway Bunny, 2021
oil on canvas
11 × 14 inches

If you become a sailboat and sail away from me, 2021
oil on canvas
11 × 14 inches

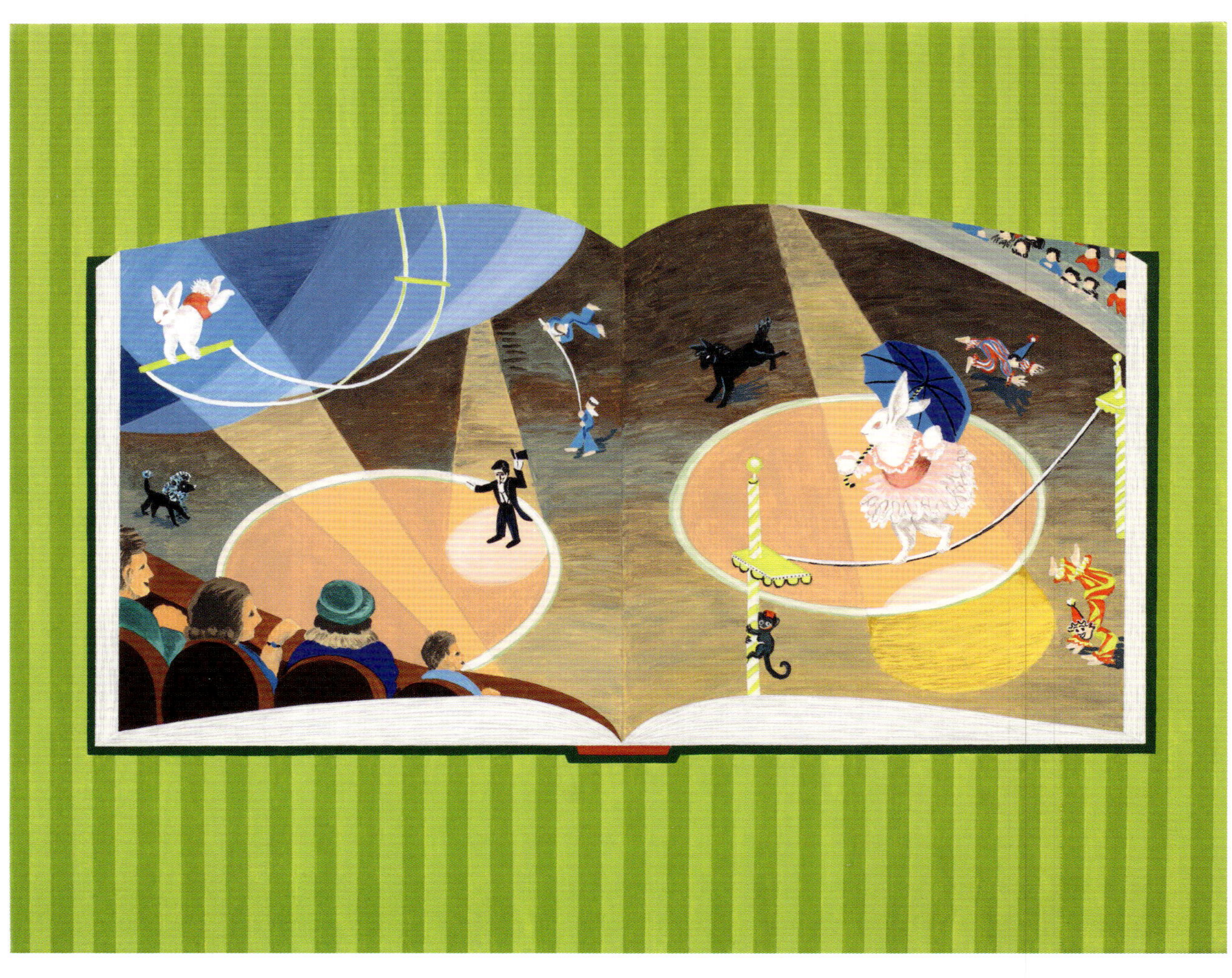

If you go flying on a flying trapeze, 2021
oil on canvas
11 × 14 inches

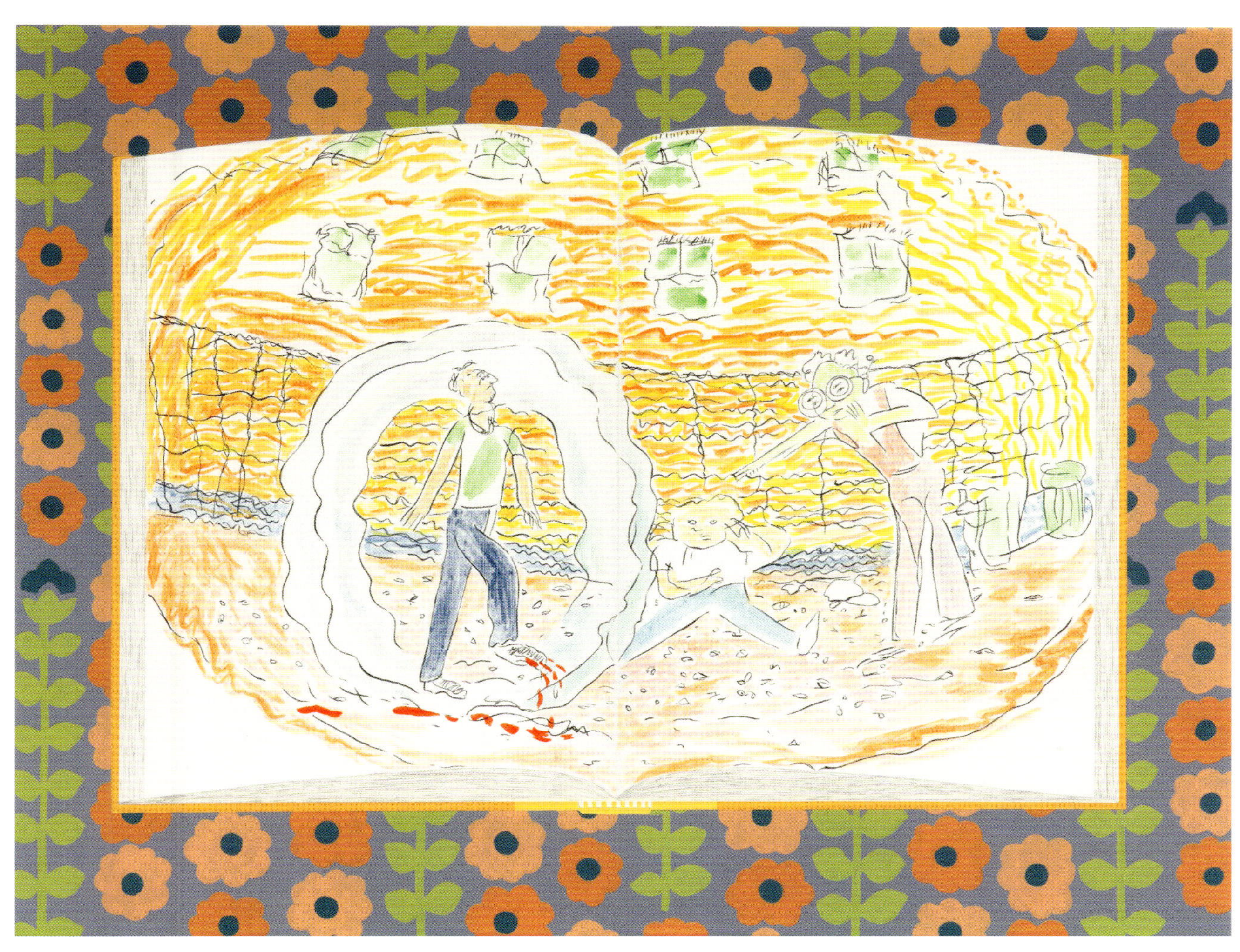

WT, TJ, and Blinky, 2020
oil on canvas
14 ⅛ × 18 inches
Museum of Fine Arts, Boston.
James N. Krebs Purchase Fund for
21st Century Paintings

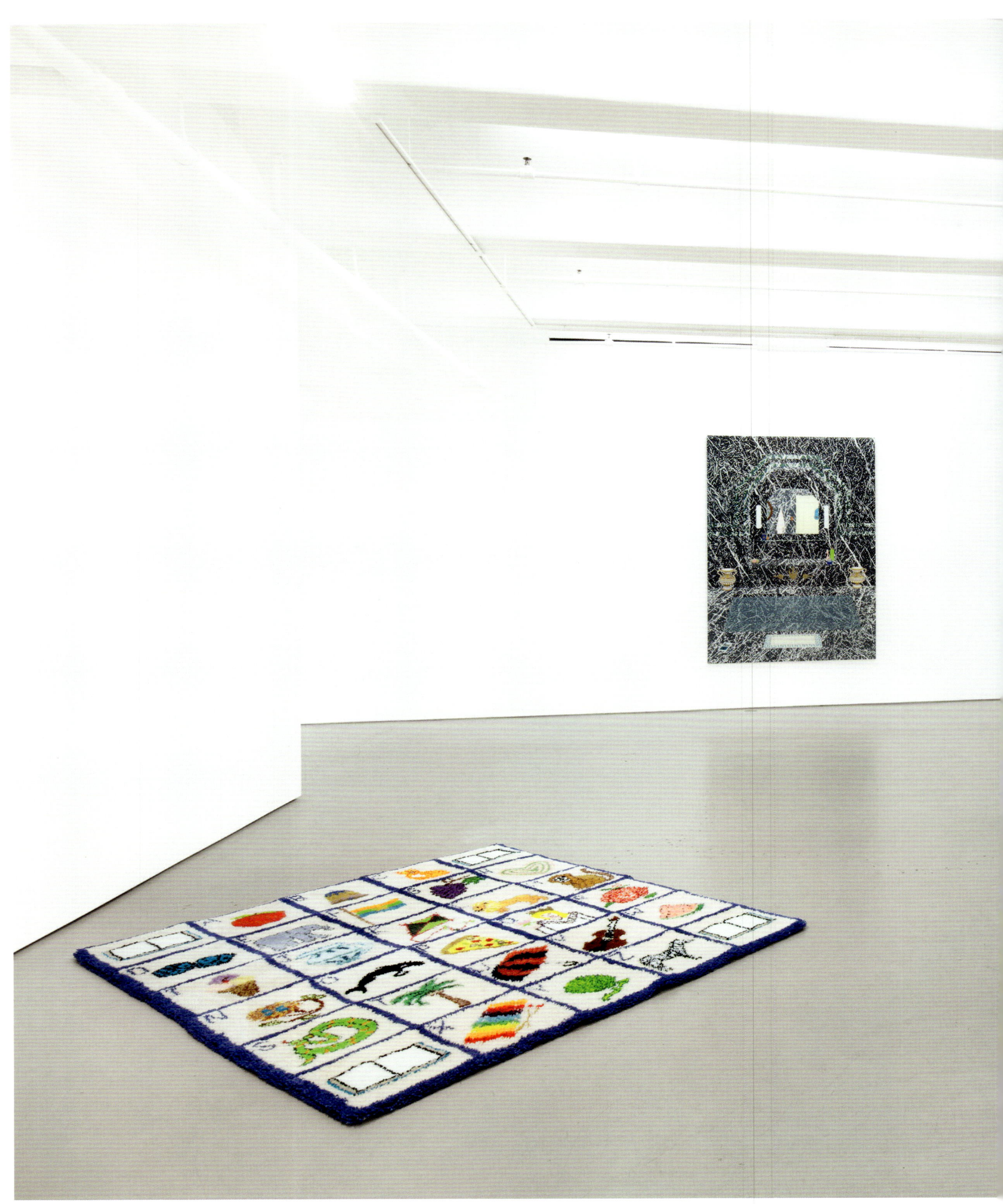

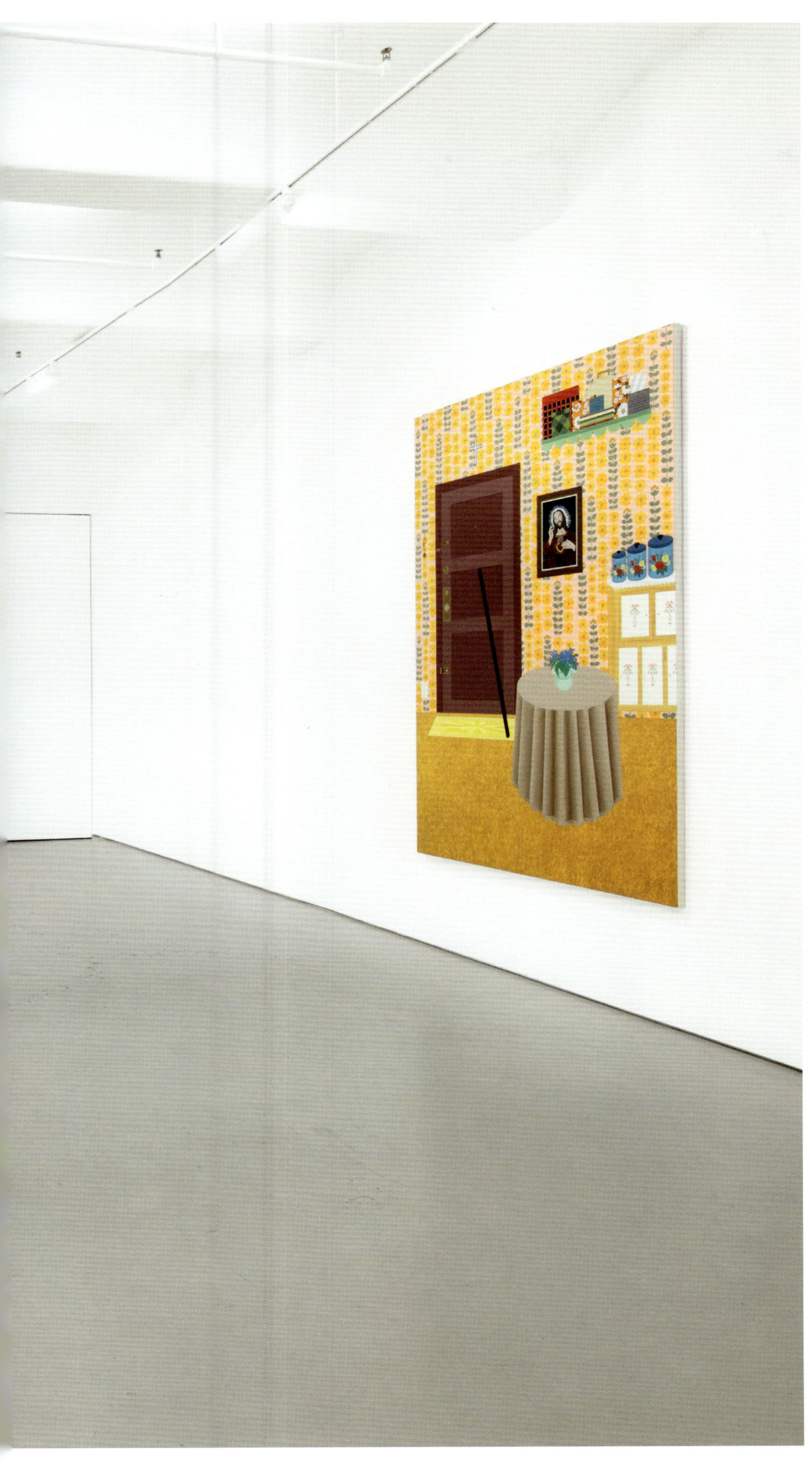

Installation view of *Where They Are*,
Jack Shainman Gallery, New York, 2020

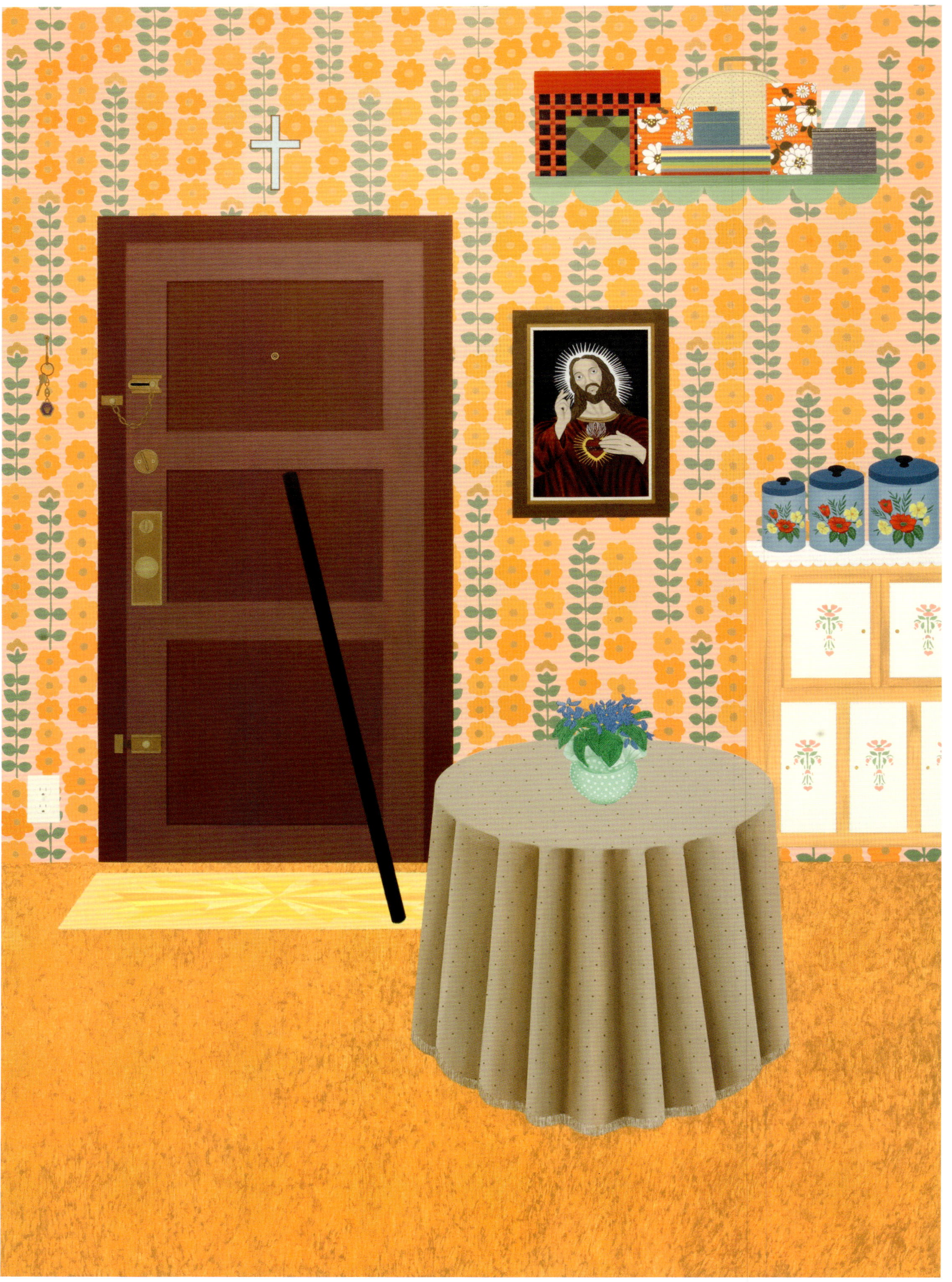

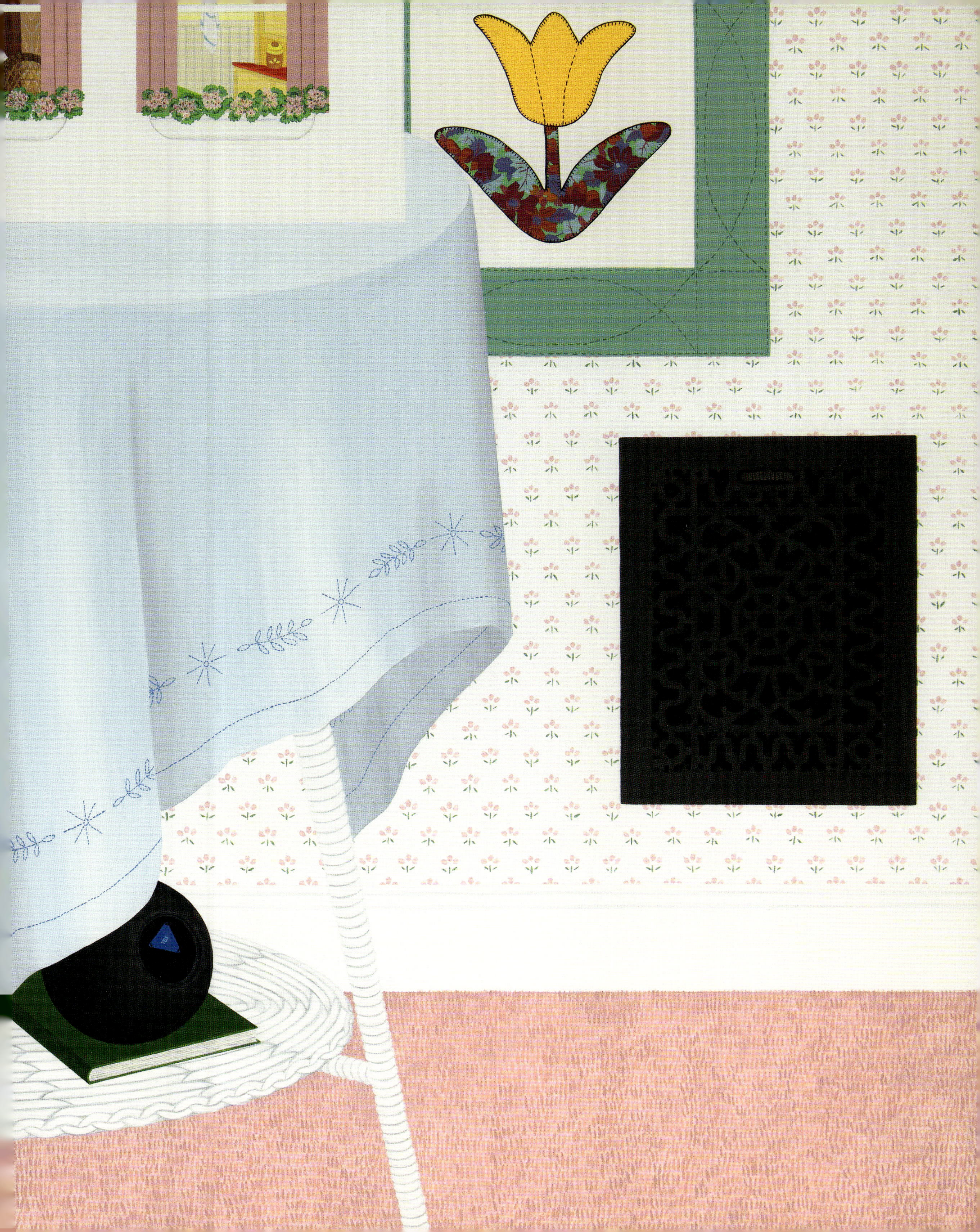
YES

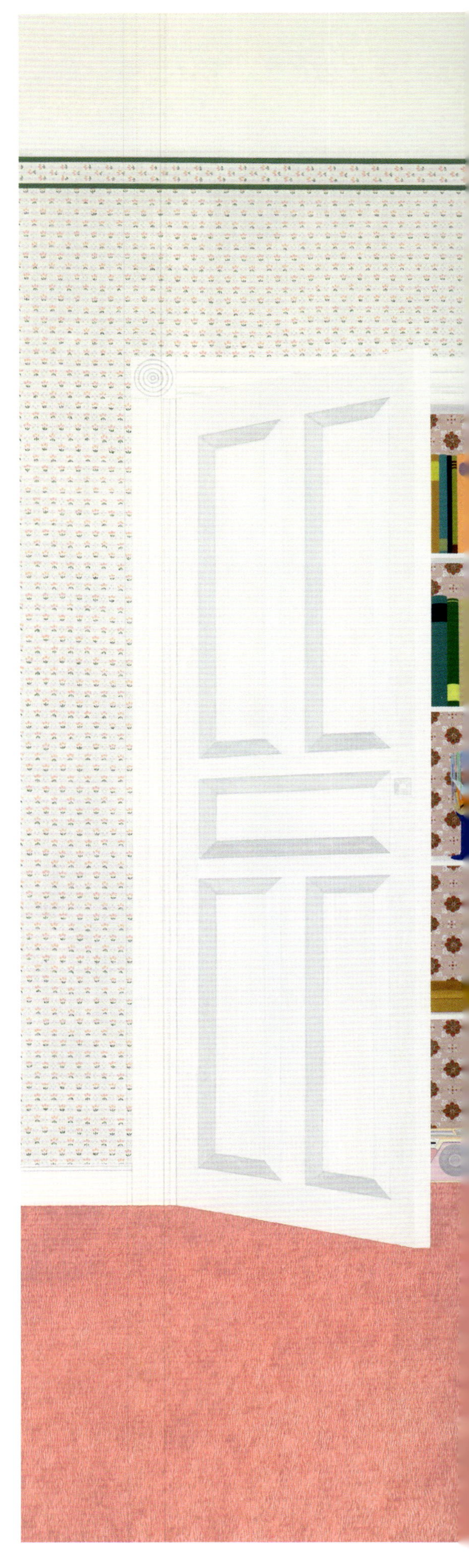

8 Greenwood Place (1988-93), 2021
oil on canvas
72 × 84 inches

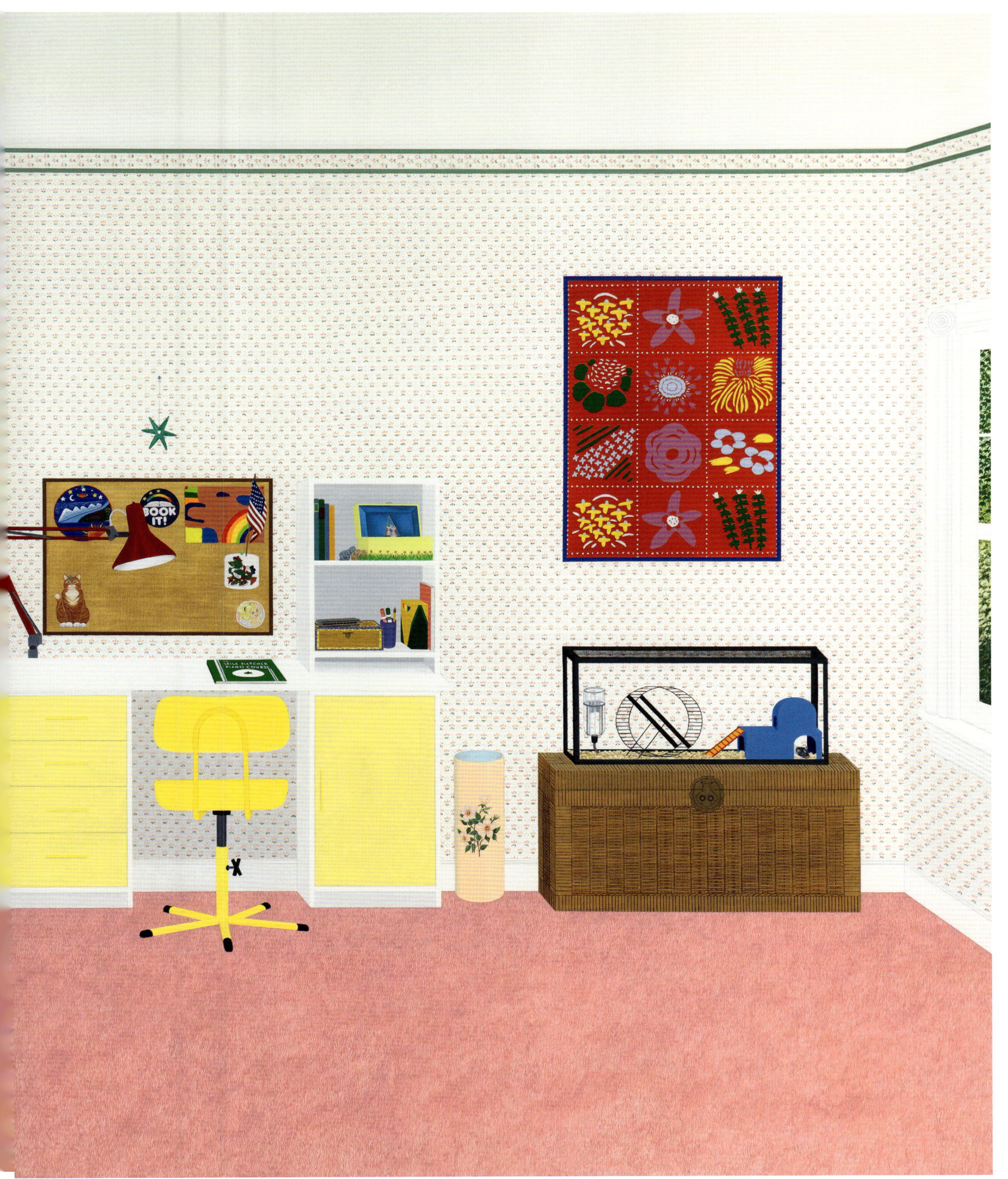
BOOK IT!
LEILA FLETCHER
PIANO COURSE

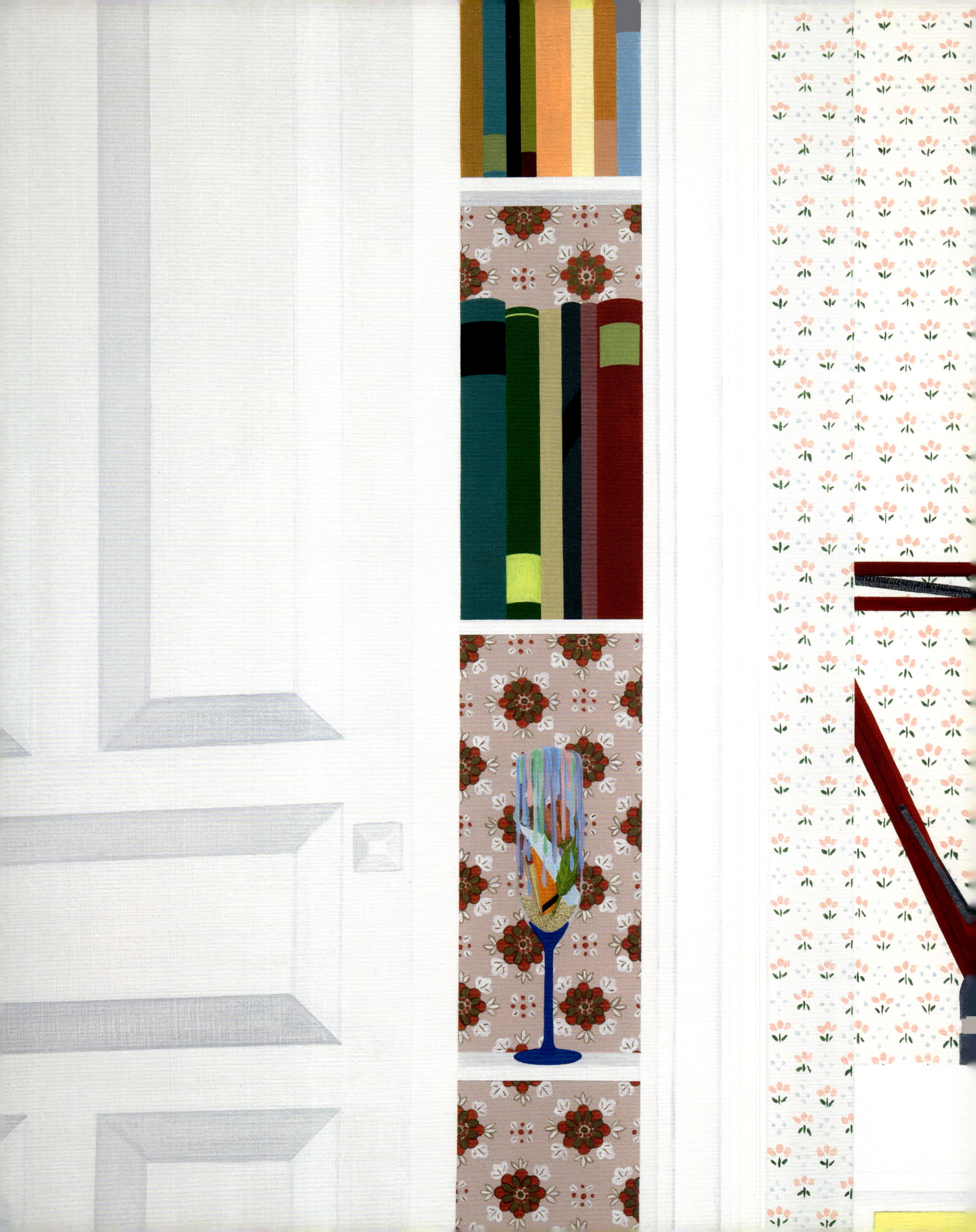

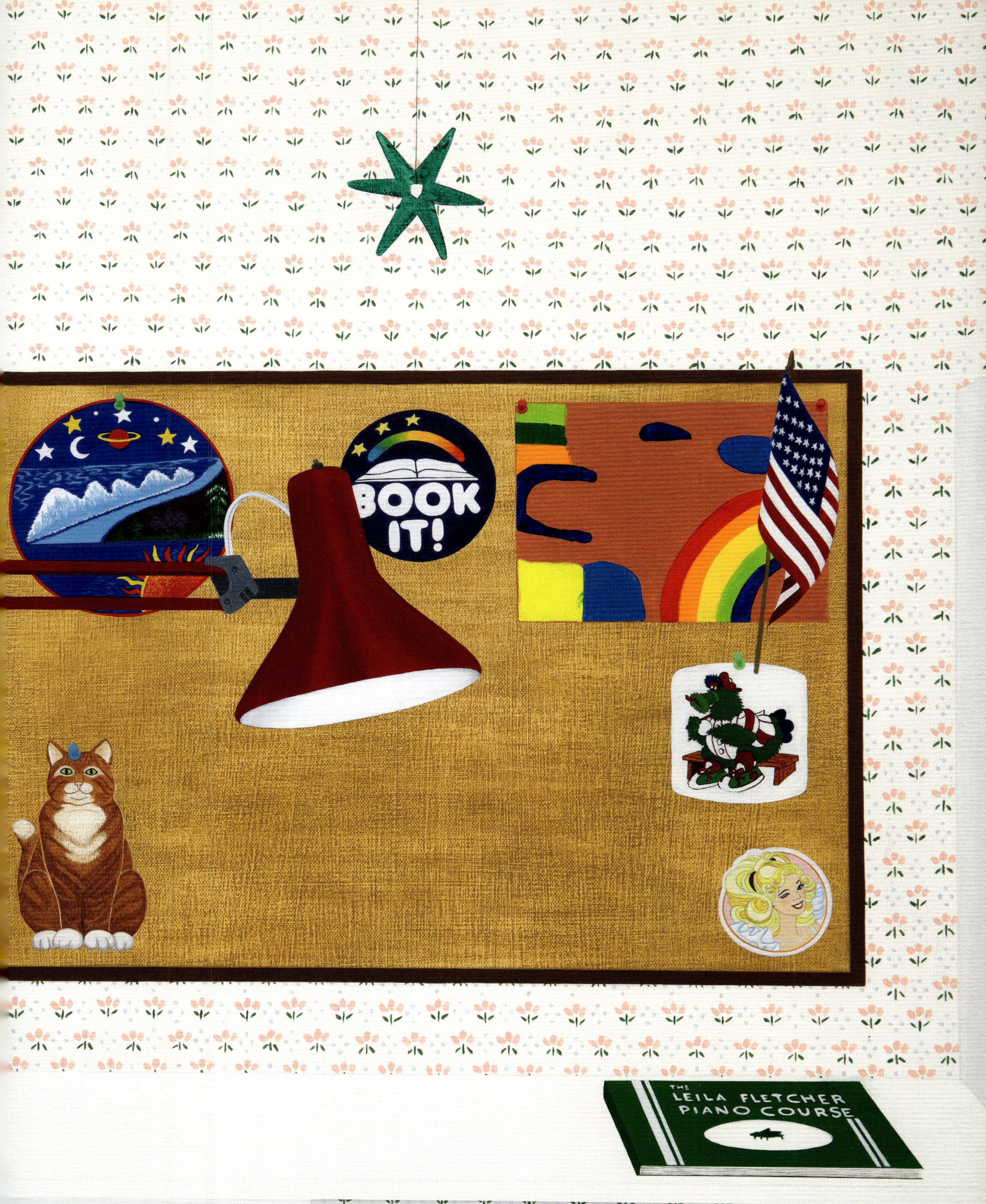
BOOK
IT!
THE
LEILA FLETCHER
PIANO COURSE

8 Greenwood Place (my bedroom), 2020
oil on canvas
84 × 60 inches

following pages
Installation view of *New Grit: Art & Philly Now*, Philadelphia Museum of Art, 2021, artworks by Becky Suss and Alex da Corte
Courtesy of the Philadelphia Museum of Art. Photo by Tim Tiebout

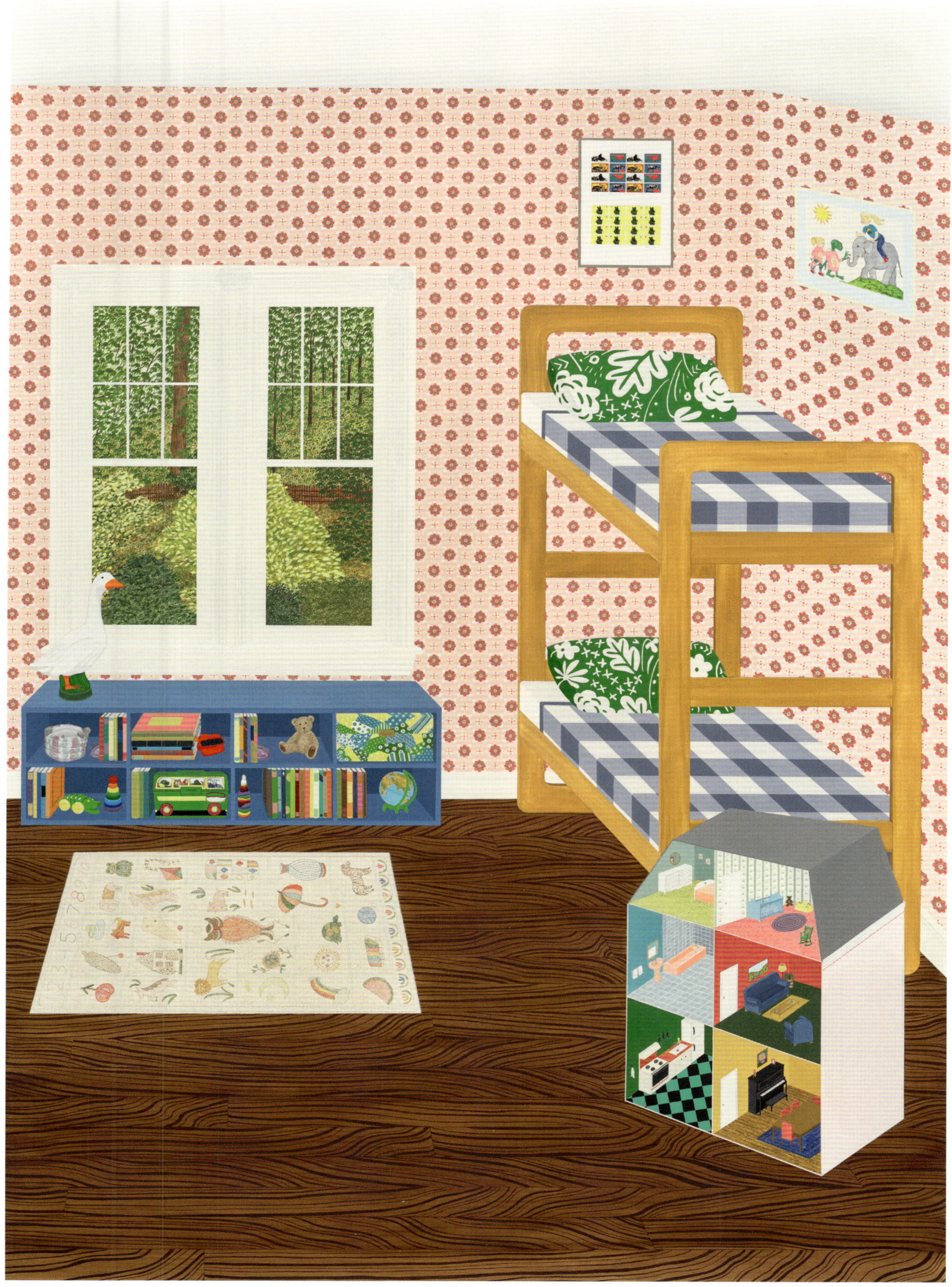

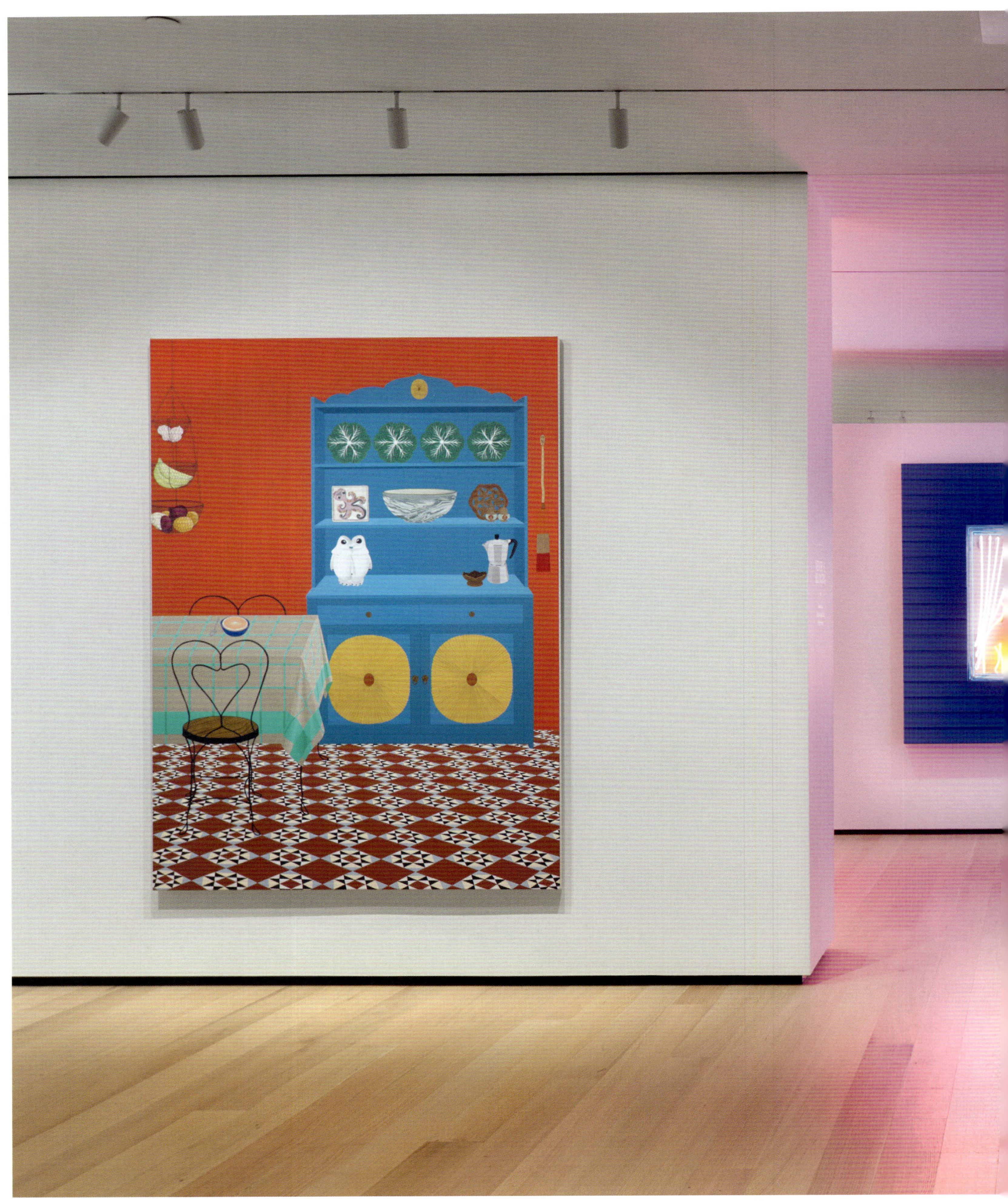

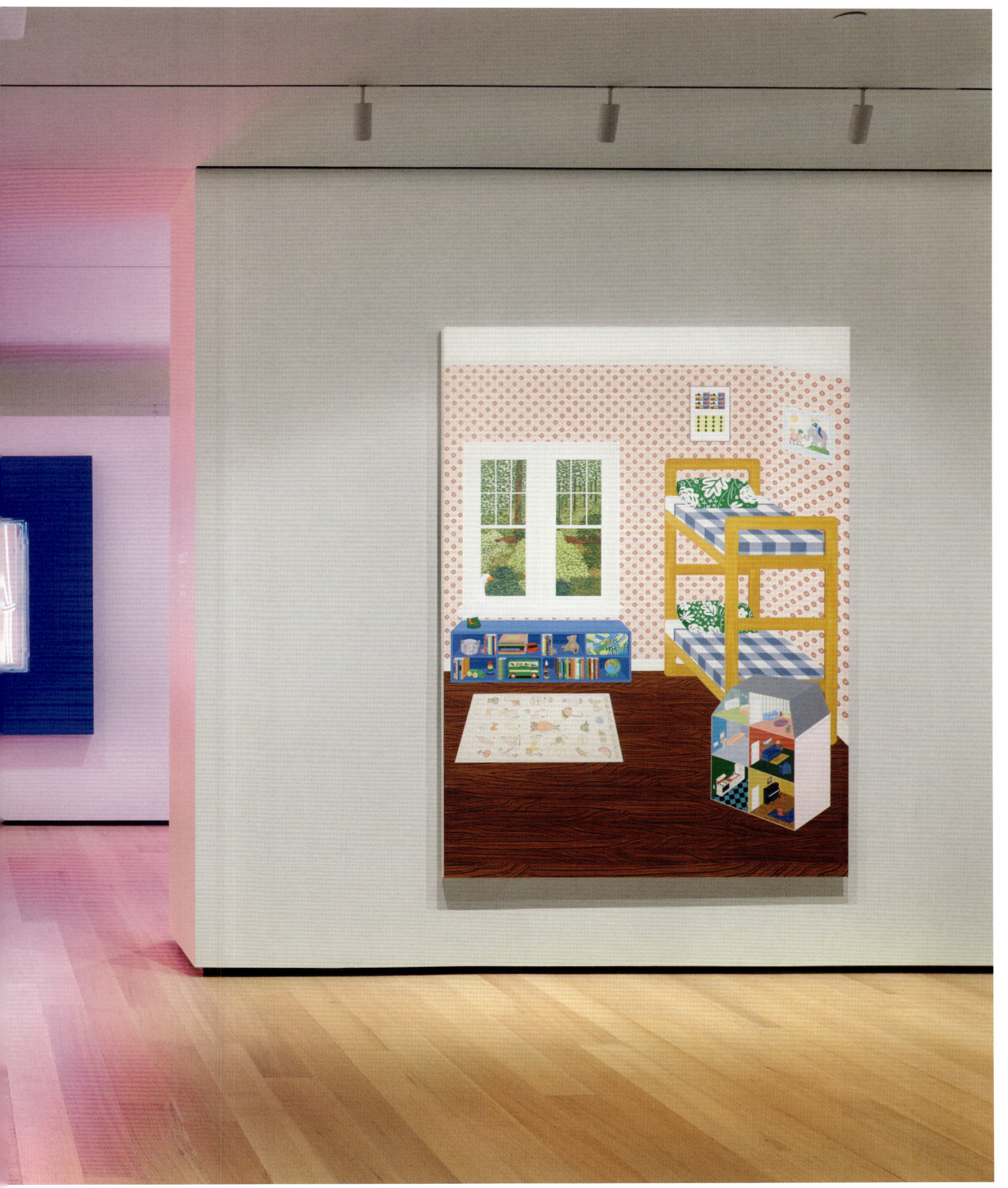

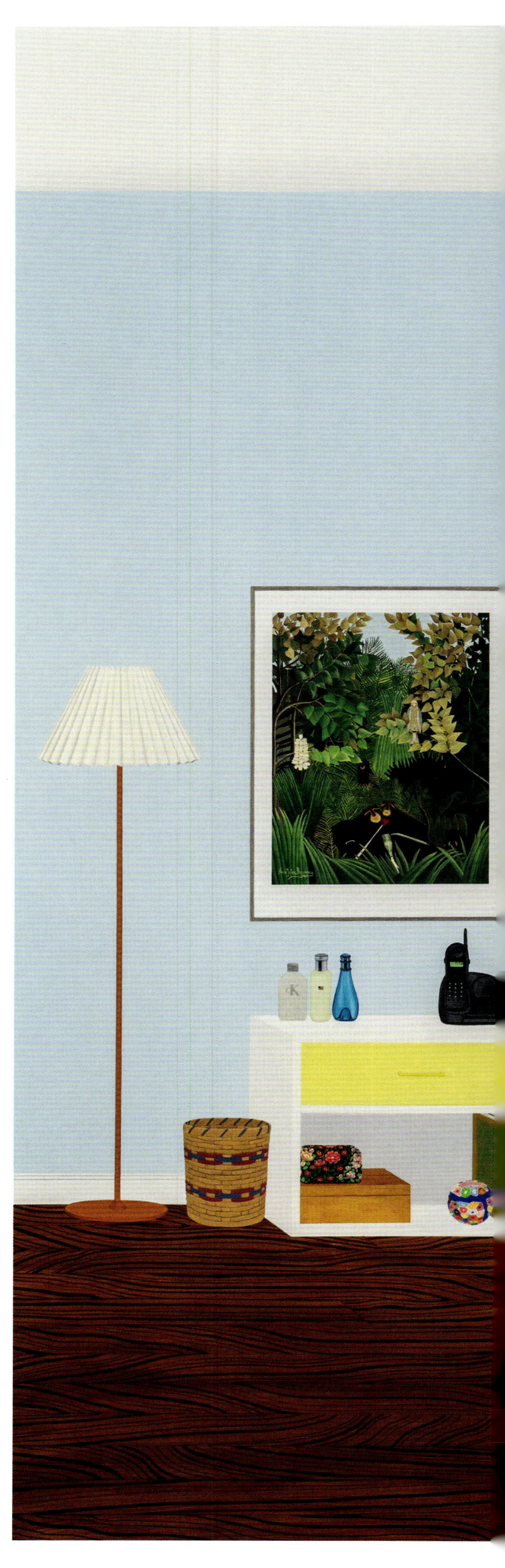

8 Greenwood Place (1997-99), 2022
oil on canvas
72 × 84 inches

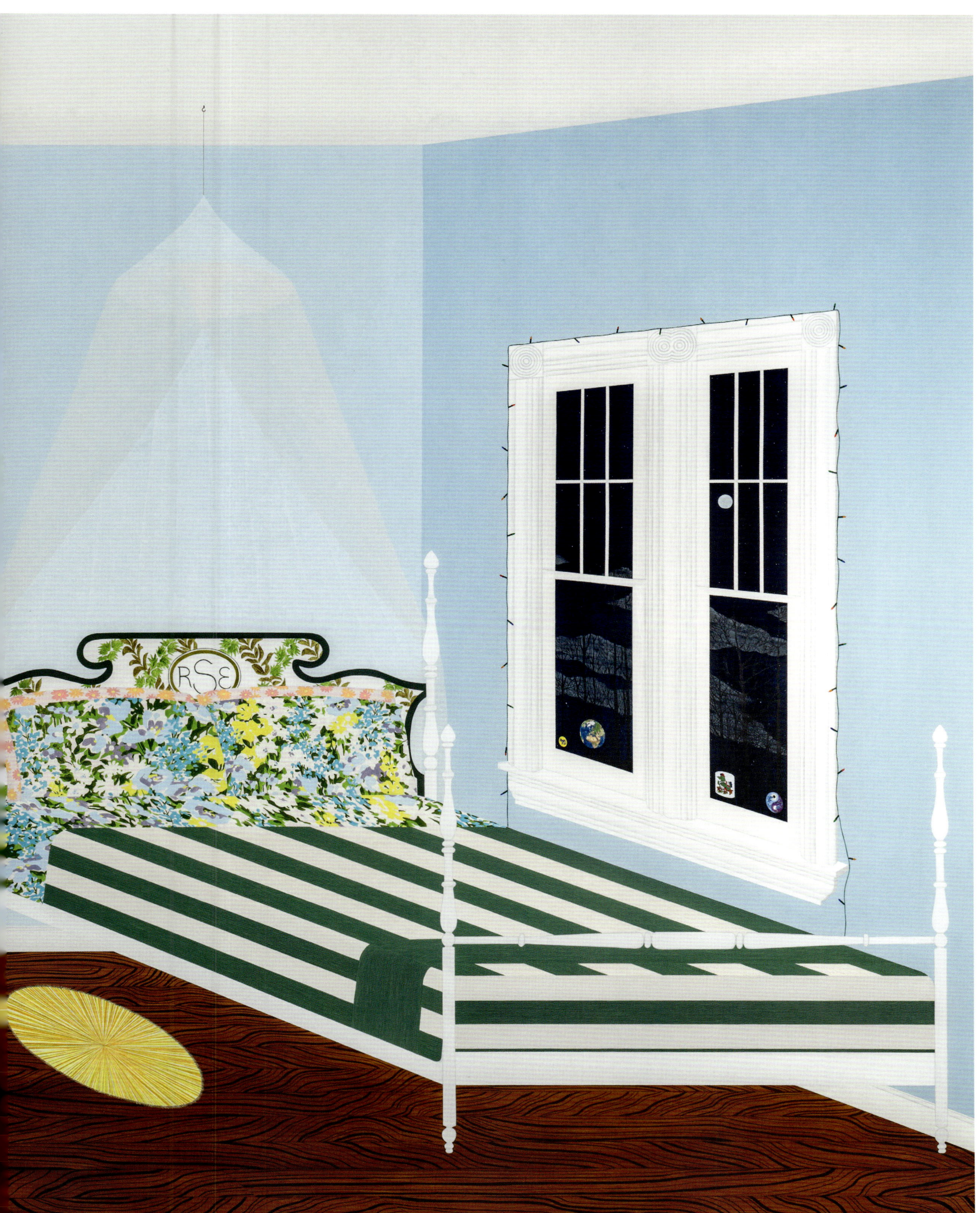

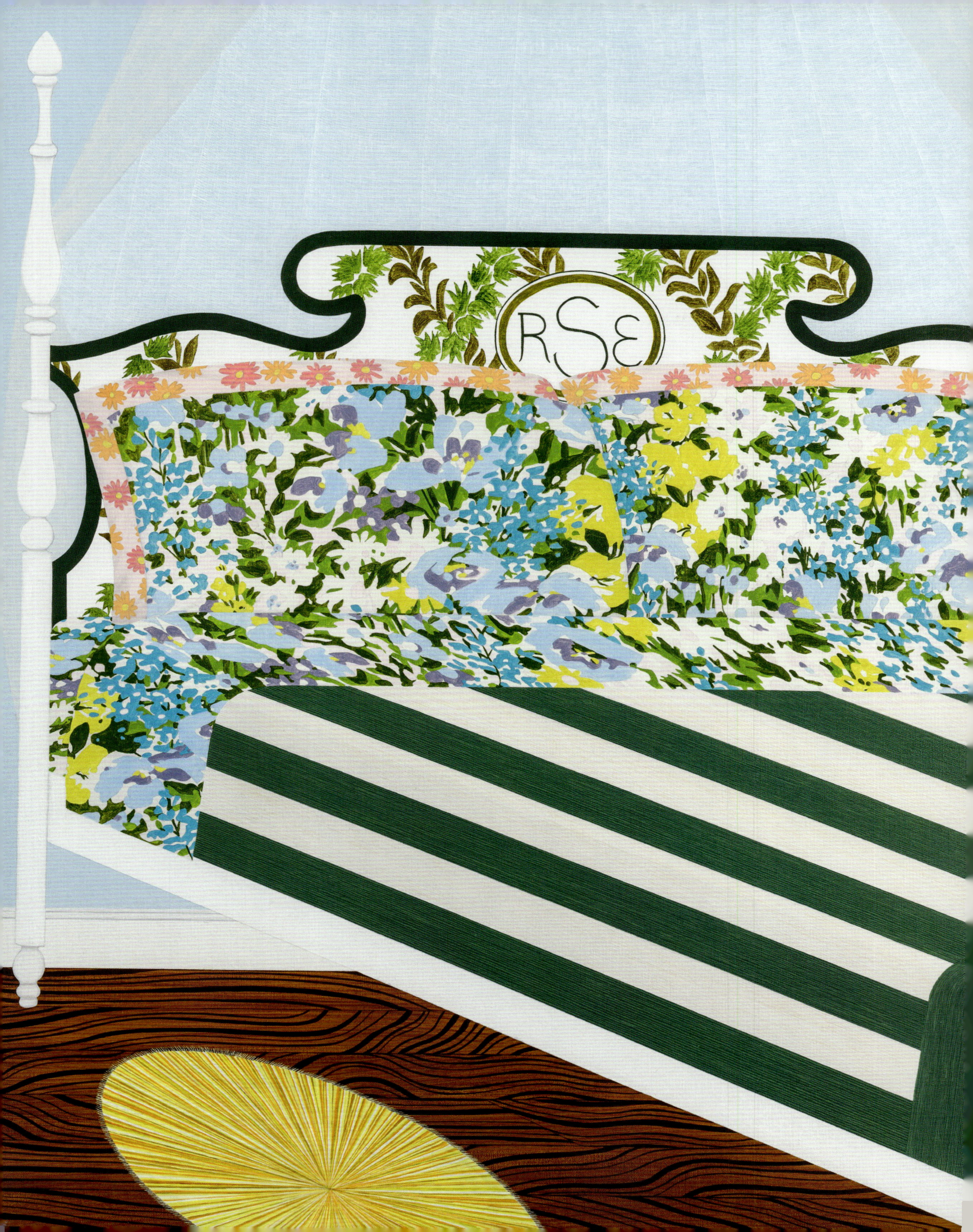
RSE

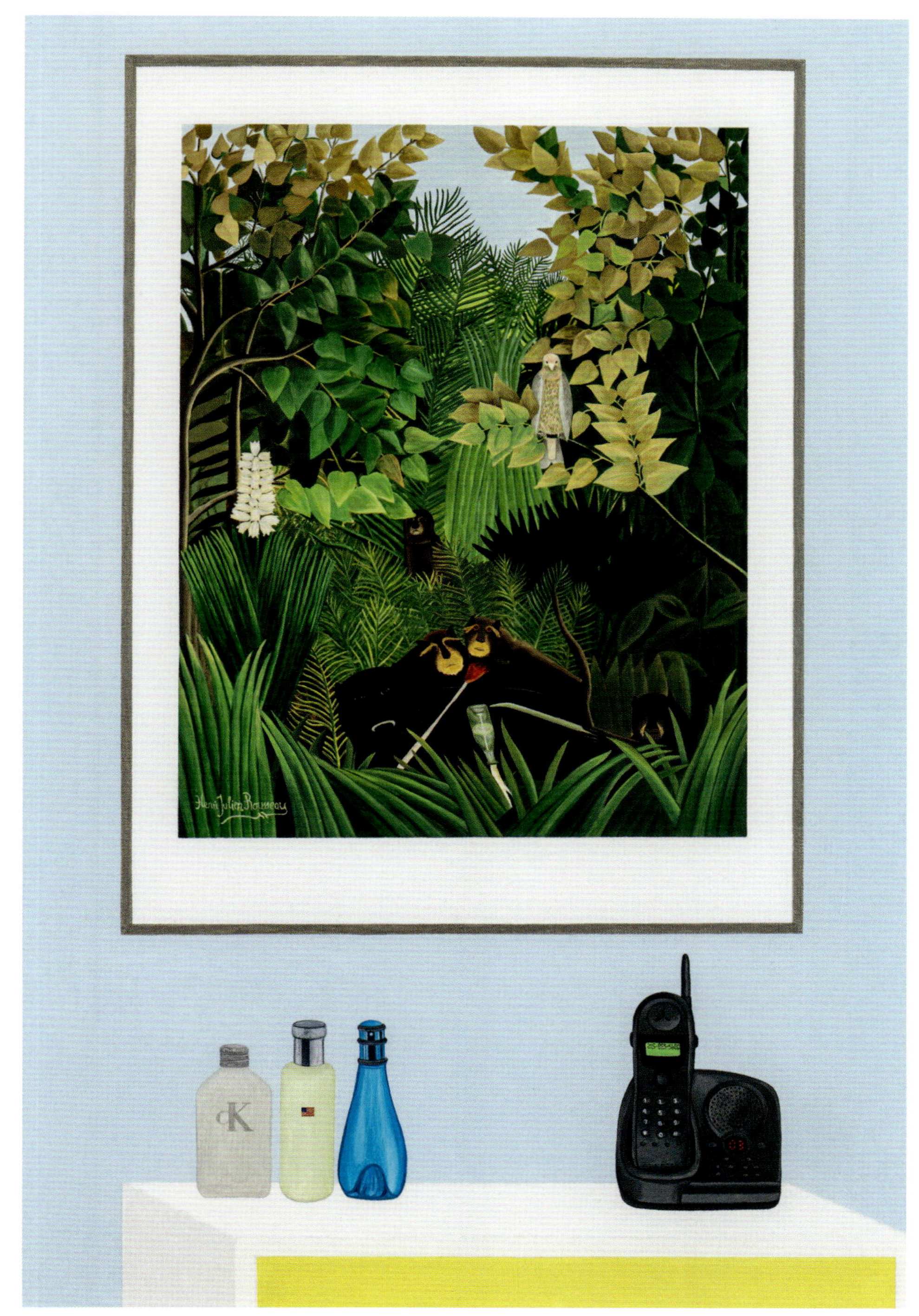
cK

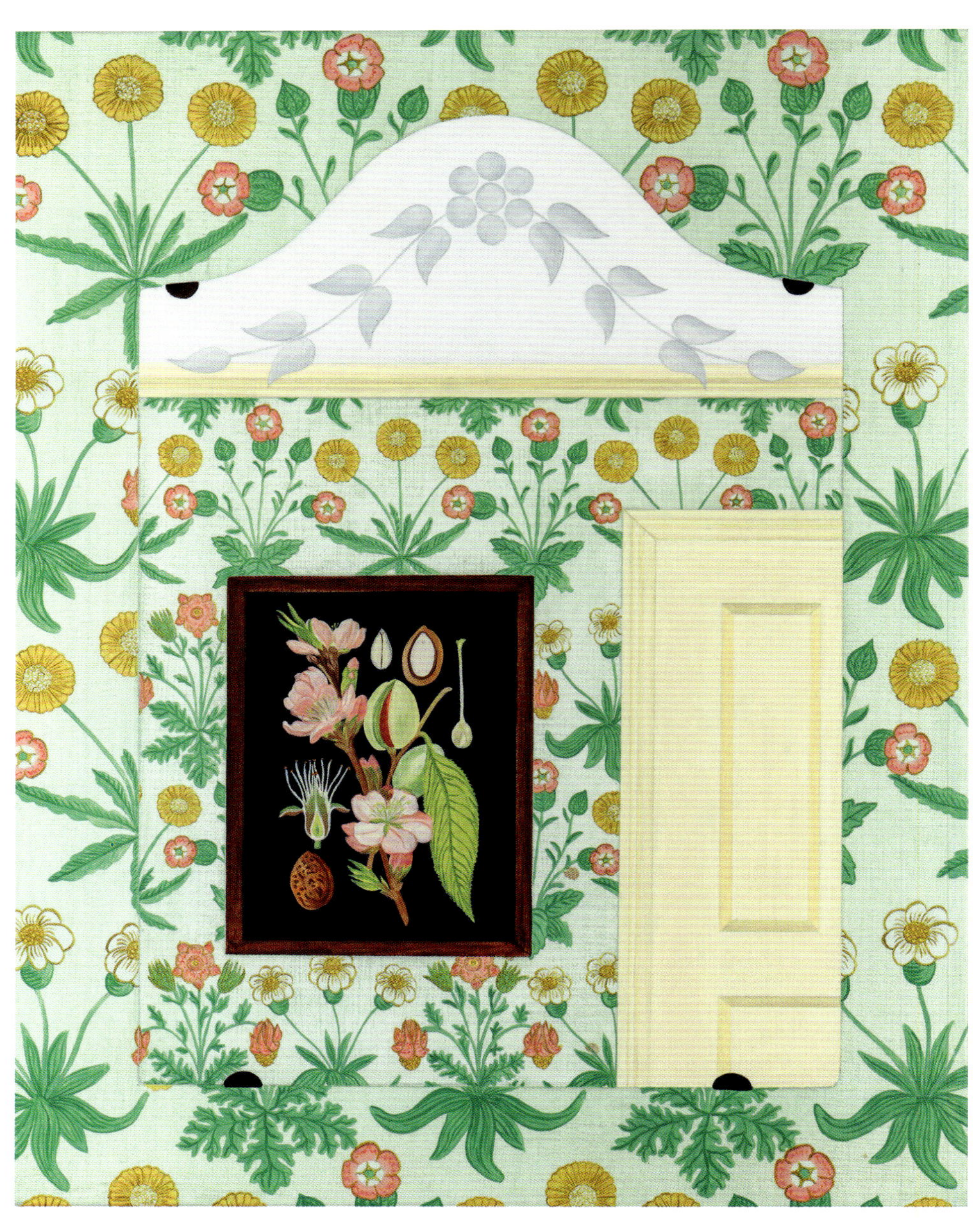

Looking Glass House #1, 2021
oil on canvas
14 × 11 inches

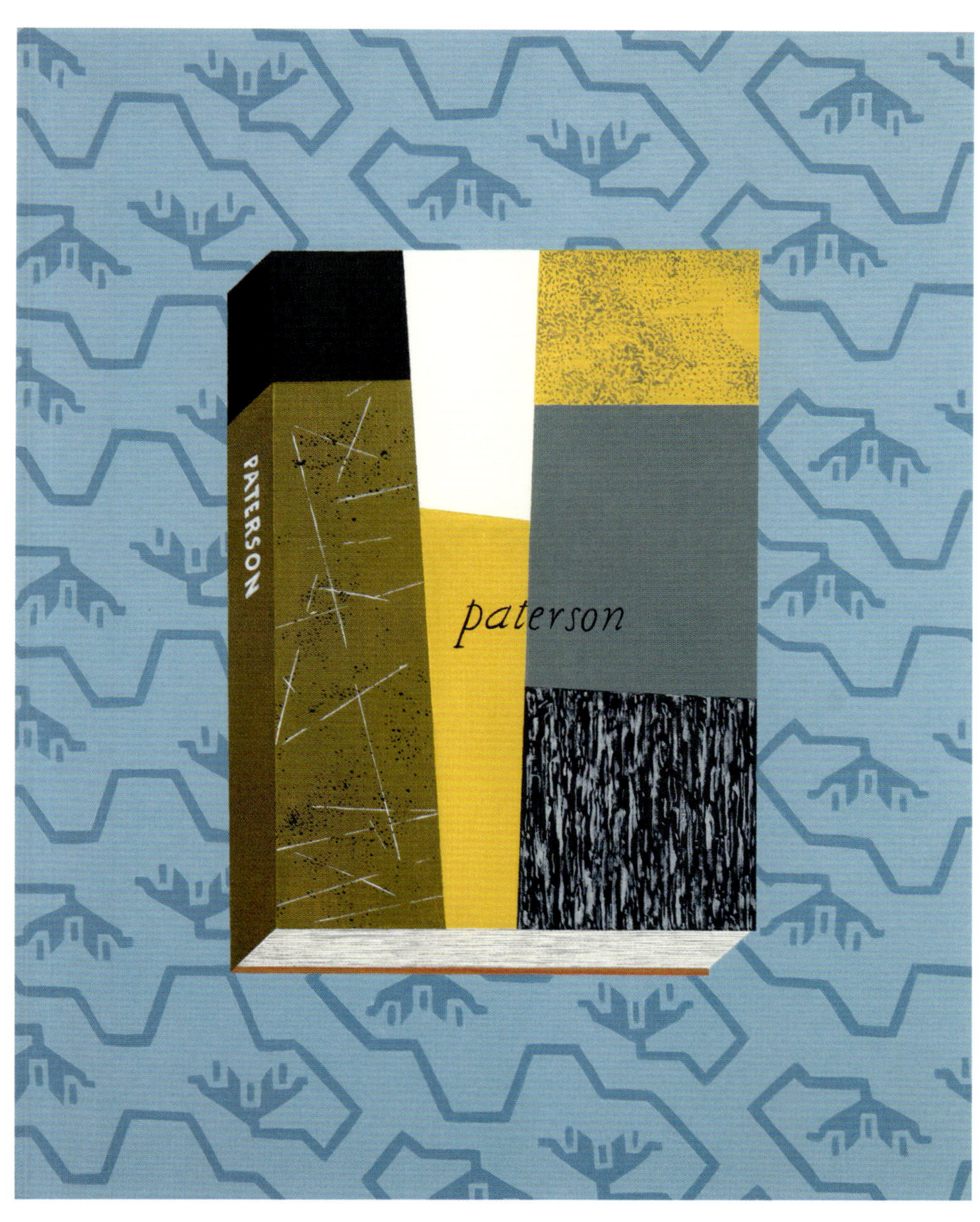

Paterson, 2021
oil on canvas
14 × 11 inches

following pages
Courtesy of the Pew Center for Arts & Heritage. Photo by Ryan Collerd

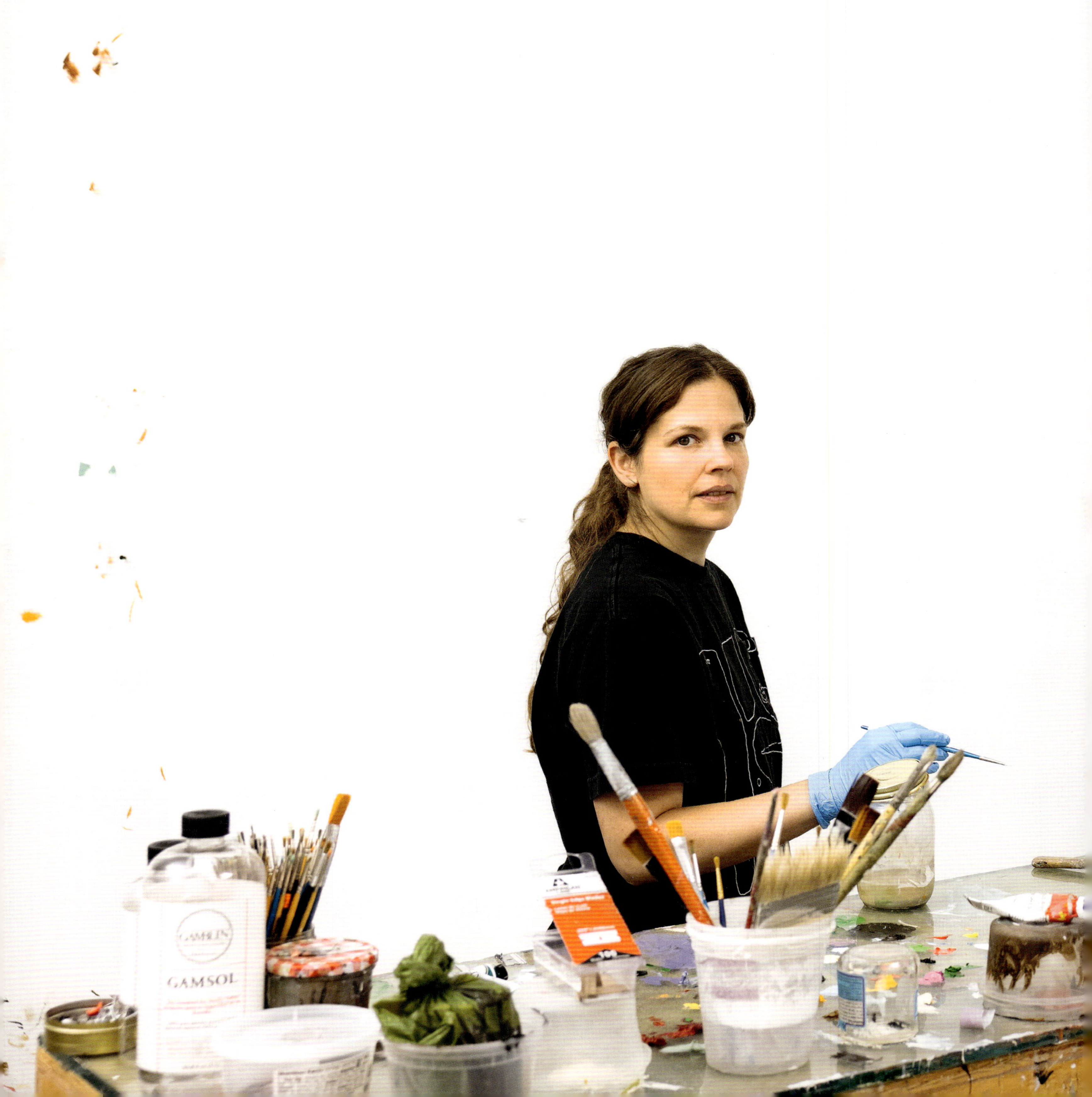
GAMSOL

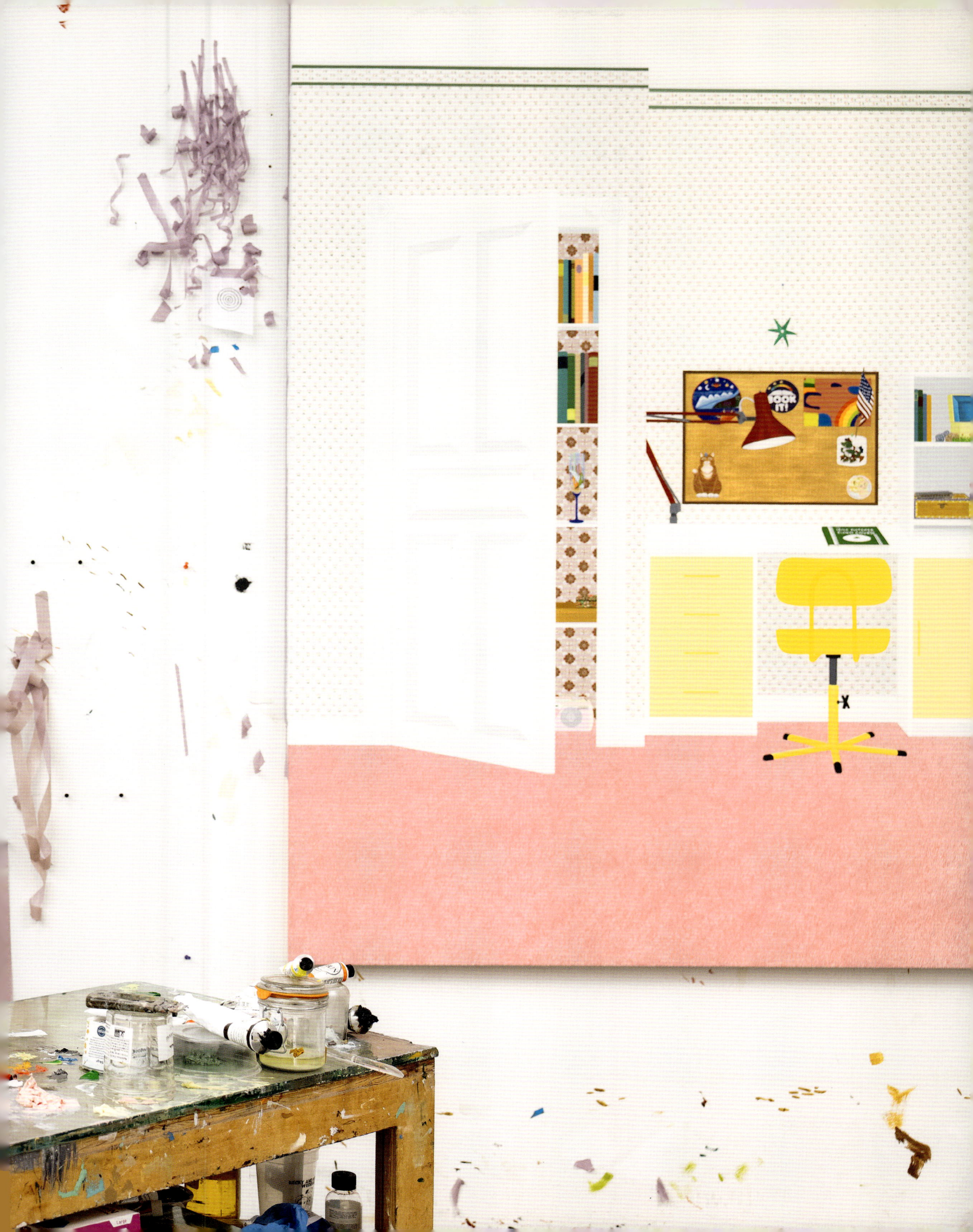

Biography and Exhibitions

Born 1980 in Philadelphia, PA. Lives and works in Philadelphia.

Education

2013
Skowhegan School of Painting and Sculpture, Skowhegan, ME

2010
MFA, University of California, Berkeley, CA

2003
BA, Williams College, Williamstown, MA

Selected One and Two-Artist Exhibitions

2020
Where They Are, Jack Shainman Gallery, New York, NY

2018–19
Becky Suss/Wharton Esherick, Fleisher/Ollman, Philadelphia, PA

2017
Homemaker, Jack Shainman Gallery, New York, NY

2015
Becky Suss, Institute of Contemporary Art, University of Pennsylvania, Philadelphia, PA

2012
Becky Suss: Wherever You Are… That's Where You Are, Snyderman-Works Galleries, Philadelphia, PA
Still Life, Vox Populi, Philadelphia, PA

2011
Cold Cold Ground, Space 1026, Philadelphia, PA
Drawings, Vox Populi, Philadelphia, PA

2009
In Let, WORK Gallery, Brooklyn, NY

2006
Homesick, Sodafine, Brooklyn, NY

Selected Group Exhibitions

2022–23
To Begin Again: Artists and Childhood, Institute of Contemporary Art, Boston, MA

2021
Dear John, Adams & Ollman, Portland, OR
Feedback, The School | Jack Shainman Gallery, Kinderhook, NY (Curated by Helen Molesworth)
New Grit: Art & Philly Now, Philadelphia Museum of Art, PA
Taking Space: Contemporary Women Artists and the Politics of Scale, Pennsylvania Academy of the Fine Arts, Philadelphia, PA

2020
Touching from a Distance, Fleisher/Ollman, Philadelphia, PA

2019
The Autotopographers, John Michael Kohler Arts Center, Sheboygan, WI
Vernacular Interior, Hales Gallery, New York, NY (Curated by Adeze Wilford)

2018–19
One Day at a Time: Manny Farber and Termite Art, Museum of Contemporary Art, Los Angeles, CA

2018
Ethics of Depiction: Landscape, Still Life, Human, Oakland University Art Gallery, Rochester, MI
In My Room: Artists Paint the Interior 1950-Now, Fralin Museum, University of Virginia, Charlottesville, VA
Orientation, Jack Shainman Gallery, New York, NY
Party in the Front, Fleisher/Ollman, Philadelphia, PA

2017
Home Room, The School | Jack Shainman Gallery, Kinderhook, NY

2016
Philadelphia Painters, Marlin and Regina Miller Gallery, Kutztown University, Kutztown, PA

2015
We Pain, LUMP, Raleigh, NC

2014
Begin Where You Are, Crane Arts, Icebox Project Space, Philadelphia, PA
do it, The Galleries at Moore, Moore College of Art and Design, Philadelphia, PA (Curated by Anthony Elms)
Good Neighbors, The Berman Museum, Collegeville, PA

2013
Reprefantasion: Abstracting Reality/Representing Fantasy, Fleisher/Ollman, Philadelphia, PA

2012
Creative Nonfiction, Kunsthalle Galapagos, Brooklyn, NY
Vox Populi, The Front Space, New Orleans, LA
Winterdown, The Icebox, Philadelphia, PA
Young Philly, Salisbury University Art Gallery, MD

2011
Call and Response, Root Division, San Francisco, CA
Wish You Were There, University City Arts League, Philadelphia, PA

2010
It's My World, Baer Ridgway, San Francisco, CA
No Right Angles, Berkeley Art Museum, Berkeley, CA

2009
Free Time, Worth Ryder Gallery, Berkeley, CA

2008
Cloud, WORK Gallery, Brooklyn, NY
The House that Sprawl Built, Hunterdon Museum of Art, Clinton, NJ
Sarah, Becky, Kate, Beat Jams, Little Berlin, Philadelphia, PA

2007
Art in the Style of Radical, Magic Pony Gallery, Toronto, ON
Becky Suss, Justin B. Williams, Caleb Neelon, and Alex Lukas, David B. Smith Gallery, Denver, CO
Experiences and Activities, Western Exhibitions, Chicago, IL
Exquisite Corpse, The Painted Bride Art Center, Philadelphia, PA
Locally Localized Gravity, Institute of Contemporary Art, Philadelphia, PA
No Bad Blood, Cinders Gallery, Brooklyn, NY
Peer Pleasure 1, Yerba Buena Center for the Arts, San Francisco, CA
Phooklyn, Lump Gallery, Raleigh, NC

2006
Sibling Revelry, Aftermodern Gallery, San Francisco, CA

2005
Out of Doors, Aftermodern Gallery, San Francisco, CA
Soon and Very Soon, Renowned Gallery, Portland, OR
Space 1026 Installation, Dumbo Arts Festival, Brooklyn, NY
The Urban Edge Show, The P4, Milan, Italy

2004
Beaver College, The Mockbee, Cincinnati, OH

Public Collections

The Alfond Collection of Contemporary Art, Cornell Fine Arts Museum, Rollins College, Winter Park, FL
Davis Museum and Cultural Center, Wellesley College, MA
The Heckscher Museum of Art, Huntington, NY
Institute of Contemporary Art, Boston, MA
Museum of Contemporary Art, Los Angeles, CA
Museum of Fine Arts, Boston, MA
Pennsylvania Academy of the Fine Arts, Philadelphia, PA
Philadelphia Museum of Art, PA
Rennie Museum, Vancouver, Canada

Artist Collectives and Residencies

Space 1026, Philadelphia, PA (Member, 2003–7)
Vox Populi, Philadelphia, PA (Member, 2010–Present)
Vermont Studio Center, Johnson, VT (2012)

Lectures and Teaching

2019
Exploring Personal Narratives & Storytelling through Representational Painting, Anderson Ranch Arts Center, Snowmass Village, CO

2017
Visiting artist series, Pennsylvania Academy of the Fine Arts, Philadelphia, PA

2011
Making Art Together; Collaborative and Collective Practices, Williams College, Williamstown, MA

2010
Approaches to Painting, University of California, Berkeley, CA
Introduction to Visual Thinking, University of California, Berkeley, CA

2007
In the Studio-Drawing and Painting, Woodmere Art Museum, Philadelphia, PA

Awards and Grants

2019
The Pew Center for Arts & Heritage Fellowship Recipient

2014
Coverley-Smith Prize, Woodmere Art Museum

2010
Art Practice Materials Grant, University of California, Berkeley
Eisner Prize in Art Practice, University of California, Berkeley (Nominee)
Joan Mitchell Foundation, Master of Fine Arts Fellowship

2009
Art Practice Materials Grant, University of California, Berkeley (Nominee)
Dedalus Foundation, Master of Fine Arts Fellowship

2003
Berkshire Fellowship from the Berkshire Art Association Frederick M. Peyser Prize in Painting, Williams College

Selected Bibliography

Books and Exhibition Catalogs

2020

• *Contemporary Artists (a publication during a pandemic)*. Boston: Museum of Fine Arts, 2019.

2019

• Baker, Alex. *Becky Suss/Wharton Esherick*. Philadelphia: Fleisher/Ollman, 2019.

• Teixeira de Freitas, Luiza. *There'll Never Be a Door You're Inside: Works from the Coleção Teixeira de Freitas*. Santander: Santander Art Gallery, 2019.

2018

• Farber, Manny and Helen Molesworth. *One Day at a Time: Manny Farber and Termite Art*. Los Angeles: Museum of Contemporary Art, 2018.

2016

• Kraczon, Kate. *Becky Suss*. Philadelphia: Institute of Contemporary Art, University of Pennsylvania, 2016.

2013

• Baker, Alex. *Reprefantasion*. Philadelphia: Fleisher/Ollman, 2013.

Periodicals

2021

• Waddoups, Ryan. "Becky Suss Recalls the Formative Interiors of Her Childhood." *Surface*, December 2, 2021.

• Heinrich, Will. "Teaching a New Inclusiveness at The School." *The New York Times*, August 12, 2021.

• Donoghue, Katy. "Helen Molesworth and Becky Suss Ask, What, Where, and How do We Learn?" *Whitewall*, July 9, 2021.

• Singer, Jill. "In Her Paintings, Becky Suss Creates Real or Imagined Interiors From Memory." *Sight Unseen*, May 19, 2021.

2020

• Coleman, Charity. "Becky Suss." *Artforum*, May/June 2020.

• Blackwood, Sarah. "The Uncanny Domestic Spaces of Becky Suss." *The New Yorker*, March 3, 2020.

• Chernick, Karen. "How a Museum Inspired a Book That In Turn Gave Birth to a Painting." *Observer*, February 19, 2020.

• Donoghoue, Katy. "Becky Suss Revisits the Captivating Interiors of Stories She Grew up Reading." *Whitewall*, January 8, 2020.

2019

• Knight, Christopher. "Review: Helen Molesworth's final show at MOCA is the anti-celebrity show we need right now." *Los Angeles Times*, October 19, 2019.

• Huff Hunter, Bea. "Becky Suss: Fleisher/Ollman Gallery." *ArtForum*, March 2019.

• Abramovich, Alex. "Termite Art and the Modern Museum." *The New Yorker*, February 28, 2019.

• Palasik, Mandy. "Wharton Esherick's Home Studio, channeled through Becky Suss's paintings at Fleisher-Ollman Gallery." *The Artblog*, January 10, 2019. Online.

2018

• Mitchell, Samantha. "Becky Suss Paints Wharton Escherick's Dream-Like Home and Studio." *Hyperallergic*, December 17, 2018. Online.

• Newhall, Edith. "Wharton Esherick, re-interpreted." *The Philadelphia Inquirer*, November 25, 2018.

• Dunlap Sathe, Jane. "'In My Room' at the Fralin lures art viewers into the great indoors." *Pulse*, May 23, 2018. Online.

• Saltz, Jerry. "Right Now Is a Blockbuster Moment in New York for Female Artists." *New York Magazine*, May 19, 2017.

2017

• Smith, Roberta. "What to See in New York Art Galleries This Week: Becky Suss." *The New York Times*, May 18, 2017. Online.

• Voon, Claire. "Paintings that Revel in the Wonder of Our Domestic Spaces." *Hyperallergic*, May 18, 2017. Online.

• Tauer, Kristen. "Becky Suss Talks 'Homemaker' Show at Jack Shainman Gallery." *WWD*, May 10, 2017. Online.

• Weiss, Haley. "At Home With Becky Suss." *Interview Magazine*, May 9, 2017. Online.

• Pogrebin, Robin. "Becky Suss's Painted Memories Have a Solo Show in Chelsea." *The New York Times*, April 27, 2017. Online.

2016

• Ayerle, Liz. "Becky Suss: The Impression Remains." *Proximity Arts*, September 14, 2016. Online.

2015

• Bury, Louis. "Speak, Memory: Becky Suss's Painterly Anthropology." *Hyperallergic*, December 19, 2015. Online.

• Butler, Sharon. "Becky Suss: The Mid-Century Modern Aesthetic". *Two Coats of Paint*, December 17, 2015. Online.

• Newhall, Edith. "Galleries: Becky Suss' art dreams mid-century dreams." *The Philadelphia Inquirer*, December 4, 2015.

• Cavitch, Max. "Becky Suss's Haunts." *Icaphila.org: Notes*, November 23, 2015. Online.

• Mitchell, Samantha. "Becky Suss." *Title Magazine*, October 18, 2015.

• Zarro, Jennifer. "Becky Suss at the Institute of Contemporary Art." *The Artblog*, October 5, 2015. Online.

• Huff Hunter, Becky. "Critic's Picks: Becky Suss." *Artforum*, September 2015. Online.

2013

• *New American Paintings: Northeast Issue #104*, 2013.

2012

• *New American Paintings: Northeast Issue #98*, 2012.

• Zevitas, Steven. "14 Must See Painting Shows: October 2012." *HuffPost*, October 16, 2012.

2011

• Jih, Diana. "Becky Suss's Cold, Cold Ground at Space 1026." *The Artblog*, May 24, 2011. Online.

Cover
Pillow #1, 2012

Design
Luigi Fiore

Editorial Coordination
Eva Vanzella

Copy Editor
Carlotta Santuccio

Layout
Evelina Laviano

Photo Credits
Unless otherwise noted, all images: Artworks © Becky Suss. Courtesy of the artist and Jack Shainman Gallery, New York. Photographs by Constance Mensh or Jeremy Lawson

Wharton Esherick 2018 images: Artworks © Becky Suss. Courtesy of the artist and Fleisher/Ollman, Philadelphia. Photographs by Claire Iltis

First published in Italy in 2022 by
Skira editore S.p.A.
Palazzo Casati Stampa
via Torino 61
20123 Milano
Italy
www.skira.net

Printed and bound in Italy. First edition

ISBN: 978-88-572-4653-6

Distributed in USA, Canada, Central & South America by
ARTBOOK | D.A.P. 75 Broad Street Suite 630, New York, NY 10004, USA
Distributed elsewhere in the world by Thames and Hudson Ltd., 181A High Holborn, London WC1V 7QX, United Kingdom.

I would like to offer my sincerest gratitude to everyone who made this book possible and who supported me on this journey. To the entire crew at Jack Shainman Gallery, but especially Tamsen Greene, Isabel Hidalgo, Anna Model, and Jack Shainman, thank you so much for making this book happen and for patiently shepherding me through this often daunting process. Thank you to the writers of these three amazing texts: Helen Molesworth, Michelle Millar Fisher, and Peter L'Official. You have all been so generous and working with each of you has been a dream. Thank you to Constance Mensch for ten+ years of reliably beautiful photographs of my work. Thank you to the crew at Fleisher/Ollman for your many years of support. A huge thank you to Liza Danges and Wendy Hitch for the loving childcare you provide Sid. Without it none of what I do would be possible.

To my mom, sister, and dad (but especially my mom), in my forty-one years you have been champions of all my pursuits, but your endless support and help with Sid and my career are the greatest gifts you will ever give me.

Finally, the biggest thanks to my husband Micah and my son Sid, for all of the Sundays and for making everything I do possible and worthwhile. I love you so much.

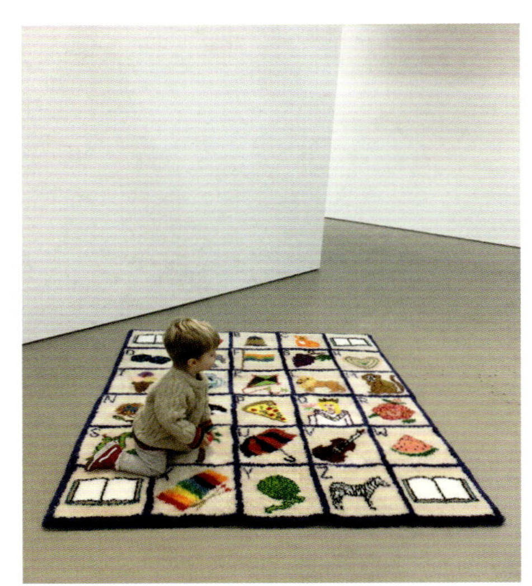